EDWARD VII'S CHILDREN

Historical biography

Frederick III: German Emperor 1888 (Alan Sutton, 1981)
Queen Victoria's family: a select bibliography (Clover, 1982)
Dearest Affie: Alfred, Duke of Edinburgh, Queen Victoria's second son, 1844–1900
(with Bee Jordaan) (Alan Sutton, 1984)
Queen Victoria's children (Alan Sutton, 1986; large print edition ISIS, 1987)
Windsor and Habsburg: the British and Austrian reigning houses 1848–1922
(Alan Sutton, 1987)

Music

Roxeventies: popular music in Britain 1970–79 (Kawabata, 1982)
The Roy Wood story (A & F, 1986)
Singles file: the story of the 45 r.p.m. record (A & F, 1987)

EDWARD VII'S CHILDREN

John Van der Kiste

ALAN SUTTON
1989

ALAN SUTTON PUBLISHING
BRUNSWICK ROAD · GLOUCESTER · UK

ALAN SUTTON PUBLISHING INC
WOLFEBORO · NEW HAMPSHIRE · USA

First published 1989

British Library Cataloguing in Publication Data

Van der Kiste, John
    Edward VII's children.
    1. Great Britain. Royal families, –
    Biographies – Collections
    I. Title
    929.7′2

    ISBN 0-86299-533-7

Library of Congress Cataloging in Publication Data applied for

Jacket photographs: front: Princess Victoria, Princess Maud and Princess
Louise by Sidney Hall, 1883 (National Portrait Gallery). *Back*: Prince Albert
Victor and Prince George of Wales by Carl Sohn. From The Royal
Collection. Reproduced by gracious permission of Her Majesty the Queen

Typesetting and origination by
Alan Sutton Publishing Limited
Printed in Great Britain by
Dotesios Printers Limited

Contents

Illustrations

vii

Nos. 63 and 64 appear by gracious permission of Her Majesty Queen Elizabeth II (copyright reserved). Thanks are also due to the following for kind permission to reproduce illustrations: BBC Hulton Picture Library (Nos. 14, 19, 22, 26, 27, 29, 31, 43, 46, 50, 55, 56, 57, 58, 65, 69, 71, 73, 74); Conway Picture Library (No. 76); Norwegian Post Office (Nos. 40, 77, 78); and Mrs R. Prior, Sussex Commemorative Ware Centre, Hove, Sussex (Nos. 9, 34, 36, 37, 38, 41, 42, 60, 72). The remainder are from private collections.

Foreword

At first glance, it is hardly surprising that the children of King Edward VII and Queen Alexandra, with the exception of King George V, have been paid scant attention by biographers. John Gore's 'personal memoir' of the latter,* undertaken at the request of King George VI and Queen Mary and published in 1941, was complemented by a similarly-commissioned work from Harold Nicolson 'chronicling his public life and attitude towards the successive political issues of his reign,' which appeared in 1952. These have been added to by Kenneth Rose's equally indispensable biography of the King, based on a wealth of material made available more recently and published in 1983; and to a lesser extent by Roger Fulford's concise character study in *Hanover to Windsor*, as well as Denis Judd's profusely-illustrated volume in the *Lives of the Kings and Queens of England* series edited by Antonia Fraser.

Of the remaining four who lived to maturity, only one – Prince Albert Victor, Duke of Clarence and Avondale – has been the subject of an individual study, that by Michael Harrison published in 1972. His brief life has been dealt with admirably in biographies of Queen Mary by James Pope-Hennessy (author of the officially-commissioned volume), Anne Edwards and David Duff, and with varying degrees of (in)accuracy and sensationalism in a host of 'Jack the Ripper' books, more of interest to the student of criminology or devotee of lurid detective fiction.

King Edward VII's daughters had only a slight impact on public life in Britain, and hardly merit biographies to themselves beyond the chapters in part-biographies such as those of all the Princesses Royal by Geoffrey Wakeford and Helen Cathcart. All the same, their lives are of interest, not least Princess Maud, who unexpectedly became Queen of Norway nine years after her marriage to her cousin Prince Charles of Denmark. Only passing mention is made of her in the two accounts of her husband King Haakon VII's life published in English, by Maurice Michael and Tim Greve. Her letters to Queen Mary, now in the Royal Archives, Windsor, most of which are published here for the first time, paint an interesting picture of life in a neutral European country during the Great War, 1914–18; they also reveal her shrewd observation of family matters from afar, particularly during and after the abdication crisis of 1936. Additional previously unpublished correspondence from her sisters Louise, Princess Royal and Duchess of Fife, and Princess Victoria of Wales, has helped to throw new light

---

* This, and all other works referred to in the Foreword, is cited in full in the Bibliography (pp. 188–90).

on members of the royal family from the latter days of Queen Victoria's reign through the turbulent first four decades of the twentieth century.

I wish to acknowledge the gracious permission of Her Majesty The Queen to publish certain material to which she owns the copyright.

I am indebted to the following copyright holders for permission to quote from published works: Constable & Co Ltd (*King George V*, by Harold Nicolson; *Queen Alexandra*, by Georgina Battiscombe); John Murray (Publishers) Ltd (*King Edward the Seventh*, by Philip Magnus; *King George V*, by John Gore); Unwin Hyman Ltd (*Dearest Mama* and *Your dear letter*, both edited by Roger Fulford); and George Weidenfeld & Nicolson (*King George V*, by Kenneth Rose).

Every effort has been made to trace and acknowledge all copyright owners, and apologies are offered to authors and publishers whose rights may have been inadvertently infringed.

My thanks for constant help, encouragement and advice during the writing of this book are due to Wing Commander Guy and Nancy Van der Kiste; Theo Aronson; Bee Jordaan; Mrs R. Prior, of the Sussex Commemorative Ware Centre; The Hon. Giles St Aubyn, and Shirley Stapley.

John Van der Kiste

Prologue

As the year 1863 dawned, London society looked forward to the wedding of Albert Edward, Prince of Wales, to Princess Alexandra of Denmark. Gloom had enveloped court and country since the Prince Consort's death in December 1861, and at last there was reason to rejoice. The marriage was to take place on 10 March, the first wedding of a Prince of Wales since the ill-starred union of Prince George to Princess Caroline of Brunswick in 1795. It was widely expected that St Paul's or Westminster Abbey would be the chosen venue for the ceremony.

However, still in deepest mourning for her husband, Queen Victoria refused to consider the idea of a wedding involving any state procession in which she would have to be seen 'alone' by her subjects – in other words, without Prince Albert at her side. She, therefore, decided that the ceremony should take place in the comparative seclusion of St George's Chapel, Windsor Castle, which had room for less than one thousand.

Punch gave vent to the national feeling of disappointment. It commented acidly that the heir's nuptials were to be held in an obscure Berkshire village, noted only for an old castle with no sanitary arrangements; already it was suspected that the castle's poor drainage facilities had contributed to the Prince Consort's fatal illness. The only announcement, it suggested, should be inserted in the marriage columns of *The Times*, and worded thus:

On the 10th inst., at Windsor, by Dr Longley, assisted by Dr Thomson, Albert Edward England K.G. to Alexandra Denmark. No cards.

Prince Albert Edward ('Bertie') was born on 9 November 1841, the second child of Queen Victoria and Prince Albert. It was ironic that although his three younger brothers all inherited, in some measure, the gifts of scholarship and temperament that their parents wished for him, he was singularly lacking in this respect. Alfred ('Affie') showed a remarkable aptitude for geography, scientific subjects, and anything mechanical or practical. Arthur was an even-tempered boy who soon became (and remained) his mother's favourite, while the delicate Leopold was a precocious reader whose love of fine arts and literature belied his tender years.

Bertie, however, was the one born to inherit his mother's throne. It was therefore vital – at least, as far as his father and the pedantic unofficial family adviser, Baron Christian von Stockmar, were concerned – that he should be subjected to an intense educational regime. Bertie, as Queen Victoria perceptively recognized, was her 'caricature'. He took after her in his Hanoverian zest for life, aversion to studying, and hasty temper. She regretted that in no way did he resemble his beloved and intellectual father.

Moreover, it was his misfortune to be overshadowed throughout childhood by his brilliant elder sister Victoria ('Vicky'), Princess Royal. She was exceptionally bright and eager to learn; only a particularly clever boy could have held his own against her. She was as ready to tease him for his stammer and lack of concentration as their parents were to praise her and scold him for his shortcomings. His childish tantrums were a disruptive influence in the nursery. When told to do something he would scream violently, stamp his feet and throw things around until he was exhausted. Only his governess Lady Lyttelton was quick to appreciate his positive qualities – his charm, eagerness to please, and readiness to tell the truth. (Vicky's 'slyness' and tendency to lie were readily forgiven by her indulgent father.) Lady Lyttelton saw that he preferred, and would always learn more from, people rather than books. Nonetheless he was certainly not unintelligent; he could speak three languages by the age of six. Fortunately his natural capacity for affection was never soured. Though he was always a little in awe of Vicky and her brilliant intellect, they remained devoted to each other throughout their lives. When he was five, Queen Victoria commented that she was 'much touched by Bertie asking me to do his little Sunday lesson with him sometimes.'

At the age of seven and a half, he was handed over in to the care of a tutor, Henry Birch, former assistant master at Eton. Six days a week his timetable was divided into five hourly or half-hour periods. Lessons were never discontinued for more than a few days at a time, but family birthdays were always holidays, and the routine was relaxed when the court moved between Windsor and London. Though Bertie resented his demanding regime, he became greatly attached to Birch, who saw – unlike Stockmar and Prince Albert – the boy's excellent memory and 'very singular powers of observation.' When Bertie was ten, Birch resigned to take holy orders, and was succeeded by Frederick Waymouth Gibbs.

On his seventeenth birthday Bertie was gazetted as an honorary colonel and made a Knight of the Garter. He was granted his own establishment at White Lodge, Richmond Park, but his freedom was curtailed by three elderly equerries and a governor, Colonel Robert Bruce. He also received a long and ponderous memorandum written by his father, warning him among other things that life was 'composed of duties, and in the due, punctual and cheerful performance of them the true Christian, true soldier and true gentleman is recognized.'[1]

Princess Alexandra ('Alix') was the second child and eldest daughter of Prince Christian of Schleswig-Holstein-Sonderburg-Glucksburg and Princess Louise of Hesse-Cassel, niece of King Christian VIII of Denmark. Prince Christian had represented the King as the bearer of congratulations from Denmark to Queen Victoria on her accession to the English throne in 1837 and again a year later at her coronation. There were rumours at the time that he might be a candidate for the hand of the young spinster Queen.

Princess Alexandra, her three brothers and two sisters, were all born and brought up at the Yellow Palace (a more humble abode than its name might

Queen Victoria and Albert, Prince Consort, at Osborne House, engraving after a photograph by Miss Day, 1859

suggest) in Copenhagen. Princess Louise was a great-granddaughter of Frederick, Landgrave of Hesse-Cassel, son of King George II of England, and her children were thus fourth cousins to Queen Victoria's brood of nine.

Like many European princes, Prince Christian was not of royal pedigree, and in nineteenth-century Denmark there was not the gulf between monarch and subject that existed elsewhere on the continent. The king ruled and lived like an old-fashioned country squire, able to walk through the streets of Copenhagen without causing a stir, and giving audiences to his subjects with the minimum of formality.

By the standards of the family into which Princess Alexandra was destined to marry, the Danish aristocracy was comparatively poor. Prince Christian received no civil list or allowance till he was nominated heir to the childless King Frederick VII in 1852, only a meagre salary as a captain in the Danish guards, which was augmented by occasional sums from the King and from his father-in-law. The children were clothed simply, the girls wore plain cotton dresses which were inexpensive to launder and difficult to spoil, and when they were old enough they helped their mother with dressmaking. Servants were a luxury the family could ill-afford, so the youngsters dusted their own rooms, and when guests were entertained they waited at table.

Prince Christian was a devoted husband and father, but devoid of cultural interests, having had a meagre education. Princess Louise was the more dominant personality, and not only did she make most of her children's clothes

3

but also taught them general knowledge, foreign languages, music and drawing. They also had English nurses, and were thus familiar with the language from their earliest years. Prince Christian took responsibility for their physical education in hand; they revelled in gymnastics and outdoor sports, especially riding.

Although lacking money, the family was a united one. All the children remained devoted to each other throughout their lives. Summers were generally spent at Schloss Rumpenheim, near Frankfurt, or Bernstorff, a hunting lodge about five miles from Copenhagen, which was granted to Prince Christian as an additional residence when he was nominated as heir. It was surrounded by a large wooded park which provided a veritable playground paradise for them all. A healthy, extroverted crowd, the Danish royal family would in years to come be renowned for its love of rough-and-tumble frolics and practical jokes. Even when they were middle-aged, no family reunion at Bernstorff was complete without the odd pillow-fight, or without the springs of a sofa having to be renewed. Guests would complain, or make the excuse, that it was impossible to write letters because of the high-spirited noise.

Only one photograph and one painting of Princess Alexandra as a child survive; both show her at the age of eleven. Likewise there are few accounts of her early life as an individual. Such as there are suggest that she was the prettiest of the sisters, extremely unpunctual, rather a tomboy, and yet wise with a sense of tact beyond her tender years.

Prince Christian of Schleswig-Holstein-Sonderburg-Augustenburg

Shortly before Bertie's seventeenth birthday, Queen Victoria and Prince Albert became increasingly concerned with choosing their son a suitable wife, enlisting Vicky (now married to 'Fritz', Prince Frederick William of Prussia) to scour the pages of the *Almanach de Gotha*. Between them they decided that the right princess would need good looks, health, education, character, intellect, and a good disposition. Bertie would not look at anyone who was too plain, and his future wife would have to be fairly strong-willed, otherwise her lot would certainly not be a happy one.

Since the Elector of Hanover had ascended the British throne as King George I, it had been traditional for the monarch to choose marital partners for his or her offspring from Germany. Stockmar backed the Queen and her husband in their quest for a German daughter-in-law, but to their disappointment all the eligible princesses were too young, too delicate, too dowdy – or Roman Catholics.

The only one who could not be faulted on these grounds was Princess Alexandra of Denmark, but political considerations made a Danish bride inadvisable. There was tension between the Scandinavian kingdom and the German confederation over the future administration of the Duchies of Schleswig and Holstein, and the British royal family was unequivocally on Germany's side. Besides, Princess Christian's relations had a reputation for immorality. Queen Victoria regarded her as beyond reproach, but not her mother and sisters – nor King Frederick VII himself. She and Prince Albert had striven hard to banish the moral shortcomings that had tarnished the Hanoverian dynasty and Coburg family, and they had no desire to see any tainted Glucksburg or Hesse-Cassel blood undo their work.

Yet she had reckoned without the influence of her Cambridge cousins. Princess Mary Adelaide of Cambridge had known Alexandra since the latter's childhood, and had played with her as a girl at Rumpenheim family reunions. She and Admiral van Dickum, Danish minister in London, were secretly trying to solve the problem for Her Majesty by pressing for an Anglo-Danish marriage.

However, it was not their influence that prevailed, but rather that of Vicky's lady-in-waiting, Lady Paget. Shortly after her wedding to the British minister in Copenhagen in October 1860 she was invited to dine at Windsor, and this gave her an opportunity to report on the charm of Princess Alexandra. Despite their initial misgivings, Queen Victoria and the Prince Consort wrote to Vicky asking her to find out more. While admitting that, as a Prussian, she would not wish her brother to marry a Danish princess, she could say nothing but good of Alexandra. Albert was likewise instantly captivated; after seeing her photograph, this most reserved of princes proclaimed that he would 'marry her at once.'

By the following spring, other candidates for Alexandra's hand were believed to be in the field. Foremost among them was the Tsarevich Nicholas. Vicky thought 'it would be dreadful if this pearl were to go to the horrid Russians.' Bertie was told of the plans being tentatively made, and reacted with restrained enthusiasm. Everyone involved had taken it for granted that a princess of such modest means would be thrilled by the prospect of becoming the Princess of Wales, but in her more impatient moods Queen Victoria secretly feared that Alexandra might not accept her son.

Albert Edward, Prince of Wales   *Princess Alexandra of Denmark*

Not surprisingly, Bertie wanted to meet his proposed bride. It was arranged that he would spend several weeks that summer in camp at the Curragh near Dublin with the Grenadier Guards. He could therefore visit German army manoeuvres in the Rhineland later, and then stay with Vicky at Baden, close to Rumpenheim, where the Danish princess would be staying. With a little subterfuge, a 'chance encounter' could be arranged without attracting the attention of Princess Alexandra's other potential suitors.

In September 1861, Alexandra and her parents set out from Rumpenheim for Speyer. She was still in ignorance about the plans concerning her. The first intimation she had that something special was happening was when she was instructed to wear her best clothes. As the three of them were admiring the cathedral, they chanced to meet the Crown Prince and Princess of Prussia and the Prince of Wales. The latter and Princess Alexandra were introduced, and though he had perhaps been told so much about her beauty that he was bound to be slightly disappointed when confronted by the reality, there was no denying that she was a lively and charming companion. They were left to wander round the cathedral together, observed at a discreet distance by the adults. Later that day, all six of them travelled together to Heidelberg, spent the night in the same hotel, and the young couple exchanged signed photographs before parting.

Much to the dismay of his parents, Bertie appeared to dread the idea of marriage and fatherhood, thus bringing an admonition from his anxious father not to indulge in 'a general vague apprehension that you might someday meet someone else you might like better,' and thereby lose 'positive and present advantages for the hope of future chances which may never occur.'[2]

In November, the Prince Consort was informed by Stockmar of 'a subject which has caused me the greatest pain I have yet felt in this life.' It was rumoured throughout Europe that the Prince of Wales had indulged in a liaison with an actress while at the Curragh that summer. Enquiries revealed that this scarcely-unexpected turn of events was true. Already feeling the strain from overwork and a succession of family deaths (notably that of his mother-in-law the Duchess of Kent, whose passing in March had left the Queen stricken with grief, and two Coburg cousins in Portugal), Prince Albert took this news badly. Suffering from the initial symptoms of what proved to be typhoid fever, he paid a visit to his son who was studying at Cambridge. They had a long frank talk, in which Bertie asked for the 'intimacies' to be kept from his mother. A few days later, Albert took to his bed at Windsor, and on 14 December he died at the age of forty-two.

Queen Victoria had not yet recovered from the shock of her mother's death, and this second bereavement within nine months brought her close to losing her reason. She was convinced that Bertie's 'fall' had broken his father's heart, and much as she pitied him, 'I never can or shall look at him without a shudder.' Where his marriage prospects were concerned, she feared that Princess Alexandra's parents would no longer accept him for their son. Princess Christian was indeed upset, not so much by the Prince of Wales's dalliance as by the belief that he was bitterly detested by his mother. If Queen Victoria really hated her son, she feared, she was bound to dislike his wife as well.

However, the Queen was determined to see her wayward son and heir married as soon as possible. A betrothal between him and the Danish princess had been one of her 'beloved angel's' dearest wishes; it was therefore her responsibility to see it fulfilled, especially as Tsar Alexander II of Russia was apparently looking at her closely as a potential daughter-in-law as well.

In September, Queen Victoria went to stay with King Leopold of the Belgians at his palace in Laeken, ostensibly to visit Coburg as a personal pilgrimage to her husband's childhood home, but really to meet Prince and Princess Christian and their two elder daughters. The Queen was immediately impressed with Alix, whom she found 'lovely', with 'such a beautiful refined profile, and quite ladylike manner.' After a long conversation with her parents, the Queen left for Coburg, while the Danish family went to Ostend. Bertie joined them there later that week, and next day they went to Laeken. Everyone, suggested King Leopold, should take a stroll in the gardens, and the young couple should be allowed to lag behind. Accordingly, Bertie proposed and Alix accepted him.

That afternoon he wrote Queen Victoria a long, 'touching and very happy' letter, expressing his delight at being betrothed and his unbounded love for Alix. Fervently, he hoped that 'it may be for her happiness and that I may do my duty towards her.' At the same time, he wished that 'our happiness may throw a ray of light on your once so happy and now so desolate home. You may be sure that we shall both strive to be a comfort to you.'[3]

Bertie was despatched on a Mediterranean cruise with Vicky and Fritz, while Queen Victoria demanded the presence of her future daughter-in-law at

Osborne and Windsor. Prince and Princess Christian protested in vain at their daughter being sent to England 'on approval'. For Alix it was an unnerving prospect, but she coped admirably with the experience. Queen Victoria quickly warmed to this attractive, unsophisticated yet serious girl. Though not a great reader, Alix brought a small collection of books with her, all well-worn copies of religious works heavily underlined with her own comments in pencil. When the Queen asked why she always appeared at breakfast in a jacket, Alix explained that it was such an economical garment; any skirt could be worn with it, and she owned very few dresses as she had to make them herself.

Alix was soon accepted by the Queen's other children. She formed a strong bond with Affie, who had half-hoped that his elder brother might lose interest in her, so that he could marry her himself. He mischievously persuaded her that it was polite to ask Mama every afternoon if she had enjoyed her forty winks.

As much as the Queen admired her, she still informed Alix that she must put her country and family behind her, and not attempt to influence her husband in any political questions that might arise.

Fêted enthusiastically by the people of Copenhagen, Princess Alexandra left her old home at the end of February 1863. She crossed the North Sea and sailed up the Thames on board the royal yacht *Victoria & Albert*, receiving the Mayor of Margate, his deputation and his address of welcome on a scroll with becoming dignity. After their backs were turned, she was seen to hit her brother Prince William with it, both laughing helplessly at the solemnity of the occasion. Yet despite her youthful high spirits, she was astonished by the thousands of people who welcomed her as the yacht drew alongside the pier at Gravesend. When the Prince of Wales stepped onto the deck to give her a hearty embrace, the crowds applauded ecstatically.

Early on the morning of 10 March, Queen Victoria took the bride and groom to the mausoleum at Frogmore where her husband's remains had been interred three months previously. They stood before the tomb as she joined their hands together, informing them solemnly that '*He* gives you his blessing.'

Still in deepest mourning, her black dress relieved only by the Garter star and blue ribbon, the Queen attended the wedding in St George's Chapel more as an observer than a participant, watching from the Royal Closet above the chancel. Vicky had spoken excitedly of her delight at the ceremony, only to be chided by her mother who asked how she could possibly rejoice, 'when at every step you will miss that blessed guardian angel?' Ladies of the royal family and household were instructed to wear half-mourning of white, grey, mauve or purple, but the other guests were permitted to wear such colour and jewellery as they wished. Although Duke Ernest of Saxe-Coburg Gotha, the Prince Consort's elder brother, had initially opposed the match and described it as a 'thunderclap for Germany,' he entered graciously into the spirit of the occasion, sharing with Fritz their duty of supporting the groom.

As for the latter, in his general's uniform with the mantle and decorations of the Garter, he was noticeably pale and nervous. The bride wore a dress of white satin trimmed with Honiton lace and orange blossom. Their responses to the Archbishop of Canterbury were so muted that they could only be heard by those

The Prince and Princess of Wales on their wedding day, photographed by Mayall, 10 March 1863. The Prince wore the Mantle of the Garter over a general's uniform; and the Princess's dress was of white satin and Honiton lace with festoons of orange blossom

close to them. Nonetheless, Lord Clarendon remarked that the Prince 'looked very like a gentleman and more considerable than he is wont to do.' To Charles Dickens, the bride appeared as 'not simply a timid shrinking girl, but one with character distinctive of her own, prepared to act a part greatly.'[4]

The couple spent a week's honeymoon at Osborne, moving into their London residence, Marlborough House, on their return to the mainland. Easter was spent at their Norfolk estate, Sandringham, and in the spring both threw themselves wholeheartedly into society life. The Prince of Wales made his first public speech on 2 May at the Royal Academy of Arts annual banquet, and his wife held her first drawing-room at St James's Palace a fortnight later. On 7 June they paid a state visit to the City of London, and the Freedom of the City was conferred on the Prince. After a banquet and ball, the Princess opened the dancing with the Lord Mayor. 'Her manner,' commented *The Spectator*, 'so English in other respects, was un-Englishly cordial.'

For society, this new era had dawned not a moment too soon. With his marriage to Queen Victoria, Prince Albert had brought a staid influence to bear on social events at which royalty was present. Since his death, and his widow's protracted mourning, these had virtually ceased. Now this Prince and Princess who looked, in Disraeli's elegant words, 'like a couple in a fairy-tale,' brought back a long-departed *joie de vivre*.

Queen Victoria's gratitude for this favourable effect 'his sweet wife' had had on her son and heir was shortlived. She was accurate in her judgement that Alix 'quite understands Bertie and shows plenty of character,' even though she was certainly not clever. By June, she was complaining that they would both 'soon be

The Prince and Princess of Wales, from a print by Knight produced for general sale to the public, commemorating their engagement and marriage

nothing but two puppets running about for show all day and night.' Already she feared that the Princess's health was not up to the demands that her position and her husband were making of her. She was beginning to look sallow, overtired, and – most serious of all – at drawing rooms, people noticed that she seemed hard of hearing. She had inherited from her mother a tendency to deafness, which was to increase with each ensuing illness and eventually become total.

The Prince and Princess of Wales were giving the monarchy a higher profile that proved popular with London society. The Prince Consort's earnestness of purpose and his widow's seclusion had been ill-received in many quarters, and Queen Victoria could not but be jealous of her son's and daughter-in-law's success in an area where she and her husband had failed. Yet she was seriously concerned for their health. Though Bertie insisted that he was anxious to take care of his wife, his mother deplored their 'going out every night till she will become a skeleton, and hopes there cannot be!'[5]

By mid-summer, Alix was expecting a child. Her marriage and impending motherhood were not the only dramatic events for the Danish royal family that year. In June her second brother William was elected King of the Hellenes, taking the style of King George I, and in November their father succeeded to the throne of Denmark as King Christian IX. He immediately laid claim to the Duchies of Schleswig and Holstein, while Duke Frederick of Augustenburg, son of Queen Victoria's half-sister Feodora and a friend of Fritz from college days, proclaimed himself head of their government on King Frederick's death. In this he was supported by Queen Victoria, Vicky, and Fritz.

'The duchies belong to Papa,' Alix declared defiantly, and Bertie sided wholeheartedly with her. Family harmony at Windsor was shattered when Vicky, Fritz and Feodora (who were all staying in England at the time) joined them. Alix was five months pregnant, and she revealed a steely side to her character which nobody had yet seen. Goaded almost beyond endurance by quarrels, Queen Victoria took her uncle King Leopold's advice and forbade any further mention of Schleswig and Holstein in her presence.

Alix expected her child to be born in March or April 1864, and as there was still much decorating to be done at Sandringham, she and Bertie spent Christmas at Frogmore House in Windsor Park, the former home of the Duchess of Kent. There was a severe frost, which made for excellent skating on Frogmore Lake. Alix enjoyed skating herself, but as her condition made participation inadvisable she had to content herself with watching her husband and their friends from the comfort of a sledge-chair on the ice each afternoon.

On 8 January, although she had been suffering some twinges of pain, she was determined not to be left indoors. The party returned to the house at dusk. Only then did her lady-in-waiting Lady Macclesfield, herself the mother of thirteen children, realize that the time had almost come. Nothing was ready, so she had to go to the local draper for some flannel.

Bertie did all he could do encourage and comfort his wife, and at nine o'clock that evening she gave birth to a son. Despite weighing only three and a half pounds, he appeared to be strong and well.

Sandringham House at the time of its purchase by the Prince of Wales, 1862

GRANDCHILDREN OF THE QUEEN 1864–1901

1 The Wales Nursery

When the baby prince was three days old, Queen Victoria reported to Vicky that he was 'quite healthy and very thriving. It [*sic*] has a very pretty, well-shaped, round head, with very good features, a nice forehead, a very marked nose, beautiful little ears and pretty little hands.'[1] As he was second in line to the throne, she maintained that the only names possible for him were Albert Victor, after herself and her late husband. Much as the Prince and Princess of Wales respected her decision, they felt that the choice should have come from them and not from her. Bertie was sufficiently moved to complain that six-year-old Beatrice had told Lady Macclesfield that Mama had settled the issue herself.

The first few weeks of Prince Albert Victor's life, or 'Prince All-but-on-the-ice', as he was irreverently dubbed by contemporary wags, were overshadowed by the threat of war in Europe. There was little doubt that his mother's anxiety concerning the plight of Denmark had contributed to his early arrival.

On 16 January, Prussia sent the Danish government an ultimatum to evacuate the duchies within twenty-four hours. The latter refused, and on 1 February a combined Prusso-Austrian force crossed the frontier into Schleswig. On behalf of the British government, Foreign Secretary, Lord John Russell announced that there was no question of going to war single-handed. Much to the Princess of Wales's distress and her husband's anger, 'thinking everyone wishes to crush Denmark,' the great powers were not prepared to intervene in order to rescue King Christian and his domains from inevitable defeat. Within a few weeks, Schleswig was in German hands, apart from the stronghold of Dybboel.

Denmark's waning fortunes overshadowed the christening of Prince Albert Victor Christian Edward at Windsor in March. He roared throughout the ceremony, his mother looked thin and unhappy, and at luncheon afterwards the Prussian Ambassador, Count Bernstorff, declined to drink King Christian's health. Though the war grieved Queen Victoria, her German sympathies were not dented one iota by Alix's unhappiness. She could only remark, how terrible it was 'to have the poor boy [Bertie] on the wrong side.' If only he had married 'a

The Prince and Princess of Wales with Prince Albert Victor, photographed by Vernon Heath, 1864

good German and not a Dane.'[2] She was honest enough to admit that her daughter-in-law's parentage had been a barrier to their intimacy, though as time would prove, this was only temporary.

None of this reflected on the infant prince. Despite her oft-expressed aversion to the frog-like physical characteristics of tiny babies, at the age of ten weeks he was pronounced by his grandmother to have a pretty little mouth, 'a well-shaped head and a great look of dear Alix . . . a very pretty, but rather a fidgety baby.'[3]

In July 1864 Denmark was forced to relinquish her sovereignty over the Duchies of Schleswig and Holstein. King Christian IX had reigned for a mere eight months before losing more than half his kingdom. This humiliation made Alix more determined than ever to return to her parents for a holiday, something she had longed to do anyway in order to show off her son, and to introduce her husband to Copenhagen. Fearing political repercussions, Queen Victoria wanted to forbid the visit, but her ministers raised no objection. In the end, she gave her permission as long as her son and daughter-in-law promised to remain incognito, did not allow political discussions in their presence, included Germany in their itinerary before returning, and sent the baby prince back to Balmoral on their departure from Denmark.

13

This last condition was not made out of mere possessiveness, for the queen had her doubts that Bertie and Alix were fully aware of their parental responsibilities. On seeing the baby at Abergeldie that September, she was shocked at his frail appearance.

When he met his daughter's family at Elsinore, King Christian declared that it was the happiest day he had known since his country was invaded. The Princess of Wales was equally delighted to be 'at home again,' though her husband was soon bored. He found their rooms at the Danish palaces uncomfortable, the food monotonous, and the evenings of small-talk and games of loo unbearably tedious. When a member of the household dared to tell him in exasperation that there was nowhere on earth more boring than Fredensborg Palace, the Prince of Wales pretended to be furious. 'How dare you say that!' he retorted, adding after a pause, 'I remember, of course, you have not been to Bernstorff yet.'

After frequent requests for his return, Eddy was sent home on the royal yacht in the care of Lord and Lady Spencer. It was with a heavy heart that Bertie allowed his infant son back across the North Sea, writing to Queen Victoria that Alix hated being compelled for the first time to part with 'her little treasure' against the doctors' advice.

Queen Victoria continued to watch her grandson's progress with interest and affection – all the more so as her other grandchildren, the sons and daughters of Vicky, now Crown Princess of Prussia, and Alice, married to Prince Louis of Hesse, lived in Germany and she saw them only rarely. To Vicky, she wrote (27 January 1865) that Eddy was:

> a perfect bijou – very fairy-like but quite healthy, very wise-looking and good. He lets all the family carry him and play with him – and Alix likes him to be accustomed to it. He is very placid, almost melancholy-looking sometimes. What is not pretty is his very narrow chest (rather pigeon-breasted) which is like Alix's build and that of her family and unlike you all with your fine chests. He is decisively like her; everyone is struck by it.[4]

By now it was evident that there would soon be a second child in the Wales's nursery. Like his elder brother, he was impatient to make his entrance into the world. On 2 June 1865 the Princess of Wales appeared at an afternoon concert, but at the last moment she excused herself from attending a dinner-party at Marlborough House that evening. At one-thirty next morning she gave birth to a second son. Queen Victoria was roused from her sleep a couple of hours later with the arrival of two telegrams from Bertie; one to say that Alix had been taken ill, and one to announce the baby's arrival.

The Queen was most put out at being unable to attend her daughter-in-law's second confinement as well as the first. 'It seems that it is not to be that I am to be present at the birth of your children, which I am very sorry for,'[5] she complained to her son. Queen Louise struck a happier note with her message of congratulation, though in writing to her son-in-law she could not omit her own element of feminine solidarity: 'How proud you must be, two boys, don't you grow more attached to Alix at every present thus brought to you in pain and anguish?'[6]

Remembering their experiences with the eldest child, Bertie and Alix had chosen names for their second son well in advance. Writing to his mother on 11 June, the Prince of Wales said that they had agreed for some time that if they had another boy he should be called George, 'as we like the name and it is an English one.' The second name, he added, would be Frederick, as used regularly by his wife's Danish forebears.

To Queen Victoria, however, this was not good enough; 'George only came in with the Hanoverian family.' (She had conveniently overlooked the name of England's patron saint.) Though she had hoped for 'some fine old name,' she approved half-heartedly of Frederick, and hoped they would call him so; 'however, if the dear child grows up good and wise, I shall not mind what his name is.'[7]

George Frederick Ernest Albert was christened at St George's chapel, Windsor, on 7 July. Thereafter, within the family, he was always known as 'Georgy'.

The pride in which Bertie and Alix held their two elder children was tempered somewhat by the shadow of the Queen, and her insistence on a major say in their upbringing. As early as 11 March 1864 she had made plain, to King Leopold, that 'Bertie should understand what a strong right I have to interfere in the management of the child or children; that he should never do anything about

The Prince and Princess of Wales with Prince George (in her arms) and Prince Albert Victor, 1865

15

the child without consulting me.'[8] The Prince knew that it was useless to protest, but Alix resented her mother-in-law's domination. When Georgy was a few months old, Queen Victoria lamented that the two women could never be as intimate as she had hoped; 'she shows me no confidence whatsoever especially about the children.' Such expressions were invariably exaggerated, as Vicky, usually the recipient of her mother's complaints, always recognized.

Though by now widowed for four years, the Queen was still jealous of her son's married bliss, and of his and Alix's popularity in society; the latter, she insisted, was making her 'haughty and frivolous'. It was clear that Eddy and Georgy would not receive an upbringing even remotely like that to which Bertie and his brothers and sisters had been subjected under the eagle eye of Prince Albert and Stockmar. Indeed, this was the last thing that the Prince of Wales wanted. He had vowed that no children of his would be condemned to a Stockmar regime.

Lord Melbourne's warning to Queen Victoria on behalf of her eldest son not to be 'over solicitous about education,' as 'it may mould and direct the character, but it rarely alters it,' went unheeded at the time. Yet the son whom the late Prime Minister had had in mind endorsed such philosophy without hesitation. His childhood memories, unlike those of the Princess of Wales in her comparatively humble yet carefree parents' home at Copenhagen, were not the happiest. It was no wonder that they resented Mama's watchful eye and continual fault-finding. Up to the day of her death both were always in awe of Queen Victoria. Bertie readily, if reluctantly, appreciated that as sovereign she had a 'right to interfere' in the formative years of two children so close to the throne, but Alix did not. This undoubtedly explained her occasional 'want of softness and warmth' which her mother-in-law deprecated at the time.

Such criticisms were generally made in moods of mild exasperation which soon passed. Yet it was in no small measure due to Vicky, the inveterate family peacemaker, that resentment was ironed out before it had time to take root. Could Mama not make an effort to see more of Alix on her own, she suggested in her letters from Germany; it would please her and Bertie so much, for she was so devoted to her, even though 'she knows and fears she bores you.' The advice was taken at once, and Queen Victoria invited Alix to Windsor for luncheon, followed by a walk and drive alone. 'Nothing could be nicer or dearer than she is,' she wrote to Vicky afterwards.

By now Alix was pregnant for the third time; her condition prevented her from accompanying Bertie to St Petersburg for the wedding of her sister Dagmar to the Tsarevich, later Tsar Alexander III of Russia. It would have been better for his reputation and popularity if she had been able to go too, for reports soon reached English society, and his family, that he was paying too much attention to Russian beauties while away.

Soon after Christmas, it was evident that the Princess was unwell. On 15 February 1867 she complained of severe pains and a chill, but the Prince was sufficiently unperturbed to carry out his engagements at Windsor, a steeplechase and dinner. While he was away, Alix stayed in bed at Marlborough House where the doctors diagnosed rheumatic fever. Only after three telegrams, each one worded with more urgency than the last, did her ever-socializing husband return. Over the next five days she suffered acute pain in her leg and hip. The doctors thought it too risky to administer chloroform during her confinement, which ended on 20 February with the birth of a first daughter, Louise.

Though Alix had withstood the confinement better than expected, neither her rheumatic pains nor fever showed any signs of abatement. All the doctors feared that her condition could soon become serious. Queen Victoria was cheered by her son's letters that Alix had been unwell, but was bearing up bravely. When she arrived at Marlborough House a week after the baby's birth, she was horrified to see just how ill Alix was. Her solicitude and that of Lady Macclesfield were her constant comfort; her husband's perpetual absence was a sore trial.

How much the orders of Lady Macclesfield and the doctors, who banished him from the sickroom, were responsible, can only be guessed at, but his apparent reluctance to cut down on social engagements did nothing to create the impression of a devoted or gravely worried husband. One night Alix asked not to be given her sleeping draught, for Bertie had promised to be home by one o'clock and she wanted to be awake – albeit in great pain – on his return. When he came back two hours late, he received a scolding which he did not forget in a hurry. His thoughtlessness was condemned by the Queen and her cousin the Duke of Cambridge, and the public were angry that he should be out amusing himself so much at sporting events, dinners and theatres, while his popular and beautiful young wife lay at home in agony.

In his defence, however, it must be said that he was not wanted perpetually hanging around in the sickroom and getting in everyone's way. Although he did have his desk moved in beside her bed, so that he could attend to his correspondence and share her company at the same time, he realized that she was in good hands and there was little else he could do. Restless by nature, he was easily bored, and time hung heavily on his hands.

It was late April before Alix could be wheeled to the window for a sight of the spring weather. On 10 May the infant princess was christened Louise Victoria Alexandra Dagmar, though her mother was still in a wheelchair, one leg completely stiff and prone to swelling. The rheumatic fever left her permanently lame, a depressing prospect for a young woman whose leisure activities eagerly embraced dancing, riding and skating, rather than artistic or intellectual interests. Worse, it exacerbated her deafness and thus cut her off increasingly from her husband's ever widening circle of friends. As her hearing worsened, so she relied more and more on a small group of close confidantes, her children, and animals.

It was inevitable that the Princess of Wales and her energetic, undomestically-minded husband would gradually drift apart. While Prince George was still a baby, Queen Victoria had noted sadly that Alix's unpunctuality and lack of organization were not calculated to make her husband's home life comfortable. Both, she observed, regularly breakfasted alone; his crowded schedule of engagements made no allowance for a wife who was rarely out of her room before eleven in the morning. All the same, despite his infidelities, indiscreet attention to ladies in St Petersburg, and associations with 'some of the female

Paris notorieties' (he departed for the opening of the Paris International Exhibition a few hours after Louise's christening), Alix had the consolation of knowing that 'he always loved me the best.'

Louise was a sickly infant, and in view of Alix's prolonged convalescence, a respite from childbearing would have been beneficial. Yet by Christmas she was expecting again. On 6 July 1868 she gave birth to a second daughter, named Victoria Alexandra Olga Marie. Queen Victoria greeted the arrival of this 'mere little red lump' with ill-concealed boredom. She told Vicky that this seventh granddaughter and fourteenth grandchild 'becomes a very uninteresting thing – for it seems to me to go on like the rabbits in Windsor Park!'[9] She had conveniently overlooked her even more prolific motherhood, having brought four children into the world within her first four-and-a-half years of marriage.

Alix's surgeon-in-attendance, Sir James Paget, suggested that his patient's rheumatism might have been partially caused by dampness at Sandringham, and Lady Macclesfield remarked on how unbearably cold it was in Norfolk during the spring. In any case, Bertie had realized that considerable alterations to the house would be needed. Shortly before Princess Victoria was born, he was advised that the premises would have to be demolished and rebuilt. In the meantime, the family would spend winter on a tour of Egypt, stopping *en route* in Denmark, Berlin and Vienna.

The Princess of Wales was thrilled to have a chance of showing her children off again to her family. Louise, named after her Danish grandmother, would accompany them for the first time, although baby Victoria was too young to travel overseas; and in this Alix's decision was supported by Paget. She asked Queen Victoria for permission to take the three children, and back came a reply that the boys might go, but it was extremely selfish of the Princess to risk the health if not life of her elder daughter, to gratify her own foolish whim. The young mother burst into tears at this peremptory missive, and the Prince of Wales wrote Queen Victoria a blunt yet tactful letter himself. He pointed out that Alix had tried to meet her wishes in every way on so many occasions, and was thus hurt and pained at accusations of selfishness and being unreasonable. As Vicky and Alice came to England so regularly with their children, which were just as strong as his, it seemed rather inconsistent 'not to accord to the one what is accorded to the others.' He won his argument, and Queen Victoria had to content herself with grumbling about the composition of their suite.

Accordingly they left for Paris in mid-November, and afterwards spent six weeks with King Christian and Queen Louise. After a cheerful family Christmas, on 15 January 1869 they saw their children off from Hamburg to England on the royal yacht. Though pleased to welcome them home, Queen Victoria wrote to express her concern that no governess had been appointed to discipline them. While the Prince of Wales agreed to consider the question of a governess on their return, he took issue with her strictures about discipline. If children of that age were too severely treated, he answered, 'they get shy, and only fear those whom they ought to love; and we should naturally wish them to be very fond of you, as they were in Denmark of dear Alix's parents.'[10]

Bertie and Alix returned to London in May, full of the wonders of Egypt and the Orient. That autumn they travelled to Wildbad for further treatment of

Alix's rheumatic knee, then to Balmoral before returning south for the winter. On 26 November, at Marlborough House, a third daughter was born, and named Maud.

As a result of Queen Victoria's seclusion and her son's profligate behaviour, by the time of Maud's birth the monarchy in England was not popular. Gladstone expressed the prevailing mood; 'The Queen is invisible and the Prince not respected.' The Princess of Wales was the only member of the family held in high esteem. In February 1870 the Prince of Wales was subpoenaed as a witness in a divorce case between Sir Charles and Lady Mordaunt, who had confessed to committing adultery with him and several others. Insanity was proved against Lady Mordaunt, and the prince emphatically answered in court that there had never been 'any improper familiarity or criminal act' between them; his assertions of innocence were firmly supported by his mother and wife. Nevertheless, it only served to diminish further the throne's standing at large, and Queen Victoria deprecated her son and daughter-in-law for leading far too frivolous a life, and being too close to 'a small set of not the best and wisest people who consider being fast the right thing.'[11] When Alix appeared in a box at the theatre she was loudly cheered, but when her husband joined her, cheers turned to hisses.

Some of the Princess of Wales's own Danish relations had not been noted for their fidelity. All the same, it had been made apparent to all and sundry that the Prince of Wales was not the most faithful of husbands. He had been indiscreet enough to write rather affectionately and call in person on an attractive young married woman, and he had done little to curtail his social engagements during his wife's serious illness.

The Franco-Prussian war and overthrow of Emperor Napoleon III only intensified growing demands for a republic in Britain, and it is tempting to wonder how much more support British republicanism would have commanded if the Princess of Wales had not been so popular. By autumn 1870 she was pregnant again, and in contrast to previous occasions she tired quickly and became easily depressed. Yet she insisted on leading a normal life as far as possible, taking her place by her husband's side as much as she could – perhaps to keep a closer eye on him.

On 6 April 1871 she gave birth to a third son. As in her other confinements, the birth was easy, but the baby arrived before time, and it was evident to the local doctor in attendance that he was not well. Hastily christened Alexander John Charles Albert, this sixth Wales infant lived for only twenty-four hours.

Both parents were bitterly distressed at this family tragedy. Alix's grief surprised nobody, but the household were moved by the reaction of her husband, with tears rolling down his cheeks as he put the child's body into the coffin himself, carefully arranged the white satin pall and piles of white flowers. She was not thought well enough to attend the funeral, and she watched the unhappy little procession to Sandringham church from her bedroom window, Bertie hand in hand with their two elder sons in grey kilts, crepe scarves and black gloves.

Not even the Princess of Wales's popularity could save the family from vicious attacks by the radical press, who did not stop at using the Crown's unpopularity as an excuse for castigating court mourning for this prince as 'sickening mummery at Sandringham'. *Reynolds' Newspaper* announced Alexander John's birth under the heading 'Another Inauspicious Event', and his death the next day as 'A Happy Release'. The paper took great satisfaction, it remarked, in informing its readers that the infant prince died shortly after its birth, 'thus relieving the working classes of England from having to support hereafter another addition to the long roll of State beggars they at present maintain.'[12]

The Princess of Wales reproached herself as being responsible for her son's death because she had not taken care of herself properly during the preceding months. While Queen Victoria was tempted to agree, she was tactful enough to take the Prince of Wales to task for encouraging his wife to neglect her health. He promised to take better care of her in future, but pointed out that she was 'naturally very active in mind and body,' so a sedentary life would not suit her.

This sad experience of childbirth was to be Alix's last. There would be no more infants in the Wales's nursery.

Before he ascended the throne, it was suggested from time to time that some of the sons and daughters of the Prince of Wales's closest friends bore a remarkable resemblance to His Royal Highness. Sometimes this was mere coincidence, occasionally not. For the most part he conducted his liaisons with the greatest discretion, and it is unlikely that more than a small amount of documentary evidence indicating illegitimate children exists.

One such case is that of Lady Susan Pelham-Clinton, who was one of the Princess Royal's bridesmaids in 1858 and who married the alcoholic Lord Adolphus Vane-Tempest in 1860. Four years later he died after a violent struggle with his keepers. In due course the widowed Lady Susan became a close friend of the Prince of Wales, and in September 1871 one of her confidantes wrote to advise him that 'the crisis' was due within two or three months. Nothing is known of the child born of this union, and Lady Susan, who died in 1875, carried the secret with her to the grave.[13]

The art collector Edward James maintained that his mother Evie, born around 1871, was the Prince's illegitimate daughter. She left her son a bundle of over a hundred letters, mostly from King Edward VII, with a few from King George V, and he said they made it obvious that the former knew he was her father; 'evidently he had had a tumble in the heather with her mother in Aberdeenshire and she was the result of it.'[14] Although the letters apparently confirmed this ancestry, the first time he heard of it was when his cousins showed him a walking stick, inscribed with a penknife by the Prince of Wales to Sir Charles Forbes (believed by everyone to be Evie's father) 'in token and appreciation of his understanding.' This, he explained, was the Prince's way of thanking his friend for helping to keep the matter secret. He advanced his claim further by describing how he once took a photograph of his mother and adding a beard to her face, stated that the disfigured likeness 'looked the image of George V.'[15]

By the time Edward James went to Eton in the early 1920s, the story had somehow leaked out. He was humiliated by the housemaster, a dour Presbyterian, who lectured his young charges on religious instruction each Sunday, inveighing against immorality at the court of the late King Edward VII and looking coldly at James as he spoke, while the other boys nudged each other and giggled.

Such is the evidence that James used to proclaim his descent from royalty on the wrong side of the blanket. His credibility, however, is tempered by a readiness to believe in rumour. He boasted of having a certain amount of Jewish blood, as the Prince Consort was the illegitimate son of a Jewish banker. This refers to the story that Prince Albert had been born of a liaison between his mother and her lover, the Jewish court chamberlain, Baron von Meyern. History's dubious authority for this information came from the memoirs of Caroline Bauer, a German actress who had been the mistress of King Leopold I of the Belgians before his elevation to the new kingdom's throne. Callously rejected by her princely lover after a liaison lasting several years, she had no reason to remember the Coburgs with anything other than hatred, and her allegations about the parentage of Prince Albert were without foundation. The truth of Edward James's claims are likewise open to doubt.

Bearing in mind the number of mistresses whose company Bertie enjoyed during his long years as heir to the throne, it would have been surprising if there were never any illegitimate children. The annals of nineteenth-century royalty in Britain are strewn plentifully with rumours of children born out of wedlock. Only one, Jeanne-Marie Langtry, born on 8 March 1881 to Lillie Langtry and Prince Louis of Battenberg (by then conveniently on naval service several hundred miles away), appears to have been authenticated. If malicious gossip and vivid imaginations are to be believed, Queen Victoria had a child by John Brown in widowhood, and her childless daughter Louise, Duchess of Argyll and Marchioness of Lorne, had offspring by Louis's younger brother Henry, by then married to her sister Beatrice, and also by a canon of Windsor. Fantasy is often more exciting than fact, but it requires more than a Hanoverian chin and protuberant eyes to prove that children born between 1860 and 1890 to female friends of the Prince of Wales were grandchildren of Queen Victoria.

2 'Such Ill-bred, Ill-trained Children'

As parents, the Prince and Princess of Wales were passionately fond of their children. Bertie was not domesticated by nature; his love of high society and rich, amusing friends made such a contrast, Queen Victoria noted sadly, to the home-loving Prince Albert, but he did adore his sons and daughters.

The upbringing of all five was typical of that for any upper-class family of the time. They enjoyed a happy, comparatively carefree country childhood spent mostly on the Sandringham estate, riding ponies and looking after pets, learning the names of birds and wild flowers in the Norfolk countryside. Their routine was only broken when the Prince of Wales's household moved from Marlborough House to Osborne Cottage immediately after the London season and before the Cowes Regatta. In mid-August they moved to Abergeldie on the Balmoral estate, before returning to Norfolk in the autumn.

Eddy and Georgy were always devoted to each other, though the difference in their characters was soon discernible. Although seventeen months younger, Georgy was stronger and more high-spirited. He was amusing, inquisitive and hot-tempered, took the initiative in pranks, and showed himself a born leader in the nursery. Although shy, he had an easy-going manner and was naturally neat and orderly. Close observers thought that he was very like his father at a similar age.

Eddy took more after his mother. He was taller, more diffident, lethargic, and lacked his brother's healthy complexion. Not surprisingly he was his mother's favourite, and she seemed to regard him with greater sympathy than did his father, who tended to be impatient with his apathetic manner – an impatience which became more evident as this elder son approached maturity.

Alix was often seen driving around London in a splendid barouche, drawn by bay horses, a son on either side. When friends asked her why she perched on such an uncomfortable seat while allowing the Princes a far more favourable position, she answered good-humouredly that the occasion demanded a buffer state between the warring elements. Personal chastisement had no place in her book. Twenty years earlier, Queen Victoria had dealt with any tendency to a display of 'warring elements' from her sons with a sharp clip on the ear in public.

Observations of the children's early years by outsiders are few and far between. Among those which have been handed down are those of Annie de Rothschild at Holkham Hall in December 1869. 'The Royal babies,' she wrote to her mother, were 'very nice little boys, rather wild, but not showing signs of becoming too much spoiled; they make very ludicrous attempts at being dignified.' Another day, Annie related, she had:

> a fearful romp with the little Princes, we taught them blind man's buff, and ran races with them. The eldest is a beautiful child, the image of the Princess, the second has a jolly little face and looks the cleverest. The Princess said to me: 'They are dreadfully wild, but I was just as bad.[1]

About four months later, shortly before Georgy's fifth birthday, he was playing with a long-standing royal servant, Mr Collins, and kicked him on the shin. Mr Collins ordered him sharply not to do that again. The Prince immediately did so out of sheer defiance, and was rewarded with a good spanking. He went bright red but did not cry; but the lesson was learned. In future Mr Collins, evidently a man of his word, was always obeyed.

The children visited their grandparents regularly. Queen Victoria's attitude to them was one of indulgence tempered with exasperation. One day, they were 'very amusing' or 'very merry in my room'; another time, she might call them 'such ill-bred, ill-trained children I can't fancy them at all.'[2] Princess Victoria in particular she found extraordinarily naughty and disobedient. The Princesses seem to have attracted less attention than their brothers, though Lady Somerset described them as 'rampaging little girls', and unlike Queen Victoria, thought 'Toria' 'very sharp, merry and amusing.' The Queen thought Alix too lenient with her children and 'neglectful' where their education was concerned, but praised her for insisting on 'great simplicity and an absence of all pride.' In fact, this and the Princess of Wales's constant admonitions to Prince George not to quarrel with his brother were her guiding principles. In Denmark, 'Apapa' and 'Amama' (King Christian and Queen Louise) always spoilt them outrageously.

When Eddy was a fortnight old, Charles Fuller was engaged as his personal attendant, or 'nursery footman'. He served both young Princes throughout adolescence, and remained a regular correspondent with the family until his death in 1901. By the time the boys were aged seven and six respectively, plans were in hand for their regular education. Queen Victoria's influence was considerable, but the danger of Eddy being dominated by his more lively brother also played its part. The Prince of Wales was adamant that their tutor should be of a liberal nature, of a character that would encourage and instruct them without dampening their natural high spirits. His choice fell on the Revd John Neale Dalton, aged thirty-two and recently appointed curate to Canon Prothero, Rector of Whippingham, near Osborne.

Every detail of the Princes' education was discussed between the Prince of Wales and Dalton, who stayed with them for fourteen years. Both men agreed that the boys' childhood should at all costs be a happy one. No deference should be paid to their rank, and as far as possible they should work hard, receive plenty of encouragement, a generous measure of free time, and never be denied the companionship of their contemporaries.

Their regular timetable made provision for them to rise at 7 a.m., studying geography and English before breakfast. At 8 a.m. came a Bible or history lesson, followed by algebra or Euclid at 9 a.m. Next came an hour's break for

The Wales children, 1875. From left: Princess Louise; Princess Maud; Prince Albert Victor; Prince George; Princess Victoria

games, then French or Latin till the main meal at 2 p.m. More games or riding followed till tea, then English, music and preparation. Bedtime was at 8 p.m.

Dalton kept two large albums recording their daily progress and noting general points of conduct each week. While he did not shrink from criticism when it was merited, remarking on faults such as 'silly fretfulness of temper and general spirit of contradiction', or 'too fretful; and inclined to be lazy and silly this week', he inspired affection in his charges which seemed a world away from the remorseless pedantry of Baron Stockmar.

Later in life, King George V would remember fondly the point in the grounds around Sandringham where his tutor taught him and Eddy to shoot with bow and arrow, and show friends the path where he ran as he allowed the boys to shoot at him as the running deer.

As was to be expected, Dalton inculcated in them both the value and duty of daily prayer and Bible reading, something they had already learnt from their mother who had always read aloud to them from the scriptures from a very early age. His efforts to interest them in art and architecture were less successful. They had inherited the natural Hanoverian tendency to philistinism, rather than the late Prince Consort's pronounced sense of the aesthetic.

Queen Victoria naturally took a keen interest in the upbringing and education of these grandchildren in direct line of succession to the throne, and Dalton regularly reported to her. One such report, dated 31 January 1874, informed her that the Princes were:

both in the enjoyment of the most thorough good health and spirits, and also daily prosecute their studies with due diligence and attention. Their Royal Highnesses live a very regular and quiet life in the country here, and keep early hours both as to rising in the morning and retiring to rest at night. . . . The two little Princes ride on ponies for an hour each alternate morning in the week, and take a walk the other three days, in the afternoon also their Royal Highnesses take exercise on foot. As regards the studies, the writing, reading, and arithmetic are all progressing favourably; the music, spelling, English history, Latin, geography, and French all occupy a due share of their Royal Highnesses' attention, and the progress in English history, and geography is very marked. . . .[3]

To keep the children's home quiet, unpretentious and comfortable, while at the same time help to maintain it as an appropriate place of entertainment for the Prince of Wales's 'fast' society friends, would have been a daunting task for most princesses. Somehow his wife managed to achieve this. When the babies were small, she was content to don a flannel apron and bath them, then go downstairs resplendent in her evening clothes and jewellery to offer hospitality to Bertie's guests.

Those whom she liked particularly might be invited to a special treat – to see the infants in their nursery, or being bathed the following night. The dictum that 'children should be seen and not heard' went unnoticed in the Wales household. Guests were be astonished, if not a little shocked, by the manner in which these high-spirited children were encouraged to mix with them.

The closest playmates of the Wales children were their near-contemporaries the Tecks. Princess Mary Adelaide of Cambridge, who had been one of the first to canvass the claims of young Princess Alexandra to be Princess of Wales, had married Prince Francis of Teck in 1866. The Teck family, which by 1874 included four children, lived at White Lodge, Richmond, and when the Waleses were in residence at Marlborough House, both families saw each other regularly. Mary and Alix remained lifelong close friends, though the relationship between Mary and Bertie was an uneasy one. As the late King Leopold had put it kindly, Princess Mary Adelaide had 'grown out of compass', and the Prince of Wales (who was hardly thin himself at the best of times) could not resist making jokes at the expense of her vast girth. In addition, his boisterous love of playing practical jokes on his friends verged at times on the cruel, and this she could not abide.

Fortunately this antipathy between both adults was not reciprocated in the next generation, and the Wales children were devoted to their Aunt Mary. At Marlborough House and Sandringham she was always a welcome guest, and wrote to her family of watching the 'dear little trio' of Wales princesses riding their ponies to hounds for the first time, or in the nursery where 'Looloo, Victoria and sweet tiny Maudie' showed her their picture books, after which she assisted at their tea.

The eldest Teck child and only girl among them was Victoria Mary, known in the family as 'May' (but usually by the contemporary press as Princess Victoria of Teck, until her marriage), born three months after her cousin Louise. Her

The Princess of Wales with Prince Albert Victor and Prince George, 1876

brothers were Adolphus ('Dolly'), born in 1868, Francis ('Frank'), born in 1870, and Alexander ('Alge'), born in 1874. Within a few years, differences between both families would become marked, but before distinctions of education and rank supervened, all the children played together happily as equals. The boys loved to amuse themselves in the garden or on the lake, pushing wooden boats around, while their sisters played with battered, much handed-down dolls.

Eddy, it was noted by everyone within and outside the family, was always a melancholy, wistful-looking child. Whenever he smiled or laughed, there was ever something of the delicacy of his mother's manner rather than the heartiness of his father and brother; in his apathy, it was said that he 'never seemed to mind what he did or what happened to him.' The others soon developed a love of their father's practical jokes, although in their case it thankfully stopped short of stubbing out cigars on people's hands, or filling the pockets of maids' uniforms with custard. George's passion for animals, flora and fauna was matched by his sisters' devotion to collecting – animals made of bronze, china or stone, miniature vases, tiny photograph frames containing pictures of each other, watercolours of gardens, royal homes and palaces, portraits of friends, favourite dogs and horses, and the like. While the girls might revel in romping around indoors or sliding downstairs on tea trays, there was a strangely gentle side to them. According to Princess Marie of Edinburgh:

> The Wales cousins had a special way of adding 'dear little' or 'poor little' to everybody they talked about. They always, if I can so express it, spoke in a minor key, *en sourdine*. It gave a special quality to all talks with them, and gave me a strange sensation, as though life would have been very wonderful and everything very beautiful, if it had not been so sad.[4]

In the autumn of 1876, the Prince of Wales considered that it was time to put in motion the next stage of his sons' education. They must leave home, he had decided, for a period of undisturbed study and proper discipline. They were becoming undisciplined, regularly interrupting adults in conversation, playing havoc with games of croquet, and delighting in using bad language, picked up in the stables.

Even their indulgent father felt that enough was enough. Queen Victoria wished them to go to Wellington College, in which the Prince Consort had taken such a special interest. Dalton had to answer that, in his frank opinion, neither boy was educated well enough to make a good showing with his contemporaries at public school. Moreover, it had always been the intention that Prince George should adopt the Royal Navy as his profession. He had shown a strong interest in naval matters, as had his Uncle Alfred from an early age, and soon after his twelfth birthday he passed the entrance examination to Dartmouth without difficulty.

When Queen Victoria suggested that Eddy could attend Wellington College, she was told that he could not be separated from his brother. Prince Albert Victor, Dalton advised, required the stimulus of his brother's company to induce him to work at all. Difficult as his education was already, it would be even more so if his brother was to leave him; 'Prince George's lively presence is his mainstay and chief incentive to exertion; and to Prince George again, the presence of his elder brother is most wholesome as a check against that tendency to self-conceit which is apt at times to show itself in him.'[5] He urged, therefore, that both Princes should be entered as naval cadets on board HMS *Britannia* at Dartmouth, a scheme to which their grandmother again found objection. The very rough sort of life to which boys were exposed on board ship, she answered, was not calculated 'to make a refined and amiable Prince, who in after years (if God spares him) is to ascend the throne. It would give him a very one-sided view of life which is not desirable.'[6]

In spite of these objections, Bertie persuaded his mother to approve both Princes being sent to sea as 'an experiment'. Her understanding that Dalton would continue to supervise them was the main condition. In September 1877 Eddy and Dalton joined George, who had already enjoyed a trip abroad to Ostend, on board *Britannia* for a spell of two years. They had a cabin to themselves, but apart from having the watchful eye of Dalton on them, they were treated just as their fellow two hundred-odd cadets.

It was no surprise that George made friends more quickly among the other cadets than the reserved and diffident Eddy. He also took more of the knocks; as he would recall in later life, the other boys made a point of 'taking it out' on them on the grounds that it would be their only chance. There was an unwritten rule that any cadet challenged by another to fight had to accept, and as he was small for his age he was often made to challenge the larger ones. After coming off decidedly second best on several occasions, he suffered a heavy blow on the nose which made it bleed profusely. From then on, the doctor forbade him to fight again.

There was a tuck shop at Dartmouth, where the boys could buy sweets as long as none were brought back on board ship. The bigger ones regularly asked George to bring them back something, but in this respect as in other things, he was allowed no privileges. Everybody was searched on their return to ship, and he was always punished if caught out as well as having his sweets confiscated. One shilling a week pocket money never went far enough, especially as nobody ever paid him back, assuming that where royalty was involved there was always plenty more where that came from.

Notwithstanding these drawbacks, George, or 'Sprat' (a nickname derived from the diminutive of W(h)ales) made excellent progress in mathematics, and showed particular promise in the practical aspects of sailing and handling of boats. Dalton's first report to Queen Victoria from on board *Britannia*, dated 14 November 1877, informed her that the boys were in good health and very happy. At the same time, he noted that Eddy was not pulling his weight; there was no danger of 'the elder Prince working too hard, or overtaxing his powers, as Your Majesty seems to fear: in fact he might work harder than he does without any risk of detriment.' No less importantly, 'there is no fear of their home affections being in any way weakened by a residence here.'[7]

Holidays from *Britannia* were spent at Sandringham, with occasional visits to Osborne and Abergeldie. It was at Osborne that George began to keep a diary, the first entry being made on 30 July 1878, recording a game of croquet with his Aunt Beatrice and then watching a cricket match between the household and the royal yacht. That same diary ended on 12 August, a fortnight later, but he began a new one on 3 May 1880 and kept it faithfully, dictating to his mother, sisters or wife when seriously ill, until three days before his death fifty-five years later.

George seemed more at ease in the outside world than his brother and sisters. The rest, outsiders considered cynically, were a mutual admiration society in their own exclusive world at Sandringham. They believed that they had been poured direct from the salt cellar of God. Visits to Amama and Apapa in Copenhagen were relished, but not so the prospect of seeing Grandmama at home. On one occasion as they were getting ready with great reluctance to leave Sandringham for Balmoral, the girls were in floods of tears, while 'little Harry' declared at the last minute, 'I won't go!' stamping her foot. 'Little Harry' was the family nickname for the tomboy Princess Maud, named after her father's friend and their hero Admiral Harry Keppel. To their closest friends, Louise was 'Toots', Victoria 'Gawks', and Maud 'Snipey'.

Typical of their correspondence was a letter written by Louise to their father's private secretary, Francis Knollys, while he was in Ireland:

> . . . you must notice that Toots is practising her steps for the tiresome court ball, that Gawks is going to bed instead like Cinderella, and that Snipey is trying to console herself with a song instead of singing her hymns in Church as she ought to do. You little *humbug*! We believe you are enjoying yourself very much in Ireland, in spite of oranges and onions thrown at your head as we see by the papers. We are afraid you won't be at all glad to see us *country bumpkins* again, as we shall have nothing to talk about but cows and cowslips.[8]

At that time Louise was eighteen years of age.

Luckily their written communications with their grandmother showed a more mature turn of phrase. A thank-you letter from Louise after her eighteenth birthday refers not only to her party at Marlborough House, but also to war in the Sudan. Queen Victoria had been shattered by the news of General Gordon's murder at Khartoum a few days earlier, and an additional relief force had just been despatched to North Africa:

> This morning early we drove to the Wellington barracks, with dear Papa, Mama, brothers, and Aunt Louise, to see the Scots Guards off. Your kind telegram was read out to them, and they all cheered and seemed delighted. We then went to Waterloo Bridge and saw them start in different steamers. It was a very sad sight, many poor wives and friends cried. I hope that it will not be a very long campaign, but I fear the poor soldiers will have many hardships to bear.[9]

In 1879 the training of Eddy and George on board *Britannia* finished, and it was agreed by his grandmother, parents and tutor that George would ultimately make the navy his career and spend the next two or three years cruising around the world. Henry Frederick Stephenson, a nephew of Keppel, was appointed his equerry. After consulting Keppel and Stephenson, the Prince of Wales decided that his sons should go on a cruise together for eight months. Queen Victoria supported this plan, and she was indignant when W.H. Smith, First Lord of the Admiralty, expressed doubts as to the wisdom of risking the lives of both princes, second and third in succession to the throne, to the dangers of the sea. Smith's fears were shared by the majority of his cabinet colleagues, and Queen Victoria rebuked him indignantly in a letter to Disraeli. The Prince of Wales, she told him, was extremely annoyed at Smith raising in cabinet a matter which had been settled within the family.

Not the least of everyone's reasons for wanting the Princes to accompany each other was Eddy's persistent lethargy. Dalton had spoken to the Prince of Wales about Prince Albert Victor's 'abnormally dormant condition of his mental powers', and believed that a further spell of naval routine, with the added stimulus of sea air and foreign travel, might give him the challenge he needed.

On 17 September 1879 the warship HMS *Bacchante*, with both Princes and Dalton on board, set sail from Spithead for the Mediterranean. With a few interruptions, this four-thousand-ton corvette was to be their home for the next three years. Their first break came when she returned home in May 1880. The boys spent a few days at Marlborough House, then went on to the Duchy of Cornwall, before putting to sea again later that summer. George's first letter from on board ship to 'Motherdear', dated 19 September 1880, gives vent to his feelings of homesickness: 'I think this last parting was horrid and I think what you said was true that it made it much worse, us having to wait in the hall till dear Papa came, because none of us could speak we were all crying so much . . .'[10]

As in *Britannia*, the Princes were granted few privileges; they were expected to work just as hard as the other midshipmen. The bulk of ceremonial duties – visits to Government Houses, official tours and inspections – was allotted to the less robust Eddy, while George was expected to 'rough it' with the others. This he did with relish, throwing himself wholeheartedly into the rota of duty on deck for several hours at a time, or skilfully removing weevils from the ship's biscuit ration.

It was during this cruise, too, that he was given a chance to develop his shooting skills, play cricket, tennis and polo. In Australia, which his Uncle Affie had visited as a young man, there were such fascinating diversions as journeys into the Bush, and a descent down a gold mine. Whenever the squadron was in harbour, balls were arranged, and George was seen to be dancing energetically until three or four in the morning.

Despite his right royal rebuke, W.H. Smith's apprehensions were soon justified. In May 1881, between South Africa and Australia, *Bacchante* ran into a severe gale. Her rudder was wrenched sideways and almost broken off at the shaft, and for five days she lost touch with the other ships of her squadron. George's first letter to his mother after the episode, written shortly after they anchored in sight of the town of Albany, dismissed their adventure in a couple of lines. Yet neither Prince was oblivious to the dangers of life at sea. Only weeks before, seamen in the squadron had fallen to their deaths on two successive days as they sailed across the south Atlantic.

Although George eagerly joined in the rather barbaric sports of baiting and killing sharks and albatross, he showed a touching concern for wild creatures by taking on board a tame baby kangaroo from Australia. It became a great favourite in the mess at mealtimes. But his hopes of bringing it back as a present for his sisters at Sandringham were dashed when it fell overboard into the Pacific.

The Prince of Wales, c. 1880

The Princess of Wales, photographed by Downey, 1883

At home their progress was followed with great interest, though inevitably there were misunderstandings from time to time. After a cruise to the West Indies, a newspaper reported that the boys had been tattooed on the nose while ashore in Barbados. 'How could you have your impudent snout tattooed?' the Princess of Wales wrote to her son. Taken to task by the Prince, a harassed Dalton had to assure them that a journalist had greatly exaggerated matters. The boys had gone to see and sniff some lilies in botanical gardens at Barbados and emerged with pollen on their noses, but soon wiped it off.

These three years at sea were recorded in precise detail in Dalton's two-volume, 1,500-page *The Cruise of the Bacchante, 1879–1882*. The editor tried to reassure his readers that the massive work was based on the Princes' diaries and letters, and that he had resisted the temptation to improve upon the spontaneous vigour of the original text. Interspersed grandly with quotations from the Bible, Browning, Shakespeare and others, the *magnum opus* is obviously the work of its editor. Four pages dealt with a visit to an ostrich farm at Cape Town, observations on the birds' diet and aggressive habits, artificial incubation of eggs, and the last ostrich census. It may be doubted whether Eddy made any written comment on this event, while George laconically noted in his diary on 2 March 1881 that 'we then passed an ostridge farm, and saw a good many ostridges [sic].'[11]

The Princes emerged from their 'education' on board *Bacchante* in August

1882. Among those who greeted them on their return was Queen Victoria, who noted perceptively that Eddy had grown taller than his father, but was still 'very slight.' George, however, still had 'the same bright, merry face as ever.'[12] Later that week they were both confirmed in the church at Whippingham, after being 'examined' by Dalton in the presence of their parents and Archbishop Tait.

But the boys' educational standards were still a sore subject. By comparison with their public school contemporaries, they were woefully ill-educated. George had largely made up for this deficiency by a ready ability to apply himself to the practical aspects of seamanship and navigation, but his spelling, grammar and syntax were poor. Eddy had none of these compensating qualities. Unlike his brother he was as listless and vacant in conversation as with the written word. Sir Henry Ponsonby, the Queen's private secretary, noticed that in speech his sentences trailed off in mid-air, as if he had forgotten what he was going to say, or was not concentrating. He had shown a marked tendency to drink heavily, and to enjoy disappearing while in port to frequent the underworld with the wilder element of his fellow midshipmen.

Soon after returning from *Bacchante*, both were sent to Lausanne, Switzerland, for six months under the supervision of Dalton and Monsieur Hua to learn French. Their progress was almost non-existent. Even as a grown man, King

Princesses Louise (standing), Maud and Victoria, with their grandmother Queen Louise of Denmark, 1882. The boat is a studio 'prop'

George V's French was alleged to be 'atrocious', and he could not speak a word of German. Beside him his father, who (like the rest of Queen Victoria's children) was fluent in both tongues by the age of five or six, was a veritable scholar.

The girls' upbringing was likewise a liberal one tempered with occasional strictness. None of them was allowed to read a novel until the Princess of Wales had given formal permission, and plays had to be censored before they were allowed to watch. They were not permitted to form close relationships with any of the youngsters with whom they were casually brought into contact. Presents could not be given by or received from anybody outside the immediate family, and they had few dolls between them.

Despite their mother's detestation of Germans, a German governess, Fraulein Nowel, was employed and it was she who taught not only her young charges, but also the Princess of Wales herself, how to spin. In addition there was a French governess, Mademoiselle Vauthier, who remained a great favourite. After her marriage and departure to a large country house near Exeter, she maintained regular contact with them, and her house was one of the few where Maud was allowed to stay overnight unaccompanied by either of her parents. Canon Teignmouth Shore prepared them for confirmation, and when they were at Marlborough House, Alix always accompanied her sons and daughters to children's services at Berkeley Chapel, Mayfair. Afterwards they would drive off to the children's hospital at Great Ormond Street, to distribute gifts in person.

At Sandringham and Abergeldie, the Princesses were well known to the tenantry on their father's estates. They frequently accompanied their mother on visits to the cottagers, to enquire after or help the sick and infirm. Their education included the rudiments of housework, as well as making cheese and butter in the Sandringham dairy. Out of doors they enjoyed riding, fencing and golf, though where the latter was concerned, they doubtless took after 'Motherdear' in her enthusiasm for the game but blatant disregard of the rules. Maud became an accomplished linguist, almost alone among members of the royal family in being fairly fluent in Russian. She was also an enthusiastic chess player, and collected sets of chessmen. As a young woman she became a patron of the Ladies International Chess Congress.

Fortified by regular letters from his family and from Dalton, to whom had been allotted the less welcome task of supervising Eddy at Sandringham and later Cambridge, George quickly advanced up the ladder of his profession. While serving with the North American squadron he was promoted to sub-lieutenant, and then returned to England for further training at the Royal Naval College, Greenwich. After completing a course on HMS *Excellent*, a shore-based school at Portsmouth, he was appointed to serve in the battleship *Thunderer*, which formed part of the Mediterranean fleet.

The Prince of Wales was proud of his son's progress, which must have been some consolation for Eddy's lack of progress. *Thunderer* was commanded by Captain Henry Stephenson, and the Prince wrote to him (July 1886) to entreat him that 'in entrusting my son to your care I cannot place him in safer hands only

The Princess of Wales with her children, photographed by Downey, 1883. Children, from left: Princess Victoria; Prince George; Princess Louise; Prince Albert Victor; Princess Maud

Cycling party, 1883. Group includes, from left: Princess Victoria; Prince George; Prince Albert Victor; Princess Louise; the Princess of Wales; Princess Maud

don't *spoil* him *please*! Let him be treated like any other officer in the Ship and I hope he will become one of your smartest and most efficient Lieutenants.'[13]

The Mediterranean fleet was based on Malta, the social life of which island the Prince of Wales deplored; to him it was nothing but gossip, tittle-tattle and what he called 'coffee-housing'. George enjoyed little luxury during this time, but he did have the consolation of family company. His uncle the Duke of Edinburgh had been appointed Commander-in-Chief of the Mediterranean squadron earlier that year, and the Edinburghs did much to alleviate George's homesickness. He spent Christmas 1886 with them, and Affie encouraged his nephew's growing interest in philately. He also noticed with approval the relationship that seemed to be forming between George and his eldest daughter Marie, or 'Missy'. Although ten years separated them, the cousins became more than good friends. To her, he was a 'beloved chum', but on his side she meant rather more.

While George continued his naval service, preparations were made for Eddy to attend Cambridge University and then enter the army. One of his tutors, James Stephen, thought the former plan, a least, a waste of everyone's time as the Prince could derive little benefit from attending lectures; 'he hardly knows the meaning of the words *to read*.'[14] Ironically Stephen, a cousin of the novelist

Prince George and Prince Albert Victor, 1886

Virginia Woolf, was to develop a close relationship with Eddy. In view of Stephen's 'cultivated taste and a natural bent towards dainty and exquisite language,' and his subsequent history of mental derangement, his influence may not have been a good one on the impressionable prince almost twelve years his junior.

The tutors who descended on Sandringham to prepare Eddy for university did their best, and in due course Prince Albert Victor was enrolled as a student at Trinity College. Those who had deplored his lack of manliness soon learnt, if rumours were to be believed, that their words had taken on a hitherto-unsuspected meaning. In November 1883 *Punch* boldly published a cartoon of Eddy standing on a balcony with two undergraduates gazing up at him fondly. One was asking, 'Isn't it beautiful?' and the other replying, 'Too lovely to look at.'

Did the Prince of Wales ever appreciate how ironic it was that his father had also paid him a visit at Cambridge in desperation after hearing of his immoral behaviour? Perhaps the coincidence was lost on him, but in fury he took Eddy away from college.

Soon afterwards the young man was gazetted a lieutenant in the 10th Hussars. In one aspect he proved himself his father's son; he was obsessed with fine uniforms. Otherwise, as a soldier he was a failure. His great-uncle George, Duke of Cambridge and Commander-in-Chief of the army, found him charming and 'as nice a youth as could be,' but 'an inveterate and incurable dawdler, never ready, never there!' He could not master the theory and practice of arms, or even elementary drill movements on the parade ground. In turn he thought the commanding officers were 'lunatics', and resented the rigours of military discipline.

Under the circumstances, Queen Victoria's journal entry for his twenty-first birthday, 8 January 1885, seemed rather wide of the mark:

> It seems quite like a dream, and but so short a while ago, that I hurried across from Osborne to Windsor, or rather Frogmore, to find that poor little bit of a thing, wrapped in cotton! May God bless him and may he remain good and unspoilt, as he is![15]

The Duke of Cambridge blamed Eddy's shortcomings on 'stupid Dalton', who had taught him '*absolutely nothing!!*' One night at dinner, conversation turned to the Crimean war, and the Duke was astonished to find that Eddy knew nothing about the campaign. All the same, the Duke later discovered that all was not lost. The young Prince was not totally ineducable; he had his father's dislike of books, 'but learns all orally, and retains what he thus learns.' A drill instructor appointed to take charge of him at Aldershot found that with patience he could teach Prince Albert Victor a certain amount, so that 'under the circumstances his papers are infinitely better than he dared to expect.'[16]

Nonetheless it was a relief to all concerned that George made sterling progress in the navy. In May 1883 he was appointed to the corvette HMS *Canada* on the North America and West Indies station. On the eve of his eighteenth birthday, he was separated not only from his parents and sisters, but also from his brother and tutor. The Princess of Wales wrote consolingly, to remind him he could find reassurance in his Christian beliefs; 'Remain just as you are – but strive to get on in all that is good – and keep out of temptation as much as you can – don't let anyone lead you astray . . .'[17]

Prince George might yield to temptation, as did most other young sailors of the day, but he had sufficient strength of character not to let it become his undoing.

3 'The "One" Wish of Louise Herself'

It had been Prince George's good fortune to leave the Sandringham nest at a comparatively early age. Eddy too had his freedom – perhaps too much – at Cambridge and then with the army. No such privilege was accorded to their sisters.

The most perceptive account of 'their royal shynesses', and the effect of their mother's influence on them, is that of biographer Anita Leslie.[1] Alix never ceased to amaze her guests and courtiers with her unaffected girlishness and a sense of fun in which she could indulge without losing dignity. This remained an essential part of her character until old age.

It all had an unfortunate result where her daughters were concerned. They could not emulate her; she was always the centre of attention, and it is doubtful whether she wanted them to try and copy her any more than they did. According to contemporaries their facial features were striking, though it must be admitted that very few photographs of them in adolescence support this claim. Nobody ever told them they were attractive, for everyone was too busy praising the eternally lovely 'Motherdear'. Had they not had such a beautiful and elegant mother, they might not have gone down to posterity as the plain creatures of popular legend. It was Maud who inherited a measure of their Mama's striking looks (instead of their father's bulging eyes) and vivacity, and she had the most personality. Others would laugh at her cheery schoolboy slang; people were 'rotters', 'bounders', or 'funks'. Not surprisingly, she was always her father's favourite daughter, and perhaps he could foresee that she was the one most suited to play a rôle in public life as an adult.

Although well instructed in music, the Princesses' education was otherwise inadequate. Queen Victoria was not the only person to complain that her son and daughter-in-law hardly ever opened a book, let alone read one properly. It was regrettable that their daughters had little chance to develop sufficient intellectual stimulation, such as that afforded to their cousin May of Teck. By the time they reached adolescence the girls – even Maud – had a reputation for being 'stupid and shallow', stiff and tongue-tied in the presence of strangers. In retrospect, though, this seems unjustified. Girls were encouraged to 'speak out' in those days; May of Teck was similarly ill at ease and quiet outside her own circle, yet nobody ever dared to suggest that she was in the least stupid.

They maintained a regular correspondence with Queen Victoria, though their letters were inclined to be wooden and stilted. Typical of these is a note from Maud, written from Fredensborg (25 September 1885):

> We are enjoying ourselves very much here with all our dear relations and we go for long walks everywhere. The other day we went to Copenhagen and Mama laid the foundation stone of the English Church, the ceremony went off very well. The English ambassador made a very nice speech which was answered by dear Papa. We then went on board the 'Osborne' where there was a big lunch. In the evening we went to the opera and saw 'Mephistopheles' which was really beautiful.[2]

In similar vein is a letter from Louise, while staying at the Hotel Victoria, St Moritz (1 September 1887):

> This is a charming place, the weather has been beautiful and I am feeling better. We have been for several amusing expeditions and the country is lovely. One day we climbed up a mountain and all found some Edelweiss of which we were very proud, and I am sending you a little piece for luck, which I picked myself, and we have to go up a great height to get it. I trust that you are well and enjoying yourself in Scotland, and are having as fine weather as we are.[3]

The young Waleses academic shortcomings increased the gulf between them and their neighbouring cousins the Tecks. In adolescence, Princess May of Teck and her brothers were lively and intelligent, albeit inclined to be serious. They were the complete opposite of the Waleses, with whom they could find little in common. Perhaps Queen Victoria was justified in calling her son's children 'poor frail little fairies', and 'puny and pale'.[4] Her namesake Princess Victoria was the most frequently ill, and for the longest stretches of time, but the brothers and sisters also suffered from more than their fair share of 'fever and fatigue', neuralgia, abscesses in the teeth, cysts on the head and eyelids, colds and influenza. W.H. Smith had been right to shudder at the possibility of some disaster overtaking HMS *Bacchante*, for if the princess predeceased their father, 'Queen Louise' would have hardly cut an imposing figure as monarch.

Despite their indifferent health, the Wales Princesses continued to revel in boisterous fun and games. In particular May of Teck privately deprecated their pillow fights and similar unladylike pastimes, and they found her rather a prig. This, and her father's morganatic blood, made her the butt of endless teasing as she was deemed less royal than were they. 'Poor May, with her Wurttemberg hands!' Louise would mutter disdainfully to the end of her days. The Duchess of Teck's extravagance later necessitated a move to Florence for some years, for the family an ignominious self-imposed exile which added to May's lack of self-confidence as a young woman. Helping at a bazaar in Kew Gardens with her cousins one day, she sold a fan and the purchaser asked her to autograph it. She seemed unable to believe that such an honour should be asked of her. 'With pleasure,' she replied, blushing, 'but aren't you mistaking me for one of my cousins of Wales? I am only May of Teck.'[5]

May could never comprehend her cousins' childish behaviour. She commented with disdain to her Aunt Augusta, Duchess of Mecklenburg-Strelitz, on a children's party for Louise's nineteenth birthday in February 1886. It was 'too ridiculous,' she wrote, adding that everybody else enjoyed themselves, but she was 'shy and bored.'

It had been traditional for descendants of the British sovereign to seek their spouses from German courts, though the Prince of Wales's marriage and that of his sister Louise, who married the Marquess of Lorne in March 1871, had weakened this tradition. With the ascendancy of Chancellor Bismarck, and the tragic death of the Prince's favourite brother-in-law Emperor Frederick from cancer of the larynx in June 1888, imperial Germany was no longer the unquestioned ally of Britain that she had been in previous years. Moreover, the Princess of Wales had never forgiven Germany for her conquest of Denmark in the war of 1864. No daughter of hers, she declared vehemently, was going to marry a German. In fact, why should her dear girls marry at all? Life at Sandringham gave them fine horses to ride, dinner with the world's most eminent statesmen, and a chance to play duets on the piano with their Mama. What else could they possibly want? Those who were tempted to argue with her to the contrary soon found that she did not hesitate to use her deafness as a weapon.

Despite her mother's possessiveness, Louise became betrothed at the age of twenty-two. Although she was the eldest daughter of the heir to the throne, 'little Louise' could hardly be regarded as a great catch. The plainest-looking of the trio, she was so tongue-tied that strangers considered conversation – or efforts at same – to be a penance. The most that could be said of her was that she was an accomplished musician, sometimes playing the organ in services at Sandringham church.

Her husband-to-be, the Right Honourable Alexander William George Duff, was born on 10 November 1849 and educated at Eton. He could claim a tenuous descent from royalty, for through one family line he was a great-grandson of King William IV and his mistress Dorothy Jordan.

In January 1874, he fought the parliamentary constituency of Elgin and Nairn, which had returned a Tory member unopposed for forty years, and won it for the Liberals. Five years later he resigned the seat on succeeding his father as Earl of Fife and Viscount Macduff, but he maintained an active career in the House of Lords speaking regularly on agricultural matters. Initially he was a close supporter of Gladstone, and represented the Home Office in the Lords, but when his party leader declared for Irish home rule he resigned his presidency of the Scottish Liberal Association, and became a fervent member of the Liberal Unionist grouping. In 1882 he was sent on a special mission by Queen Victoria to invest King Albert of Saxony with the Garter, and in turn he was awarded the First Order of Saxony. He was a founder member and vice-president of the Chartered Company of South Africa, resigning his seat on the board after the Jameson raid in 1896, and a partner in the banking firm of Sir Samuel Scott & Co. As befitted a man of his wealth, he owned fourteen country houses, and more than 100,000 acres of land in Elgin, Banff and Aberdeen.

For some time, he had been a close friend of the Prince of Wales, who was only eight years his senior. He had introduced the prince to Sir Charles Dilke, then Under-Secretary for Foreign Affairs (until a divorce scandal cost him his

Alexander Macduff, Earl of Fife, and Princess Louise at the time of their engagement, photographed by Downey, June 1889

career) and a valuable source of information for items of political and diplomatic knowledge which Queen Victoria refused to share with her son. Ironically this was the same Dilke who had clamoured so fervently for a British republic in 1871 at the height of the Crown's unpopularity, and had been anathema to the Queen ever since. Macduff, as he was known in the family, was a regular companion of the Prince of Wales and his sons on shooting expeditions in the Highlands and Norfolk. George's early letters made regular references to going out shooting with 'Papa and Eddy and Lord Fife.' On visits to Sandringham he had been a cheerful victim of April Fool jokes and apple pie beds.

Queen Victoria, always a partisan of Scotsmen, also liked him; he was one of the few sporting friends of her son to win her full approval. Her opinion was not widely shared, for to some he was strikingly reminiscent of the family's *bête noire* John Brown, her late Highland ghillie. He was ill-mannered (a trait sometimes put down to shyness), often selfish, and his language was more suited to the barracks than the drawing-room. Where drink was concerned he took after his father, who never went on sporting expeditions without what looked like a pair of telescopes. On close examination, these were seen to be two bottles, one containing brandy, the other whisky.

The engagement was announced in June 1889, almost four years after the couple's first meeting at Princess Beatrice's wedding, where Louise had been a bridesmaid. There was criticism at court where it was thought to be wrong for a princess to marry someone of less than royal blood, and the unhappy marriage of Queen Victoria's daughter Louise to a Scotsman – coincidentally, also a former Liberal member of Parliament – had set an unfortunate precedent. May of Teck, who was probably Louise's closest friend at the time, expressed her reservations to her Aunt Augusta; 'for a future Princess Royal to marry a subject seems rather strange.' Moreover, Fife's disagreeable character was well known. How could this shy, ill-at-ease princess be happy with such a man, almost old enough to be her father?

But Louise was perfectly content. She was tiring of her over-protective mother and longed to escape, yet without having to make a 'grand marriage' to a European prince who would sweep her away to an alien court on the continent.

Would Fife make a suitable Prince Consort, if the worse came to the worst? Already it was feared (if not hoped) that the dissipated, sickly Prince Albert Victor would not outlive his father and grandmother. George, like his brother, had narrowly escaped drowning on naval service, and as he was still in the Royal Navy the risk remained. Too few lives stood between the throne and 'whispering Louise', who had obviously barely a shred of her Grandmama's force of character.

Such objections, however, were firmly brushed aside. The Prince of Wales warmly approved of the man with whom he had much in common. The Princess of Wales, whose father had become King of Denmark only because his wife was in direct line of royal descent, readily dismissed such petty distinctions of lineage. Despite Macduff's associations with the abominable Dilke, Queen Victoria respected him. She considered that Louise had long looked on him as an elder brother.

She recorded in her journal (27 June 1889):

Bertie, Alix and the girls came to luncheon, but they asked specially to speak to me before and I was still on the sofa. He said he had something very important to communicate, viz. to ask my consent to his Louise's marriage with Lord Fife! I was much pleased, and readily gave my consent, and kissed her and wished her all possible happiness. They all seem so pleased, as it was the *one* wish of Louise herself, and he also had long cared for her. We were a large party at luncheon. Bertie telegraphed to 'Macduff', as Fife is always called by his friends and by Bertie and little Louise. Just before dinner, Bertie brought Lord Fife into the Audience Room, that I might wish him joy, and he thanked me for giving my consent. He was very nervous when he kissed my hand, but seemed very pleased.[6]

Later that day Queen Victoria wrote to Macduff, signing herself 'your very affectionate future Grandmama':

... I love my granddaughters dearly and they are like my own children; their happiness is very near my heart. Dear Louise will, I am sure, be happy with you, whom I have known and liked from your childhood. That my dear beloved grandchild should have her home in dear Scotland and in the dear Highlands is an additional satisfaction to me![7]

Though he had a reputation for parsimony in his dealings with individuals, Macduff was a generous landlord. He graciously declined to allow his Scottish tenants to make Louise and himself any wedding present. While touched by the cordial feelings which prompted them to make such an offer, he felt that it was not appropriate for them to devote their resources to any unnecessary expenditure during an agricultural depression. Among gifts that the couple did accept was a diamond necklace for Louise from the English ladies at court. Subscriptions, limited to a maximum of £10 from each contributor, were collected by the Duchess of Abercorn and a small committee.

The wedding took place on 27 July 1889 in the private chapel at Buckingham Palace. Guests included Crown Prince Frederick of Denmark, the widowed Louis, Grand Duke of Hesse, and King George of the Hellenes. Among the bridesmaids were Louise's sisters and their cousins, the daughters of Prince and Princess Christian of Schleswig-Holstein.

At the wedding breakfast Queen Victoria announced her intention to elevate the bridegroom from the Earldom of Fife to the dukedom, at the Prince of Wales's request, though she thought such arguments about distinctions of title rather unnecessary. The marriage ceremony was notable in that Barnby's hymn 'O Perfect Love' was used thus for the first time.

Queen Victoria thought Louise very pale and 'too plainly dressed,' and had her veil covering her face 'which no Princess ever has and which I think unbecoming and not right.' However Marie Adeane, recently appointed lady-in-waiting to the Queen, thought the bride 'looked her very best', and commented on her charming manner; after signing the register, 'she shook hands with everyone and simply beamed with joy.' The groom, she commented rather curiously, looked 'a nice man and he behaved very well, his manner to the Queen being particularly good.' The responses of both were almost inaudible to the guests, and Macduff lost his way in the 'To have and to hold' sentence so the archbishop had to repeat it, and there was 'a good deal of fumbling with the ring but there were no tears and very little agitation.'[8]

With scant regard for the sensibilities of its Scottish readers, *The Illustrated London News* remarked that:

> There is no doubt that the marriage of the Prince of Wales's eldest daughter to an Englishman is more popular than could have been any Royal wedding to a foreign Prince, had he been even as distinguished and as deeply loved as the late Emperor of Germany [*sic*]. We are a clannish people – as, indeed, any people that is to hold together and to do any good for itself must needs be; and we are glad that the Prince of Wales has chosen his first son-in-law from among the old English houses whose history is bound up with the nation's life.[9]

The same writer insisted that 'we are all Englishmen,' and that any 'North Britons' who did not recognize as much might as well campaign for Scottish home rule.

Bride and groom spent most of their honeymoon at Mar Lodge and Macduff's other estates in Scotland, joining the royal gathering at Braemar in September. The Shah of Persia paid a visit to England early in July, necessitating much lavish and tiresome entertaining which the Prince of Wales would have gladly foregone. His wife was not amused when the Shah offered his palace in Teheran for her daughter's honeymoon, her patience having already been sorely taxed when he assumed that her ladies-in-waiting were members of her husband's harem and suggested that the uglier ones should be executed.

The 'immensely rich' Macduff and his young wife spent their married life in an enviable array of homes. Their main English base was Sheen Lodge, a white ivy-covered mansion to the north of Richmond Park. This would always be their favourite home, and it was here that their children were born. In Scotland they had a choice between Duff House, Banff, and Mar Lodge, Aberdeen, as well as houses at 11 Portman Square, London, and Chichester Terrace on the Brighton seafront.

This first departure from the family group was keenly felt, as Princess Victoria commented to the Queen (6 August 1889): 'It is indeed sad to think Louise will not be at home on my next birthday but it is so charming to think she is not far from us and so happy too.'[10]

Louise was glad to escape from the eternal nursery at Sandringham, and despite her husband's sporting interests they shunned the glittering gaiety of the Marlborough House set. They rarely travelled abroad except on family visits to their Danish relatives at Copenhagen. Louise's obituary in *The Times* many years later appropriately commented that 'her natural reserve, added to a certain delicacy of health, made her shrink from publicity.'[11]

Indeed, it did not escape comment from some quarters that they seemed to play no part in the public affairs or ceremonial duties regularly expected of royalty. Theirs was a relatively simple household, with Louise declining an offer of ladies-in-waiting. Yet guests were never allowed to forget that she was the eldest daughter of the heir to the throne. Shyness did not stop her from preceding company into dinner each evening.

Married life had a remarkable effect on Louise. Relations and neighbours who had known her as a shy, tongue-tied princess, overshadowed by her mother hardly recognized the vivacious Duchess of Fife, 'looking so mischievous and happy.' The Duchess of Teck found her and her husband so contented 'that it does one's heart good to see them.'

Shortly after her arrival as a young bride at Mar Lodge, Louise wrote enthusiastically to Queen Victoria of their reception, as well as of a mild accident to their carriage (17 August 1889):

> I have had so much to do the last two days since we arrived here that I have not had a moment to do anything except to write to Papa and Mama. I was just sitting down to write to you when I received your kind telegram. The accident to our carriage was of course much exaggerated in the papers, only one of the wheels became heated and refused to turn round. We soon got another carriage and arrived here about 7 o'clock having been delayed barely an hour. It rained a little at first but cleared up at 5.0 and was then lovely and quite mild and the country looked beautiful. The clan all met us at the gate with four pipers, there were a great number of them, who preceded the carriage and all looked very smart. They gave us a grand reception, and the whole thing was a fine sight. The weather has been showery but not cold since we came. I am delighted to be here in my Highland home, but having had so much to do and arrange have unfortunately not had time to go about yet much. Macduff went out stalking before luncheon today and killed five stags, which were all very good.[12]

Louise and Macduff took eagerly to that wonderful if not altogether dignified new invention the bicycle on the South Downs and in rural Scotland, and indulged their love of fishing to the full. One autumn Louise landed seven large salmon, a feat then unprecedented on Deeside by a lady angler.

Among regular guests to the Fife domain was Edward Hamilton, a treasury official and Gladstone's private secretary for some years. He wrote to them regularly until his death in 1908, and generally sent Louise books as presents on her birthday or after staying with them, as one of her letters from Mar Lodge (25 October 1894) shows:

> I cannot thank you sufficiently for the charming fishing book you have so kindly sent me. It arrived yesterday and I am delighted with it. The weather has been so much against fishing this year that I fear I shall not be able to make any entries in it for 1894, but I shall begin by recording last year's sport. It has been raining here for the last two days, so I hope I may be able to get one or two fish before we leave, which we unfortunately do very soon.[13]

Before her marriage, Louise's chief artistic interests had been her music and the family hobby of photography. Now she discovered a hitherto-untapped talent for painting and interior design, which she initially put into practice by devising the interior decoration of their Brighton house. When a plumber left a lighted candle under the floor and fire destroyed the old Mar Lodge, the new mansion (boasting one hundred and twenty rooms) was built from a rough

The Duke and Duchess of Fife with their bicycles

sketch drawn by her and elaborated on by their architect. Queen Victoria was, naturally, invited to come and lay the foundation stone of the new residence. Macduff had been dismayed at losing his collection of stags' heads in the fire, but set to work with alacrity on a new one, until three thousand skulls adorned the arched pine rafters of the vast new ballroom.

Though always happiest in the country, when in London Louise was an enthusiastic patron of theatre first nights and the opera.

A letter to Queen Victoria, written from Portman Square (15 February 1890), shows how faithful she was at remembering family anniversaries, and makes plain her new-found happiness with married life:

> I thought so much of you, dear Grandmama on the anniversary of your wedding day, which Papa told me would have been your golden one, had you not suffered the greatest sorrow which any one can experience, and which I can now thoroughly understand and appreciate. Although the day could not have been without its bad memories for you, yet I know and am glad to think you must have had many happy and tender memories too. Our house here is now very comfortable and I think we

have made it bright and pretty. This is such a healthy part of London so high, it faces the south and we get all the morning sun. We hope that you will come and see it some day. We very often go down to Sheen, which is very nice and quite country, although within a drive. I daresay you know dear Grandmama, that I do not often gush, but I cannot tell you how happy I am with Macduff. Happier *ever* than I thought I would be.[14]

Macduff particularly enjoyed attending the Balmoral servants' balls. At one, he suggested to Queen Victoria that they should dance a reel together. After a momentary hesitation she went to change, returning some minutes later in a shorter skirt. The two of them, it was said, proceeded to choose 'the kind of reel usually danced by sweethearts,' and danced 'in rather an improper way.' Yet nobody dared to tell Her Majesty that she had risked making herself look faintly ridiculous.

It was significant that Louise's health improved after her marriage, as in time did that of Maud. Now liberated from the stifling atmosphere of her childhood home, she was keen to see her brothers and sisters enjoying the benefits and freedom of married life as well.

4 'Poor Dear Eddy'

All the family looked forward to the day when Eddy would finally settle down. Though his mother's possessiveness, and perhaps the example of his father, were partly responsible for making him the man he was, it would be unfair to blame the Prince's shortcomings entirely on his upbringing. From infancy his deafness was pronounced, but as the Princess of Wales was so sensitive about this hereditary handicap, nobody ever broached the subject with her, and he was consequently never medically treated for the condition. Yet her realization that he also suffered from what she called 'beastly ears' increased the protectiveness she felt towards her first-born; as did his slowness, inability to learn, and evident lack of character, all negative qualities which irritated his father and probably caused many an argument in private between his parents. He had a piercing, high-pitched voice which others found unpleasant, and his easy-going nature bordered on imbecility. Perhaps he suffered from porphyria, an ailment in which a chemical imbalance in the blood causes symptoms such as bulging eyes and manic depression, and which had been mistakenly diagnosed as insanity in the case of his great-great-grandfather King George III.

Apparent indifference to what happened to him was recalled some seventy years later by his cousin, the Grand Duchess Xenia of Russia. While boating on Lake Fredensborg with the family one day, Eddy suddenly picked up his sisters' little dog and threw it into the water. 'Why did you do that?' asked his astonished grandfather,* pushing him in over the side. Eddy seemed quite unconcerned as he scrambled back into the boat, announcing rather unnecessarily that he was very wet. 'Of course you're very wet,' snapped his grandfather, 'you've been in the lake.' 'Why did you do that to me?' 'Because you did it to the little dog.'[1] Such feeble-mindedness is not altogether without its more comic side, but the idea of a King of England who, as Xenia said, never *minded* anything, was not something to contemplate with equanimity.

The only person who had any noticeable effect on Eddy was his father, who teased him unmercifully. 'Don't call him Uncle Eddy,' the Prince of Wales would tell younger members of the family, 'call him Uncle Eddy-Collars-and-Cuffs.' His neck and arms were unnaturally long and out of proportion to the rest of his body, and he was so self-conscious about his awkward appearance that he wore high starched collars and very wide cuffs. As his father told him none too kindly, these sartorial refinements made him look more ridiculous than ever. Eddy was afraid of this genial but sometimes demanding and terrifying parent,

---

* Possibly Tsar Alexander II, but more probably King Christian IX.

The Prince and Princess of Wales with their family on the steps of Marlborough House, c. 1889. From left: Prince Albert Victor; Princess Maud; the Prince and Princess of Wales; Princess Louise; Prince George and Princess Victoria

and unhappy at 'not being up to' what was expected of him. Far from being resentful of the stronger character of his younger and smaller brother, even in maturity he was devoted to and very dependent on George.

Queen Victoria was fond of him, but her affection was tempered by anxiety when she wondered how the young man would eventually discharge his duties as sovereign. His interest – enthusiasm was too strong a term – in all forms of dissipation and amusement, not unexpected in a bachelor army cadet of his years, was quite unrelieved by any concern with weightier matters.

In 1889 there was a scandal. The police raided a homosexual brothel in Cleveland Street, off Tottenham Court Road in central London. Among its clients was Lord Arthur Somerset, superintendent of the Prince of Wales's racing stables. The Prince had always regarded Arthur as an intimate friend, and after his initial disbelief, expressed thanks that he had been allowed to flee the country quietly in order to avoid prosecution. To that ardent royal connoisseur of female beauty, any man addicted to 'such a filthy vice' must be 'an unfortunate lunatic.' His distress was all the more acute as his elder son, also a close friend of Arthur, evidently indulged in such vices, and worse still, was believed to be a regular at the brothel. To add insult to injury, the other patrons apparently referred to him as Victoria.

Eddy's connections with the underworld of Victorian London in the 1880s were rumoured to go further than the Cleveland Street episode. Some suspected that he was 'Jack the Ripper', who savagely murdered and disembowelled several prostitutes in the Whitechapel area between August and November 1888. Such assumptions rested more on fantasy than fact. Firstly, the Prince was nowhere near London on the dates of the killings; secondly, he was far too slow-witted to commit or be closely involved with such crimes and cover up his traces. Even so, it was pointed out that he hunted deer with the family at Balmoral, and had been shown how to dissect venison and remove vital organs from animal carcases. A photograph of him in a deerstalker hat had recently been published, and excited witnesses testified to having seen a moustached man of medium height, wearing such a hat and 'collar and cuffs' leaving the scene of one murder.

A plethora of Jack the Ripper theories, which need not concern us here in detail, has since arisen. Another argument maintains that the murderer was the prince's tutor, James Stephen. Yet another suggests that the killings were part of an elaborate royal cover-up.

In 1884 Prince Albert Victor had met a Catholic commoner, Annie Elizabeth Crook (so the story went), fathered a daughter by her, and married her the next year. To prevent knowledge of this liaison from going any further Dr James Gull, who had been held in high esteem since bringing the Prince of Wales back from the brink of death from typhoid fever in December 1871, had been prevailed upon to subject Annie to an operation that left her a complete idiot, and then to arrange for her admission into an asylum, where she died in 1920 without recovering her reason. Five prostitutes who knew the whole story were judicially executed, their violent deaths being laid at the door of a mythical Jack

Prince Albert Victor, octagonal plate by Wallis Gimson & Co., 1886–87. This plate also exists with an added inscription above and below the design commemorating his visit to Burnley to open the Victoria Hospital, 13 October 1886

51

the Ripper. The daughter, Alice, survived two deliberate attempts in infancy by a cab driver to run her down, and was brought up by the painter Walter Sickert. Annie had been one of his models, and he was responsible for introducing her to Eddy. After an unhappy marriage, Alice became Sickert's mistress and bore him a son, Joseph. She outlived Walter by eight years, dying in 1950.

Those who doubted this far-fetched story were vindicated when Joseph Sickert denounced most of the facts as a hoax. Yet it speaks volumes for the young prince's character that he could even have been remotely connected with such bizarre legends. The actress Sarah Bernhardt later claimed that he was the father of her child.

Eddy's trip to India in the spring of 1890 had similarly unfortunate consequences. Tales of the way he passed his time and enjoyed native hospitality were quick to emerge. Some months after his return, the satirical radical journal *Truth* published an imaginary interview with him about his Indian tour and impressions of the country. A typical answer attributed to him read:

> You ask me what impressed me most
> Whilst Hindustan I travelled o'er?
> My answer is, A certain man
> I came across at Shuttadore.

In May 1890 Queen Victoria created her grandson Duke of Clarence and Avondale. She was as reluctant to give him a title as she had been with Macduff, but it was thought that the future King of England should have some suitably becoming designation. The last Duke of Clarence had been Prince William Henry, who ascended the throne in 1830 as King William IV. On the advice of the Garter King-at-Arms, the Dukedom of Avondale (a Scottish title held by King George II before becoming Prince of Wales) was added, as the Earldom of Clarence was a subsidiary title held by the young Duke of Albany. The Queen regretted that her grandson should be 'lowered to a Duke, like any one of the nobility which a Prince could never be,' but still thought it right that he should be a peer.[2] He took his seat in the Lords on 23 June, introduced by the Prince of Wales and the Duke of Edinburgh. From seats in the royal gallery, the ceremony was watched by the Princess of Wales and her two younger daughters.

It was evident that Eddy's way of life was undermining his uncertain health. His weak constitution, aggravated by heavy drinking and addiction to Turkish cigarettes, was further weakened by gout and possibly venereal disease. The Prince and Princess of Wales hoped in vain that Queen Victoria knew nothing of his more sordid activities. 'I ask again *who* is it tells the Queen these things?' Knollys wrote to Ponsonby in some amazement, after a letter from Her Majesty to her daughter-in-law protesting about his behaviour.

Efforts were made to interest him in two of his German cousins. In 1889 he had professed himself passionately fond of Princess Alix ('Alicky') of Hesse, but to his chagrin she turned him down, refusing what their grandmother called 'the greatest position there is.' Much as she liked him as a cousin, Queen Victoria told Vicky, Alicky knew she would not be happy with him, and as he would be unhappy with her 'he must not think of her.' As the knowledgeable Queen possibly recognized, the future Empress Alexandra Feodorovna had sound reasons for knowing such a match would not bring happiness to either partner. Her only surviving brother Ernest ('Ernie') was on embarrassingly intimate terms with their male domestic servants. His cousin Princess Victoria Melita of Edinburgh, who was later to be married to him for seven miserable years, told the family bluntly that 'no boy was safe with him.' Alicky may well have heard rumours that Eddy and Ernie were birds of a feather. Alternatively, she already knew and was possibly attached to the Tsarevich Nicholas by this time; but such knowledge as Queen Victoria had of her grandson's private life probably discouraged her from doing anything to encourage such a marriage with his Hessian cousin.

Later Princess Margaret ('Mossy') of Prussia, youngest sister of Emperor William II, was invited to stay with her cousins at Sandringham. Queen Victoria and Vicky, the Princess's mother, hoped for a marriage between them. Mossy was an attractive, if not beautiful, level-headed young woman who shared her mother's attachment to England, but neither she nor Eddy kindled a flame in each other. The Princess of Wales's staunch detestation of Germany probably played its part, although she had come to love the ill-fated Emperor Frederick and his wife, and was aware that Mossy hated her unfeeling imperial brother almost as much as Alix herself. The Waleses had had nothing but sympathy for their stricken uncle's family. 'How dreadful is it not about poor Uncle Fritz's throat?' Maud wrote to Queen Victoria (27 November 1887). 'We are all so sorry about it, poor cousins are so miserable and write us such sad letters but they pray and trust that it will be better soon.'[3]

Eddy demonstrated his waywardness by falling in and out of love with remarkable ease. The two main recipients of his affections in turn were not sufficiently royal; the first was royal after a fashion, but doubly ineligible. She was Princess Hélène d'Orleans, daughter of the Comte de Paris, Pretender to the French throne. The Orleans family had been banished from France in 1886 and had settled in England. They were on close terms with Queen Victoria and her family, and saw much of the Waleses.

In May 1890, Queen Victoria wrote anxiously to Eddy that she had heard rumours of him 'thinking and talking' of the French princess. He must therefore avoid meeting her as much as possible as it would only 'lead to make you unhappy if you formed an attachment for her.' It was impossible for him, being so close to the Crown, to marry the daughter of the claimant to the French throne; and he could not wed a Roman Catholic. Even if she was to change her religion merely to marry him, it would be 'much to be deprecated . . . and be most unpopular.'[4]

But the Princess of Wales, who was determined not to be saddled with a German daughter-in-law, unwisely encouraged the young couple; so did the Duchess of Fife, who invited them to stay at Sheen Lodge and Mar Lodge. Not content with this the romantically-minded Duchess, who appeared to have inherited her Grandmama's inveterate passion for matchmaking, invited the Comte and Comtesse de Paris and Hélène to stay at Mar Lodge in August 1890. Eddy followed in hot pursuit, and they were soon unofficially engaged. Before giving them a chance to dwell at length on the consequences of what they had

The Duke of Clarence, c. 1890

done, the Princess of Wales bundled them both into a carriage with orders to go immediately to Balmoral and tell Queen Victoria in person. Eddy was a little apprehensive at the thought of the Queen's reaction, but to his surprise she was 'very nice about it and promised to help us as much as possible.'

Queen Victoria graciously promised to find out how the obstacles could best be surmounted. What, she enquired of her Prime Minister and Lord Chancellor, would be the constitutional position of the heir presumptive if he wished to marry a Roman Catholic wife, or a wife who had renounced her religion and become a Protestant? Eddy offered to abdicate his rights to the succession, professing that he could never be happy without her.* It was rumoured at court and in society that this was a heaven-sent excuse for removing the chronically unstable Prince from the direct line of succession. However the Comte refused to countenance such a match, and ordered his daughter to retract. Tearfully she went abroad determined to seek an audience with the Pope, but he sided with her father. By early the following year, all parties concerned understood the matter to be officially closed.

---

* His nephew King Edward VIII's insistence in 1936 that he would renounce the throne to marry the equally ineligible Mrs Simpson (see below, p. 175) thus had a familiar ring.

Queen Victoria and the Princess of Wales thought that poor broken-hearted Eddy would never recover from this blow. The cynical Sir Henry Ponsonby knew otherwise. After seeing Eddy one day at Marlborough House holding forth in a lively manner, he concluded that the young man had obviously been prepared for such an outcome, and that the settlement of an impossible situation had come as a relief.

Eddy's heart was not broken, but lost again. This time the lady who inspired his temporary passions was Lady Sibyl St Clair Erskine, the nineteen-year-old daughter of the Earl of Rosslyn. Prince and lady exchanged long affectionate letters, but fortunately for the latter she was about to be engaged to Lord Burghersh. Eddy's last letter to her, written in November 1891, enquired after the rumours of her betrothal, and warned her gently not to be surprised if she heard before long that he was to be engaged as well. It would be 'a very different thing to what it might have been once,' but he was philosophical; 'still it can't be helped.'

Something had to be done about this embarrassing young man, and the sooner the better. Shortly after the Prince's promotion to the rank of major in summer 1891, his father decided that it was a waste of time his remaining in the army; he had dismally failed to acquire even a rudimentary knowledge of military subjects. His education and future had been a matter of some considerable anxiety for them all, 'and the difficulty in rousing him is very great.'[5]

The Prince of Wales had lost patience with him, but at the time he was in no position to chastise his son for bad behaviour. In September 1890 Prince Albert Edward had stayed with the shipowner Arthur Wilson at Tranby Croft, near Doncaster, and was called upon to sign as witness the confession of a fellow-guest, Sir William Gordon-Cumming, who had cheated at baccarat. Claiming that he had only signed it under undue pressure, Gordon-Cumming protested his innocence, and when the matter was made public in London society a few months later he brought a civil action in the courts to clear his name; the Prince of Wales was summoned to give evidence. Just as the wave of criticism from those who were shocked at his gambling was dying down, he became involved in the private arguments between an old flame, Frances Brooke (an unscrupulous and spoilt woman, nicknamed 'the babbling Brooke', and the one mistress of her husband that the Princess of Wales had never liked nor trusted) and his old friend Lord Charles Beresford. Lady Brooke had asked the Prince to retrieve a foolish and hysterical letter she had written Beresford, which had been opened by Lady Beresford and lodged with her solicitor in order to shut her up. Lord Charles charged the Prince with needless interference, trying to wreck his marriage, and promised to exact reparation or revenge for his role in the business. Eventually the Prime Minister, Lord Salisbury – who must have felt that more important matters had a claim on his attention – had to be called in to make peace between them all.

Embarrassed by the results of his well-intentioned if foolish actions, the Prince of Wales was not in the best of tempers that summer. For once, even his long-suffering wife was out of patience with him, and discussions on what to do about their son were conducted in rather strained circumstances. The Prince of Wales wanted Eddy out of harm's way on a tour of the more remote colonies, hoping perhaps that he would not be exposed to the same temptations as he had been in India. Queen Victoria maintained that his time would be better spent in visiting Europe, to gain a sound knowledge of continental languages, countries and political personalities; he and George were '*very* exclusively English, and that is a great misfortune.'[6] She reminded Bertie that, much as he disliked his lessons and lacked application as a boy, he travelled much, 'and with good people, and you profited immensely by what you saw, and by the number of interesting and clever people you got to know. No doubt you were much more lively than Eddy . . .'[7]

The Prince of Wales hesitated to let him loose on the fleshpots and vice dens of Europe, but was at a loss as to how to tell the Queen; 'it is difficult to explain to you the reasons why we do not consider it desirable for him to make lengthened stays in foreign capitals.'[8] The Princess, however, felt that matters could be resolved more simply; if he stayed with his regiment, she would be able to keep a motherly eye on him. Meanwhile the Prince felt there was nothing to be gained in pursuing the discussion further, and on departing for Hamburg on 14 August, deputed Knollys to let the Princess decide whether Eddy should go on a tour of the colonies; embark on a colonial and European tour; or immediately become betrothed to Princess May of Teck.

The idea of a match with this highly eligible Princess, whom Eddy had known since childhood, was not new. Five years previously, it had been discussed but ruled out, so Ponsonby thought, because in his view Prince Albert Victor had not shown any interest in her, and because the Prince and Princess of Wales disliked her parents. It seems surprising that he was unaware of the friendship between Princess Alexandra and the Duchess of Teck.

By August 1891, however, those in the know realized cynically that all the preliminaries were fairly well settled, as long as Princess May did not put up any resistance. Knollys informed Ponsonby that he did not anticipate any real opposition on Eddy's part, 'if he is properly managed and is told he must do it – that it is for the good of the country, etc.'[9]

The Teck parents made an odd couple, 'fat Mary' with her extravagance and sometimes tactless if well-meant remarks, and Francis, whose mental state had been disturbed since a mild stroke seven years previously. But their only daughter was beyond reproach. She was intelligent, well-educated, attractive and had plenty of character, although she was a little shy and lacking in self-confidence. As with many other children with disorganized or extravagant parents, she had of necessity matured quickly and exerted something of a stabilising influence among the family.

After weighing up the alternatives, the Princess of Wales chose the third; her son should marry Princess May. Having settled the daunting problem of her child's future, she departed for Denmark. Yet even here she failed to find her customary peace of mind, for rumours were circulating around London society of her husband's involvement in the Brooke–Beresford quarrel. Already upset and embarrassed by his part in the Tranby Croft scandal, she felt unable to face returning to England in October, as planned, and left instead to join the silver wedding celebrations of her sister Dagmar, now Tsarina, and Tsar Alexander III at Livadia in the Crimea.

Throughout the preceding months, May had seen much of the Waleses. In January 1891 she and her parents had been to stay at Sandringham for six days, and had also been at Sheen Lodge with Louise from time to time. Ironically the one cousin of whom she saw little was Eddy, who had been out of the limelight with his regiment at York, though he had spent a day with her at Ascot during the summer. Plans for the young couple's future were a closely-guarded secret among the elder generation, but from the state of her parents' suppressed excitement, May knew what was happening. Her suspicions increased when she and her parents met the Prince of Wales at Easton in October for three days. 'He was perfectly charming,' she told her Aunt Augusta. As she might have added, he had good reason to be.

In the last week of October, May and her brother Adolphus were commanded to visit Her Majesty at Balmoral. They caught the night train from Euston station to Aberdeen on 4 November, and this important visit to Scotland lasted ten days.

It was clear to all that this was a final inspection as to the suitability of Princess May to marry the awkward young heir presumptive, become the making of him, and in due course become Queen Consort. Queen Victoria was duly impressed with her twenty-four-year-old second cousin, noting that she had no frivolous tastes, was very carefully brought up, and was well-informed and always occupied.

Soon after May's return to White Lodge, the other central character to everyone's plans was carefully briefed. It was taken for granted that Eddy would do as he was told. His father informed him that he was about to be invited to Luton Hoo, the Bedfordshire home of the Danish minister Mr de Falbe and his family, and Princess May would be among the other guests. He must pay her particular attention and be on his best behaviour, but was not to propose marriage to her until the new year, when she and her family would be invited to Sandringham for his birthday celebrations. Eddy solemnly agreed.

At Sandringham the atmosphere was tense, for excitement had given way to severe anxiety. The Prince of Wales, still reeling from public criticism in the wake of the Tranby Croft affair and dreading repercussions from Lady Brooke's letter, had celebrated his fiftieth birthday at his Norfolk home. It was the first birthday since his marriage that he had spent without his wife, who was still at Livadia and in no frame of mind to return home. The occasion was further overshadowed for him by a fire which broke out in the house eight days earlier, destroying the top floor and damaging the dining room.

Worse was to come. Prince George, now promoted to Commander, had served on HMS *Thrush* in the North American and West Indies station, had returned to Plymouth in July 1891 and joined his family at Cowes the following month. After joining the customary Danish royal family gathering at Fredensborg later that summer and staying at Mar Lodge with Louise and Macduff to stalk and shoot, he went to Sandringham for his father's birthday party. On 10 November, he complained of a severe headache. On the 12th he was in bed with a high temperature, and on medical advice he was moved to Marlborough House where he could receive better attention from the doctors.

The Duke of Clarence and Princess May of Teck at the time of their engagement, photographed by Downey, December 1891

Typhoid was diagnosed and a telegram to Livadia brought the alarmed Princess of Wales home. Ever since the Prince Consort's death in 1861 and the Prince of Wales's recovery from the same disease ten years later to the day, when his life was all but despaired of, the word 'typhoid' had an ominous ring in the family. The crisis of his illness was reached on 24 November; on 3 December he was declared out of danger, though not till 21 December was he pronounced strong enough to leave his bed.

In George's diary for 3 December, a note appears in his mother's handwriting. It is not concerned with his illness, but with an even more momentous event; Eddy was engaged to May.

The previous day, Eddy, May and her parents were among the party at Luton Hoo as planned. In the evening of 3 December, a grand county ball was held. He waited carefully for the moment when he could take May by the hand from the crowded ballroom and lead her into the adjoining boudoir, which had been carefully left deserted for them. 'To my great surprise,' May wrote in her diary a little unconvincingly, 'Eddy proposed to me.'

Any surprise she felt can only have been at the speed with which her young suitor had taken this great step. She realized that he would have done so before long, even if she was expecting him to wait until after Christmas as bidden by his father. There had never been any question in her mind that she would shirk her duty by turning him down. She had been brought up to venerate the throne, and notwithstanding her lack of self-confidence, she knew that with the right guidance from her relations she would play her part fittingly as Duchess of Clarence and Avondale, later as Princess of Wales, and ultimately as Queen.

She had known Eddy since childhood, and shared the general opinion that he was an unprepossessing youth who compared unfavourably with his brother. Unlike George, he used to bully and tease her unmercifully. However, these unpleasant childhood memories of him counted for less than the chance of the most dazzling position any princess could hope for. She, Princess Victoria Mary of Teck, one of the impoverished royals who had been forced to live abroad for several years because of her parents' crippling debts, could look forward to becoming Queen Consort of England. Although her husband-to-be gave every appearance of being an immature, shallow, self-indulgent playboy, she had the example of her mother in making the most from marriage to a weak and unstable husband. How much she knew of his dissipated ways is open to question. Their recent meetings had been under the watchful eye of parents, his and hers. Between them, they had done their best to keep certain aspects of Eddy's life and character secret from her.

Eddy departed a couple of days later for London and Windsor to announce the glad tidings to his parents and grandmother in person. Queen Victoria had already decided how suitable May was; 'I had much wished for this marriage.' Her happiness was still tinged with compassion for the 'blighted life of that sweet dear Hélène,' Alix hoped fervently that her son had 'found the right bride this time.' 'It has indeed been like a dream to think you will be our sister!' Princess Victoria wrote to May. 'A dearer one we certainly could not wish for.'[10]

It was too much to expect that everyone would rejoice at the impending marriage. Although she eagerly accepted an invitation to the ceremony, the Empress Frederick was still disappointed that her youngest daughter was not to be the bride, for seeing Mossy brought closer to the line of succession would have been some consolation for the unhappiness she had endured in Germany. Princess Christian of Schleswig-Holstein also had an unmarried daughter, Helena Victoria, known as 'Thora', or less reverently as 'the Snipe' because of her long nose, whom she considered had a better claim than the far less royal Princess May of Teck. Thora doubtless knew enough to prefer spinsterhood – which was her ultimate destiny – to married life with such an unattractive husband. Louise, Marchioness of Lorne, whose unhappy marriage was a sore trial to the family, made predictably spiteful remarks about the impending nuptials, and May's Aunt Augusta, who loved to interfere in anything to do with her niece, felt insulted because nobody had thought to consult her about the engagement first. And although he had sent an effusive letter of congratulation, Emperor William was furious when told that he was not on the wedding list, while his mother was. To his Aunt Alix, Willy was still emphatically *persona non grata*.

These mutterings of disapproval did not concern May. What did alarm her was the revealing attitude of her future father-in-law. Still smarting from the 'many worries and annoyancies' [*sic*] which the previous year had brought him, the Prince of Wales found it impossible to keep up the pretence that his eldest son was a paragon of virtue. He was continually telling May to 'keep Eddy up to the mark,' or 'see that he does this and that.' Within a few days of the engagement, she found herself acting as his unofficial private secretary and answering most of his correspondence.

Rumours were beginning to reach her that the rest of the family had hoped and prayed would remain hidden a little longer. Gradually sober reality at what she had done began to dawn on her. 'Do you think I can really take this on, Mama?' she asked her mother in despair. The Duchess of Teck, whose married life had been clouded by the necessity of mothering and managing a loving, but difficult and now semi-invalid husband, snapped back that of course she could. Look at the man she herself had 'taken on'.

The wedding was arranged for 27 February 1892, ostensibly well before Lent, and because of Queen Victoria's insistence that long engagements were 'very trying and not very good.' Behind the scenes, though, some thought that the less time May was given to ponder her fate and change her mind – if indeed she could assert herself and say no – the better.

That Christmas a thick yellow fog descended on London, and lasted well into the new year. So did a severe epidemic of influenza claiming among others, the life of Prince Victor of Hohenlohe-Langenburg, son of Queen Victoria's half-sister Feodora. The Prince of Wales and his eldest son attended the funeral at London, and the latter came back with a heavy cold. A ball and lawn-meet of the local hunt at Sandringham, arranged as part of the celebration for Eddy's birthday early in the new year, were cancelled due to court mourning.

As guests congregated at Norfolk, illness raged. George was still convalescing from typhoid, while May and the Princess of Wales, like Eddy, were suffering from colds; Princess Victoria, Knollys, and Eddy's equerry Captain Holford had taken to their beds with influenza. Those who were well enough went skating on the lake, now frozen solid. On 7 January the Prince of Wales took the men out shooting; Eddy's cold was worsening, but no excuse was accepted for his not taking part. The ladies lunched with them at Dighton Probyn's cottage, and May noticed how unwell her betrothed was looking. She persuaded him to walk back with her afterwards; he was very pale, and complaining of dizziness and a severe headache. At the house, George took his temperature and sent him straight to bed. By now the rest of the family and guests were taking large doses of quinine to try and keep the infection at bay. So many people had influenza, and colds were so much a part of the Waleses winter at Sandringham, that nobody suspected at first that Eddy might be seriously ill.

The following day, 8 January, was his twenty-eighth birthday. He came downstairs in a dressing-gown to receive his presents, but felt so weak that he had to go back to bed immediately afterwards. Thus he missed his birthday dinner, at which the Duke of Teck solemnly proposed his health, followed by entertainment from a ventriloquist and a banjo player. George and May jointly took on the task of answering his telegrams and letters of congratulation. His mother, who loved him more dearly than anyone else, telegraphed to Queen Victoria at Osborne: 'Poor Eddy got influenza, cannot dine, so tiresome.'[11]

Next day he developed inflammation of the lungs. The Prince of Wales's physician Dr Francis Laking was summoned, and diagnosed incipient pneumonia as well as influenza. He telegraphed for Dr Broadbent, who had attended George during his typhoid, and he arrived on the 10th. Throughout this day and the next, George and May were allowed to speak to him but come no closer than peering over the top of a screen around his bed for fear of infection. The bedroom was small by royal standards; lying in bed by the window, Eddy could stretch out his arm and touch the mantelpiece with his hand.

On 12 January, his condition deteriorated so sharply that only his parents were permitted to visit; doctors urged the need for perfect peace and quiet. There was no peace or quiet from the delirious patient himself. He shouted at the top of his voice, cursing the officers and men of his regiment in strong language which he had doubtless heard from them many a time, talking wildly of Lord Randolph Churchill and Lord Salisbury, professing undying admiration and love for Queen Victoria and for his Hélène. Not once did anybody hear May's name called. His fingernails were blue and his lips vivid. In the small sitting-room next door his horrified parents, brother and sisters, May and her parents all gathered, peeping over the screen from time to time.

To the Princess of Wales it all brought back memories of her husband's attack of typhoid twenty years earlier. Queen Victoria offered to come to Norfolk, but her son was firm and replied politely that there could be no question of her coming. Ostensibly the reason given was fear of infection, a risk to which a lady in her seventies should not be exposed. Privately, though, her arrival at the Prince of Wales's sickbed in 1871 had created a stir in the household at Sandringham that those who remembered did not wish to experience a second time.

The Princess regularly sat by Eddy's bed, fanning him, stroking his hair and temples, smiling bravely as she wiped the sweat from his brow. She was buoyed up by hope that he should be spared to her as was his father. But after an all-night vigil, early in the morning of 13 January, she woke her husband in tears to tell him that the doctors had given up hope. He wandered restlessly in and out of the bedroom, while she sat by the bedside most of the day and evening. Not till after midnight could the doctors persuade her to rest. She had only just settled down on her sofa before they called her back. Her son was dying.

For several hours, as the Princess of Wales wiped perspiration from the patient's face and nurses put ice against his forehead, all that could be heard from the sickroom were the sobs of his grieving family. The little room was crammed. Three times he rallied and members of the family were sent away, only to be summoned again a few minutes later. The Prince of Wales's domestic chaplain, Dr Hervey, was called in to read prayers for the dying.

Moments before the end, the Princess turned to Dr Laking and asked, 'Can you do *nothing* more to save him?' He shook his head. At this the despairing look on her face, May later said, was the most heartrending thing she had ever seen. At 9.35 on the morning of Thursday, 14 January, murmuring, 'Who is that?' to himself, the Duke of Clarence died.

His mother found some solace in religion, telling May that his death made 'one more link with heaven.' Yet neither she nor her husband ever really got over their bereavement. Despite his faults, the Duke of Clarence had always been affectionate and amenable to his family. Just as it seemed to them that his future happiness was assured, all was suddenly over.

'Gladly would I have given my life for him,' the Prince of Wales wrote sorrowfully to Queen Victoria, 'as I put no value on mine. . . . Such a tragedy has never before occurred in the annals of our family, and it is hard that poor little May should virtually become a widow before she is a wife.'[12]

George, Duke of Cambridge had scarcely bothered to conceal his impatience with Eddy while he was alive. From his winter retreat at Cannes, he wrote with a heavy heart that his great-nephew was 'a thorough Gentleman and I never heard him say an unkind word of or to anyone.'[13]

In his letter of condolence the Prime Minister, Gladstone, then aged eighty-two, noted that he could just recall one comparable tragedy – that of Princess Charlotte of Wales, daughter of the Prince Regent, whose death in childbirth in November 1817 had made it imperative for her middle-aged uncles to contract valid marriages and produce at least one heir to the throne between them.

To Queen Victoria, the loss was 'an overwhelming misfortune!' For the second time that week the Prince of Wales had to beg his mother not to come to Sandringham.

Among correspondence in the Royal Archives, Windsor, is a volume of 'Letters and Papers relative to the illness and death of Albert Victor, Duke of Clarence'. Two examples, both from his sisters, will suffice. From Sandringham, Princess Victoria wrote (19 January) to her grandmother:

> How can I express my thanks to you for the lovely sympathetic letter I received from you this morning. In this our overwhelming grief – It is almost impossible to believe

that our beloved Eddy has really been taken from us – Just now when all his future seemed bright, it seems cruel he should have had to go. But the Lord's ways are not ours – and He knows what is best for us – How I wish dear Grandmama you could have seen him as he lay there, as a saint or knight, with a heavenly peaceful expression on his lovely face. Then and only then could we with resigned hearts say 'Thy will be done'. Those last hours of agony which we passed near his bedside will remain before me to my dying day. Thank God, the end was quite calm and they say he couldn't have suffered. I know how much dearest Grandmama you will feel his loss, you were always so devoted to him – as he was to you – dear Papa and Mama it is indeed a bitter bitter trial for them. They bear their grief with such wonderful calmness and resignation. I am so grieved to think you won't be present at St George's tomorrow though indeed I feel it would be too much for you and give double anxiety to the parents.[14]

A week later, Louise wrote, also to her grandmother:

I am so much obliged to you for your kind letter which touches me so much, as I can see how thoroughly you feel for us in our great sorrow. I have always known how fond you were of our poor dear Eddy, who certainly was in every way worthy of your affection. I can hardly realize now, that he has really gone, and it all seems like a dreadful dream, too sad to be true. His was such a gentle, kind and affectionate nature, that everyone was devoted to him, and it is some consolation to me to know that his memory will be cherished by all his relations and friends. We are all heartbroken and I am sure we shall never quite get over it. I can never forget that awful morning when he died, when we were all around his bedside and watched his dear young life ebb away, even the three skilful doctors being powerless to save him. It is too sad for words and I will say no more, except to thank you for your very kind letter which pleased me so much.[15]

A more objective note was sounded by the *St James Gazette* obituary. While admitting that it would be sycophancy to say that the late Duke was regarded with enthusiastic affection or intense personal regard by his future subjects, it remarked on the 'unassuming, retired life' which he had led and which had given him no opportunity to become a public figure; he 'may be said to have lived under the shadow of the shadow of the throne.'

Naturally it had to be left to a later generation of biographers to place the Duke's death in perspective. Some seventy years later, Sir Philip Magnus remarked succinctly that the promotion of his brother to the position of heir presumptive to the throne was a merciful act of providence.[16]

Some people believed at the time that his death was rather less than providence, and wondered why he should have taken such a turn for the worse after the doctors arrived. It was rumoured that his fingernails had turned blue while he lay in his death agony, an indication that he had been deliberately poisoned. Comments made during the Tranby Croft baccarat court case in June 1891 by the Solicitor-General, Sir Edward Clarke, about 'a tottering throne' and men sacrificing themselves to 'prop up a falling dynasty' had allegedly sent such a tremor through court circles that the only hope of perpetuating the monarchy lay in eliminating the existence of an heir presumptive who was beyond doubt unfitted to reign. Such tampering with the line of succession, it was suggested by some, had its precedent in the suspected judicial execution of Crown Prince Rudolf of Austria-Hungary (who most were convinced had committed suicide at his Mayerling hunting lodge in January 1889), because conservative elements in the dual monarchy dreaded his radical sympathies and how he would implement them when he succeeded his father, Emperor Francis Joseph.

On the other hand, members of staff on the Osborne estate were sure that the Duke of Clarence was still alive. When the Jack the Ripper theories resurfaced about eighty years later, rumour had it that he had become incurably insane like his great-grandfather King George III and was secretly confined on the Isle of Wight, surviving until 1930.

As far as the bereaved bride-to-be was concerned, the Duke of Clarence belonged firmly to the past. To the end of her long life, Queen Mary never mentioned his name once to her children.

On 15 January, the body was moved to Sandringham church, where a service was held two days later. At the foot of the coffin lay a wreath shaped like a harp with broken strings, a token to May from the ladies of Ireland. The Princess of Wales wished Eddy to be buried there beside Alexander John, and Queen Victoria sympathetically agreed to grant the sorrowing mother her request, but the Prince of Wales overruled them. To him, Windsor was the only resting place for one who had been so close to the throne.

On the morning of 20 January, therefore, the coffin was taken to Wolverton Station and thence to St George's Chapel, Windsor, May following in a carriage with blinds drawn across the windows. As the journey came to an end, guns boomed from the Long Walk and the chapel bell rang mournfully through the cold winter air. At 3.30 p.m. the procession entered the chapel. The funeral's most moving moment came when the Duke of Teck handed the Prince of Wales a replica of the bridal bouquet of orange blossom, which was laid on the coffin. The Prince sobbed throughout the service, while the Princess hid from view, watching from the 'Queen's closet' in the gallery where Queen Victoria had discreetly watched their wedding in March 1863.

The proceedings were marred by one discordant note which had its element of farce. As the Princess of Wales had expressed a personal wish that the ceremony should be as private as possible, she was displeased to see that three of her sisters-in-law (Helena, Louise and Beatrice) had come from Osborne specially to attend. After the service was over, the royal sisters could not open the door of their pew. Immediately they thought that their spiteful brother and his wife had had them locked in on purpose. In high dudgeon Beatrice complained officially to Ponsonby, who took it up with the Prince of Wales's equerry Sir Arthur Ellis. After consulting his master, Ellis sent back a reply that 'the harem of princesses' had not been locked in; the door had become jammed. All the same, none of the ladies was wanted at the funeral; the Princess of Wales had particularly requested privacy; and if Princess Beatrice was annoyed, 'it cannot be helped and she must get over it – as she likes.'[17] Rarely can a royal servant have been called upon to deliver such a terse rebuke to his sovereign's daughter.

Throughout the country a day of national mourning was observed, with businesses, music halls and theatres closed. To the majority of Queen Victoria's subjects, a dashing romantic prince had just been betrothed and then suddenly taken tragically from them. Had they known more of the late Duke's character, their mourning might not have been so intense.

Denied so much in life, the Duke of Clarence was honoured in death. The sculptor Alfred Gilbert was commissioned to design and execute his funeral monument. A recumbent effigy with a head of Mexican onyx, lying on a high table tomb surrounded by ivory weepers, was placed in the Albert Memorial Chapel at Windsor.*

---

* Alfred Gilbert had designed the Shaftesbury monument ('Eros' and the fountain) in Piccadilly Circus, but as a result of heavy expenditure on his commissions and extravagant living, he went bankrupt in 1901 and settled in Bruges, leaving the Clarence memorial unfinished. At the request of King George V he returned to England after the Great War, and soon after completing his work received a knighthood.

5 'The Frogs in the Pond'

Prince George was stunned by Eddy's death. No two brothers, he wrote to Queen Victoria (18 January 1892) in his grief, could have loved each other more than they did; 'I remember with pain nearly every hard word and little quarrel I ever had with him and I long to ask his forgiveness, but, alas, it is too late now!'[1] Still very weak after his own illness, he suffered from nightmares and insomnia. So great were fears of a relapse that a nurse who had tended him during his attack of typhoid was temporarily recalled. He was still convalescent when he accompanied his parents to Compton Place at Eastbourne, and later to Cap Martin in the south of France.

The Prince of Wales showed himself a true son of his mother by the way in which he preserved Eddy's deathbed room as a shrine to his memory. A Union flag was draped over the bed, and his dressing table was left just as it had been during his final illness, with his wristwatch, brushes, soap and comb lying on top. For many years afterwards, a fire was kept burning in the grate. On the exterior wall, under the window, his monogram and the date of his death were carved in stone.

As expected, the family reunion at Compton Place was a miserable affair. It was arranged to include 27 February, the day on which the wedding should have taken place. May, looking like 'a crushed flower', in Queen Victoria's phrase, was there with the Waleses, who presented her with a rivière of diamonds ordered by Eddy's parents as her wedding present. The Duke of Teck observed that his daughter had quite become the child of the Waleses, and foresaw that she would be 'very much taken up with them.' She went shopping with George by day, and played bezique with him during the evenings. He loved to reminisce with her about his 'darling boy', the brother of whom he had been so protective. Throughout the rest of his life he used Eddy's pen. The relationship between the two was reckoned to be no more than platonic at the time, he signing his letters to 'Miss May' 'ever your very loving old cousin Georgie'. In turn, her replies were signed, 'your devoted Cousin May'.

Louise and Macduff joined them briefly at Eastbourne, and on their return to Portman Square the former wrote to Queen Victoria (22 February) that they found everybody:

> pretty well, but of course sad. Indeed the more we all realize our terrible sorrow, the harder it is to bear. There are some things I feel, which one can never forget or get over, though they say that time is a great healer.[2]

In March the family went to Cap Martin, and from the hotel Maud wrote to her grandmother (6 April), suggesting that the change was doing them good:

We like being here immensely, it is such a lovely place and we have the most perfect weather, it is quite hot just like July and we are out almost all day. Dear Mamma seems really a little better and is very fond of this place and I think it does her a lot of good. We go for long drives every day and saw the Villa where you stayed at Mentone some years ago, the view is beautiful from there.[3]

As if the shock of the bereavement was not enough, the diffident and far from robust Prince George now found himself second in line to the throne. He was only too aware of his shortcomings in temperament for such a daunting destiny; a slight lisp and knock-knees further undermined his self-confidence. The elder generation recognized that changes had to be made in order to prepare him for the future. Accordingly he was given his own accommodation, a suite of apartments in St James's Palace, and the 'Bachelor's Cottage' in the grounds of Sandringham. Finance was no problem, for in 1889 the Prince of Wales had secured an annual grant of £36,000 to be divided among his children as he saw fit. The majority would have provided an appropriate allowance for the Duke of Clarence, but on his death the sum was re-allocated with George being the main beneficiary.

On 24 May 1892, Prince George was created Duke of York, Earl of Inverness and Baron Killarney. He wrote to his grandmother to thank her for the honour, and with characteristic honesty she replied that she was glad he liked the title 'Duke of York'. She herself begged to differ, on account of its 'not very agreeable associations'. To her, it was and would be forever connected with its last holder, her Uncle Frederick, who, as a result of his mistress', Mary Ann Clarke, illegal sale of commissions, had been disgraced as Commander-in-Chief. Until then, the title Duke of York had been one traditionally bestowed on the sovereign's second son, and Queen Victoria thus broke with tradition in 1866 when she created her son Duke of Edinburgh instead. In 1890, when the question of a dukedom for Prince George had been mooted at the same time as one for his brother, she had told Ponsonby that she wished for one for her grandson free of any ignominious associations. If a title was necessary, why could he not be created Duke of Rothesay or Earl of Chester?

On 17 June, George took his seat in the Lords, introduced by his father and the Duke of Connaught. 'Fancy my Georgie boy doing that and now being a grand old Duke of York!'[4] his mother wrote playfully.

No less important was the matter of finding a Duchess of York. It was now common knowledge that the Prince of Wales's children did not enjoy the robust health of their uncles and aunts, and that George had twice been in danger of premature death – once at sea, and once from typhoid. The spectre of a shy, listless 'Queen Louise' eventually succeeding to the throne reared its head once more.

Prince George had lost his heart to Julie Stonor, the orphaned daughter of one of his mother's ladies-in-waiting, and a granddaughter of Sir Robert Peel. 'My own darling little Julie,' as he referred to her in his diary, was a commoner and, like Hélène d'Orleans, a Roman Catholic. Unlike Eddy, he had enough sense to realize that such a marriage could never be. Julie married the Marquis d'Hautpoul in 1891, but she and Prince George remained close friends until the latter's death. To her was accorded the distinction of being the only commoner allowed to address him simply as George.

The next possible candidate for his hand was his first cousin Marie of Edinburgh. Both had remained on close terms since their days on Malta; the Prince of Wales liked her and thought her pretty (not perhaps without a twinge of jealousy, for his Edinburgh nieces were far more attractive and lively than their Wales cousins), and the Duke of Edinburgh saw his industrious, naval-minded, stamp-collecting nephew as a man after his own heart. Such a Wales–Edinburgh match, Queen Victoria recognized, was 'the dream of Affie's life.'

He had reckoned without his wife Marie, who had resented her English relations ever since being denied precedence over her sisters-in-law at court (she was a Russian grand duchess and only daughter of the mighty Tsar of Russia – they were mere royal princesses) and the Anglo-Russian antagonism of the late 1870s which had nearly led to war between both countries. No daughter of hers, she vowed, could think of marrying an English prince. Once it was evident what her mother-in-law and husband were thinking, she made Marie write George a stiffly-worded note to the effect that he must not think there was anything definite in the friendship between them. She then took her daughter safely out of harm's way by arranging for her to be introduced and engaged to the well-meaning but shy and ineffectual Ferdinand, Crown Prince of Roumania.

For a while, relations between the Prince of Wales and Duke of Edinburgh were strained. Bertie thought that Affie had snubbed him and his son, until he realized what had really happened. But Alix was relieved. If her 'Georgie boy' had to get married at all, it would certainly not be to one of the Edinburgh princesses. They were much too German, and Marie was in her estimation 'a perfect baby'. Moreover, she cordially disliked the Duchess of Edinburgh, though not the Duke. For her part, Marie had always detested Eddy, and would have treated George's wistful reminiscences about 'his darling boy' with contempt.

The simplest solution to the problem was the most obvious. While the family were at Sandringham in that doleful week of January 1892, the Duke of Teck had embarrassed everyone by wandering around muttering repeatedly, 'It must be a Tsarevich.' He was alluding to Tsarevich Nicholas, who had died of tuberculosis in 1865 shortly after being betrothed to Alix's younger sister Dagmar. His deathbed wish was for her to marry his eldest surviving brother Alexander, which she did the following year. This arranged marriage had proved very happy, and Alexander (now Tsar Alexander III) defied Romanov tradition by remaining faithful to his wife. Their mutual happiness had been commented on by Queen Victoria to one of the funeral guests. Lady Geraldine Somerset, lady-in-waiting to the late Duchess of Cambridge and mother of the infamous Lord Arthur, noted in her diary that everybody from the Queen downwards, except Prince George himself, had resolved that George would soon marry May.

Perceptively, May was well aware of the whispering that went on behind her back, and was ill-at-ease. She would have been even more worried had she known what Queen Victoria bluntly told the Duke of Cambridge, some five weeks after Eddy's funeral, when she alluded again to Tsar Alexander III's marriage; 'You know May never was in love with poor Eddy!' Dr Manby, one of the doctors at Sandringham, was to testify that it was obvious from the beginning that George and May were falling in love. While attending the Duke of Clarence in his last days, he looked out of the window and saw them pacing the gardens, hand in hand.[5]

Though George must have realized that his days in the navy were numbered, he went to sea again at the end of June soon after taking his seat in the Lords. He was given command of HMS *Melampus* for summer manoeuvres, an experience he hated. The weather was rough, and he suffered from violent seasickness. Night after night he had to remain on deck, and for six days he was unable to change his clothes. The flagship, he reported, 'made any number of mistakes and we all got anyhow. I hope I shall never be in any other manoeuvres.'[6]

It was understood that fifteen years in the navy had done nothing to give him any political knowledge. On his return to England in November 1892, a course of meetings with politicians was arranged. He dined with members of the government and opposition, and attended parliamentary debates in the upper and lower chambers. In February 1893, he was present when Gladstone introduced his second Home Rule Bill into the Commons, making what he called 'a beautiful speech' lasting two and a quarter hours, 'wonderful for a man of eighty-three.'

That same month, he started to acquire some experience himself in public speaking. He gave an address in aid of the Society for Prevention of Cruelty to Children; next day he received the freedom of the Merchant Taylors Company and had to make a reply. Afterwards he admitted that the occasion made him 'horribly nervous'.

One of the few happy events in the Wales family during the otherwise grim year of 1891 was the birth of a first grandchild. On 17 May Louise was delivered of a daughter, named Alexandra. It was a relief to all that she could produce healthy children, for on 16 June the previous year she had had a stillborn son. The death in childbirth four months later of her Greek-born cousin Alexandra, married to Grand Duke Paul of Russia, was another unhappy reminder of the hazards of pregnancy. 'For her it is a mercy,' she wrote sadly to Queen Victoria (25 September 1891), 'but it is a terrible grief for those she has left behind.'[7]

Shortly before Christmas next year, Louise informed the immediate family rather coyly that she was pregnant again. To Queen Victoria she wrote (11 December 1892):

Mama will tell you from me, that I am not very strong just now, but I like to tell you this myself, too, dearest Grandmama. You know that I do not like anyone to know this, especially long before! I am sure that you will kindly do, as you did before, and not mention this to anyone. I confess I am rather sensitive about myself and I am sure you will understand and enter into my feelings about it. We have come here from Castle Rising and shall be a little while in London now. Although I have been here, I have been obliged to take great care and have not felt very well lately. So I am sure that you will understand my not proposing ourselves to ask you to let us come to Windsor just now, as we should very much have liked to do.[8]

Louise, Duchess of Fife, with her second daughter, Lady Alexandra Duff, her mother the Princess of Wales, King Christian IX and Queen Louise of Denmark, photographed by Downey, 1893

On 3 April 1893, Princess Maud of Fife was born. However, three pregnancies had taxed her mother's health quite enough, and there would be no male heir to the dukedom.

Meanwhile, the matchmaking continued. As early as August 1892, the Prince of Wales had warned his son that Queen Victoria was 'in a terrible fuss about your marrying.' He and the Princess of Wales had at first felt that a quick engagement between George and May would be an insult to Eddy's memory, but gradually commonsense prevailed over sentimental considerations. May, it was recognized, would make an excellent queen consort-in-waiting, and they were in no position to resist ever-increasing pressure from Mama at Windsor. Bertie was not slow to see the benefits of such an alliance, as long as his son was happy with the idea. Eventually the possessive Alix realized that her one remaining son could not remain a bachelor for ever. Louise was also playing her part; while resting at Sheen before the birth of Maud, she invited May to visit her and wrote to George, telling him about it and praising her guest lavishly.

The mournful first anniversary of Eddy's death came and went, with Maud writing sympathetically to May the next day:

> My thoughts have been with you so much all these dreadful days when we spent so many sad and agonizing hours together here only a year ago! and yet it all seems so vivid in our mind that it might have been but yesterday – Sad, sad are those anniversaries when they come round and bring back all that one has lost.[9]

On 4 March George joined his mother and two youngest sisters for a Mediterranean cruise on board the yacht *Osborne*, *en route* for the Princess of Wales's family at Greece. She told everyone that he needed 'a complete change and rest before settling down in life,' though they all knew that this was her last chance to have him all to herself before he married. At the court of Athens he pondered on his future, and fortified by the encouragement of his aunt, Queen Olga, his mind was made up.

Mother and son parted at Malta, for she felt that she could not bear to be in England when the engagement was announced. After returning to London, George went to stay with the Duke and Duchess of Fife at Sheen Lodge, and on 2 May he dined with the Tecks at White Lodge. The two young people whose future was being so carefully planned were nervous and embarrassed by speculation in the press, and May had asked her parents to avoid leaving them alone with each other. But the Duke and Duchess of Teck knew that they would not have to be patient for long.

Next day, May was invited to tea with the Fifes, ostensibly to see baby Maud. Louise found an unexpected ally in the amphibian world. 'Now, Georgie,' she suggested brightly, after looking at the awkward expressions on their faces, 'don't you think you ought to take May into the garden to look at the frogs in the pond?'[10] Dutifully he led her into the picturesque gardens and made his proposal, which was accepted.

There followed an evening of excited calls and telegrams to closest relations. In her joy the Duchess of Teck telegraphed to her family and friends, 'May engaged to Duke of York.' Then she realized in a panic that Queen Victoria might be angry with her for making the news public without her express permission, and a further telegram went out to each recipient. 'Unless announced in papers keep engagement secret.' She need not have worried, for Queen Victoria gave the press permission to publish the news at once, in advance of her official announcement at a Privy Council meeting on 16 May.

To some journalists, however, the story had long ceased to be news. Three months earlier, a writer from *The Observer* had telegraphed Sir Henry Ponsonby to ask whether rumours that the engagement would be made public on 11 February were true. Ponsonby diplomatically telegraphed back: 'Thanks for the information I had not heard it before and cannot find any one in this house who has.' Queen Victoria was delighted with this 'excellent answer'.[11]

The wedding was arranged for 6 July in the Chapel Royal, Windsor, and the eight weeks between their betrothal and the ceremony proved extremely hot and oppressive. Heat was only one of the problems with which the young couple had to contend. Both shy by nature, they were distressed at their failure to communicate their feelings adequately to one another. They exchanged daily notes, expressing the sentiments they felt unable to put into speech. 'The more I feel, the less I say, I am so sorry but I can't help it,' ran one of May's apologies, while George told her he was eternally grateful that they understood each other so well, making it unnecessary for him to say how much he loved her, 'although I may appear shy and cold.'

Parental possessiveness added to the uneasy atmosphere. The Duchess of Teck was loath to leave them alone together, and made endless demands on her daughter as if nothing had changed. In vain did George suggest bluntly that May should tell her mother she would not do any more 'and that I don't wish it.' 'I hope you are quite well again,' she wrote to him a few days later, 'I am nearly *dead*.' On the other hand 'Motherdear' was less possessive than usual, though her letter of congratulation ended on a rather artless note which must have made her future daughter-in-law's heart sink; 'I hope my sweet May will always come straight to me for everything.'[12]

Staying in London during a hot summer spell, it could not be anything other than a very public engagement. The couple were obliged to receive deputations, admire and sort wedding presents (no less than 1,400) and attend gala performances at the opera and theatre. Crowds cheered with what must have seemed tiresome predictability wherever they went.

Fortunately their sense of humour did not altogether desert this unusually serious-minded Prince and Princess. On being told that less reputable elements of the press were attempting to make capital out of a rumour that HRH Prince George had been married in Malta, he told May with a chuckle that the wedding would have to be cancelled; 'I hear that I have already got a wife and three children.'

The Tecks were invited to stay at Buckingham Palace for the wedding, and Queen Victoria joined them there on 5 July. With her customary candour, she remarked that the heat was 'quite awful.' The Prince and Princess of Wales held a garden party at Marlborough House in the afternoon, five thousand guests being invited.

The Duke and Duchess of York on their wedding day, 6 July 1893

At supper that evening in the palace, Queen Victoria sat between King Christian of Denmark and Tsarevich Nicholas. The latter's great likeness to Prince George, she noted, led to 'no end of funny mistakes, the one being taken for the other!' More than once during his stay the bachelor Tsarevich was congratulated on having found himself such a splendid bride. Other royal guests included Prince Henry of Prussia, only surviving brother of the German Emperor and far more popular with his English relations, and Prince Albert of the Belgians.

At the wedding next day, George wore naval uniform. He was supported by his father and the Duke of Edinburgh, who was shortly to succeed to the Dukedom of Saxe-Coburg Gotha. After appearing with Queen Victoria on the palace balcony, he and May drove through crowded cheering streets to Liverpool Street Station, where they boarded a train to Wolverton. 'Most enormous crowds I ever saw,' the groom noted in his diary.

The honeymoon was spent, rather unimaginatively, at what was to be their home for the next seventeen years – York House, Sandringham. Given the

The Duke of York (seated) and Tsarevich Nicholas of Russia, photographed by Downey, 1893. This was taken while the latter was on a visit to England for the former's wedding, and demonstrates the similarity between the cousins

choice, May would have surely preferred a few days overseas. Not so the unadventurous George, for whom Sandringham was a haven of security. The little house was badly planned, ugly, poorly furnished, and totally lacking in privacy. May's Aunt Augusta had noted their choice of home with regret; 'it mixes them up so entirely with the present Wales surroundings.'

Less than a fortnight after the wedding, the Prince and Princess of Wales returned to the 'Big House' with their two younger daughters, King Christian and Queen Louise of Denmark, and their youngest son Prince Waldemar. Over the next few days, members of this party dropped in regularly at York House, inviting themselves to tea or breakfast, and summoning them to dinner at Sandringham and bowls afterwards. With admirable restraint, May later recalled that 'just after we were married we were not left alone enough,' adding that this denied them the opportunity of learning to understand each other as quickly as they might otherwise have done.[13]

The family's attitude towards May had now changed, and not for the better. 'Sweet May', as the Princess of Wales had called her, was now 'Poor May'. This note of disparagement was soon picked up by her two elder daughters, who seemed to resent their cousin's having taken their only surviving brother away from them. She was so unlike them in character; her reserved attitude and appreciation of things intellectual made her everything that they were not. Louise and Victoria were undoubtedly jealous of the status that marriage to the heir presumptive had given to their sister-in-law, and such jealousy spilled over into occasional resentment. 'Now do try to talk to May at dinner,' Victoria spitefully told a guest at Windsor one evening, 'although one knows she is deadly dull.'[14] Thankfully Maud, despite still being single herself, had no part in her sisters' small-minded attitude.

The Wales Princesses were not the only ones to make disparaging remarks about the Duke and Duchess of York behind their backs. As they appeared outwardly so indifferent to one another, jokes were cracked in London society about how successful the marriage would be in providing another generation of heirs to the throne. Did they recall the cynical quip of Charles Greville in 1840, commenting on how strange that the 'bridal night' of Queen Victoria and Prince Albert should be so short, and that an early walk on the morning after their wedding was no way to provide the nation with a Prince of Wales? Coincidentally, May told her mother during the honeymoon how much she and her husband were enjoying Greville's 'amusing though spiteful' memoirs.

Any fears that the Duchess of York might fail in her dynastic duty proved groundless. By Christmas it was known that she was expecting a child. The all-important question for the parents-to-be was where the birth should take place. Buckingham Palace and York House (their London residence) were both rejected as being too 'public'. York Cottage plainly lacked privacy from the Wales's. This left only one further choice – White Lodge, Richmond, where George and May thought she would find some seclusion. They had reckoned without the Duchess of Teck's persistence.

Since her daughter's marriage, a change had come over the Duchess. She had relied on May to keep the house running, assist with her charities and look after her finances. May's brothers were either too irresponsible or too young to take her place, and the Duke's health was deteriorating fast. The shock of Eddy's death and the excitement of his daughter's marriage had taken their toll on his already enfeebled mind; his temper was worsening, and he was apt to break out into fits of uncontrollable laughter and moodiness, or talk incoherently without ceasing for no apparent reason. The Duchess was sixty, and years of obesity were beginning to tell on her. She could no longer cope with the cares of running her family and looking after her pitiful husband, and she therefore found refuge in bursting in on her daughter and son-in-law unannounced. She would come for lunch without warning and stay until after dinner. Although May was used to her behaviour, George, with his naval upbringing and passion for orderly routine was exasperated by her lack of punctuality and planning. Many a time he complained bitterly to his wife, but out of pity for her mother she felt helpless to do anything about it.

During the later weeks of June 1894, with the birth expected any day, May was horrified to see large numbers of people gathering outside the gates of White Lodge each morning, hoping to catch the news of a royal happy event before the press, and perhaps see the baby as well. In the evening of 23 June a

Four generations: Queen Victoria, holding her great-grandson Prince Edward of York, flanked by the Prince of Wales and Duke of York, at the infant Prince's christening, White Lodge, Richmond Park, 16 July 1894

son was born. To the Princess of Wales, his arrival in the world was her first happiness, she said, since Eddy's death. Queen Victoria was also impressed with the 'fine, strong-looking child.' There were now heirs to the throne in three generations.

Yet again, Queen Victoria was determined that this youngest descendant should be named in accordance with family tradition. She was most anxious, she wrote to George (26 June), 'that he should bear the name of his beloved Great Grandfather, a name which brought untold blessings to the whole Empire and that Albert should be his first name.'[15]

Tactfully George wrote to reply that he and his wife had already settled on the name Edward, after Eddy, if their first-born was a prince. His parents had shown commendable lack of interference in leaving the choice of names entirely to them. Thus Edward Albert Christian George Andrew Patrick David was christened in the drawing room at White Lodge on 16 July; he was always known in the family as David, but Prince Edward to the public at large.*

Both parents left the Lodge with relief. May was at last allowed a complete change of scenery and took herself off to the Hotel Victoria, St Moritz – with her

---

* To avoid confusion, future references in this text will be to 'Edward'.

mother. George departed for Cowes, from where he wrote to say that nothing would induce him to go through six weeks of such an experience again for anything.

The next time May was pregnant, she and her husband intended that the confinement should take place somewhere else. Despite their misgivings as to lack of privacy, it was at York House that their second son was born on 14 December 1895. Coming on the doubly black-edged anniversary of the Prince Consort's death and that of Princess Alice, Grand Duchess of Hesse, in 1878, the Prince of Wales had to admit that 'Grandmama was rather distressed,' but he trusted that the new Prince's birth would 'break the spell' of the unlucky date.[16] On his suggestion, the baby was named Albert. Queen Victoria, who gladly accepted an invitation to be his godmother (and presented him with that great honour, a bust of the Prince Consort, as a christening present), answered Prince George's regret that he should have been born on such a sad day with her assurance that 'it may be a blessing for the dear little boy and may be looked upon as a gift from God!'[17]

The *Morning Advertiser* greeted his birth effusively:

The little Prince belongs to the nation as well as to his parents. He may never be called upon, as his father was, to step into the place on the steps of the throne, vacated under such sorrowful circumstances by an elder brother. But his birth is a second guarantee of the direct succession to the British Crown – that greatest of all inheritances, as Mr Gladstone once finely called it.[18]

Not until some forty years later would the irony of this editorial be appreciated.

6 'The Brightest of the Princesses'

By now speculation was rife as to who would seek the hand in marriage of the Princesses Victoria and Maud, both now in their mid-twenties. Queen Victoria told Bertie it was time that they thought of choosing husbands, but he answered sadly that he was powerless. Alix, he said, found the girls such good companions that she would not encourage them to do so, and they themselves had no inclination for married life. He knew very well that the last remark was false, especially as Maud was repeatedly grumbling at her mother for not doing enough to find her a husband, but in certain matters he had to defer to his wife. If she was to tolerate his all-too-public liaisons with Sarah Bernhardt, Lillie Langtry, Mrs Chamberlayne and others, he had to put up with her foibles. Her unpunctuality and late morning rising had to be borne as meekly as the domestic tyranny she exercised over her daughters. Not for nothing did King George V comment in later life to Queen Mary that his Mama was one of the most selfish people he knew.

In bad weather, the inhabitants of Sandringham continued to suffer from illness almost as a matter of routine. Writing to thank Queen Victoria for her Christmas present of a drawing block for sketching, Maud told her (31 December 1893) that:

> We spent a very quiet Christmas this time as dear Mama was ill and I too. This horrid influenza takes all one's strength away and it takes such a long time before one gets well. Now thank goodness dear Mama is getting on slowly but she had two very strong attacks with high fever and for some days was really very bad – I have had this dreadful abscess in my ear and have been shut up a month in my room as it has not healed yet and I am so afraid of the draughts, it has been quite agonies [sic], anything the matter with one's ears is always very painful.[1]

For once, her sister Victoria was perfectly well at that time. 'I have been doing sick-nurse to the whole family,' she wrote proudly to Queen Victoria that same day, 'so my time has been fully occupied.'[2]

'It really is not wise to leave the fate of these dear girls *dans la vague* for years longer,'[3] Vicky wrote. In the spring of 1894 her thoughts turned to her nephew Prince Max of Baden. Victoria or Maud, she felt, would suit him perfectly, an added advantage being that Max was very pro-English and would enjoy being in England as much as possible. Bertie, she realized, would favour the idea, if only Alix did not 'dislike us Germans so.'[4]

Prince Charles of Denmark, with Princess Maud and Princess Victoria of Wales, all in Elizabethan costume, c. 1895

Maud had the misfortune to fall in love with a thoroughly eligible yet at the same time quite impossible suitor – none other than May's brother Francis (Frank) of Teck. Eligible because he was a cousin, and they had known each other most of their lives, but impossible because he was such an infuriating young man. He had inherited all the fecklessness and extravagance, as well as the charm, of his parents. His gambling was indulged in to a degree that made the Prince of Wales seem restrained, and he lived on credit. Ever since he had been expelled from Wellington College for projecting his housemaster over a hedge in order to win a bet, the elder generation had silently shaken their heads over his behaviour. Maud adored him, but fortunately for her he had fallen for a married woman much older than himself, and never bothered to answer his doting cousin's letters. In order to teach him a lesson, he suffered the customary Victorian punishment of being packed off to India out of harm's way.

If there was one branch of the family into which Alix would allow her daughters to marry, it was that of her Danish kinsmen. After Frank's disgrace, there was talk of one of them being betrothed to their cousin Christian, a few months

Princess Maud and Prince Charles of Denmark at the time of their engagement, 1895

Maud's junior. This came to nothing, but soon it became apparent that his younger brother Charles was taking an interest in Maud.

Like the Teck brothers, Charles had known Maud since childhood. They had ridden their ponies, cycled and indulged in endless practical jokes on regular Danish family reunions at Fredensborg and Bernstorff. Much as the Prince of Wales might deprecate the boredom of such places, some of the younger generation thought otherwise. In particular Tsar Alexander III, a terrifying autocrat at home who dreaded the assassin's bomb and bullet which had claimed his father's life, was completely unrecognizable in Denmark. With his unrestrained enthusiasm for the schoolboy jokes which were beneath his imperial dignity in Russia, 'Uncle Sasha' was a great favourite of Maud and Charles. They giggled when he found unsuspecting victims for the watering hose and only owned up when it was apparent that otherwise they would get the blame for his misdemeanours, and at a small instrument which he kept concealed beneath the tails of his evening coat, 'making it give out a very fair imitation of certain natural noises whenever anyone paid him ceremonial reverence.'[5]

In September 1894 Tsar Alexander fell ill. Nephritis was diagnosed, and on 1 November he died at the early age of forty-nine. The family were stunned, and the Duchess of Fife was among those who went to console the sad gathering at Bernstorff just after Christmas. To Queen Victoria she wrote tenderly of her maternal grandmother's grief:

I came here to be with poor dear Amama, who could not have gone through all this sad time alone! She feels our beloved U(ncle) Sasha's loss deeply. He was a real son to her, she had seen so much of him; besides poor dear Aunt Minny's grief is very painful to her, and she is devoted to them all.[6]

Entering the Danish navy at the age of fourteen, Charles was promoted to second lieutenant in 1893. By the time he reached maturity he was six feet two inches tall, and despite a habitually grave expression he had an acute sense of humour; when amused, he would rock back and forth on his feet. For a couple of years, gossips had been talking of a secret engagement between the royal cousins who had been close since childhood, and as a cadet it was said that Prince Charles kept a photograph of Maud in his desk at the officers school. During a family reunion at Fredensborg, he proposed to Maud and she gladly accepted him; their engagement was announced in October 1895. He was almost three years her junior, and Alix wondered if the age difference might prove a barrier as far as he was concerned. While some thought him not as dashing or perhaps even as handsome as Frank, he was a much steadier character and Maud realized that he would make her a for better husband. Moreover, with her love of yachting and the sea, it was fitting that her husband should be a sailor.

Initially Maud and her parents were apprehensive lest the Duke and Duchess of Teck should feel that they were snubbing their son. May tactfully assured them that there need be no fear of that; Frank had behaved so foolishly that they had given up any thoughts of another Wales–Teck alliance. The Duchess of Teck admired Charles and thought him quite charming, though he looked so much younger than Maud. She maintained that he ought to enter the British navy, but heard that Queen Louise of Denmark was violently opposed to the idea. Her one great fear was that Maud did not 'care for him enough to leave England for his sake and live in Denmark and I dread her finding this out when too late.'[7]

From a worldly point of view, it was suggested that the granddaughter of Queen Victoria could have done much better for herself than 'a newly-commissioned sub-lieutenant in a miniature navy'. It was undoubtedly a love-match, and Maud was more than happy to make what gave promise of being a modest marriage. Some years earlier, it was said, she had turned down the hand of Prince Constantine of the Hellenes, as she could not envisage life in a foreign court, and eventually a consort's crown. The second son of a crown Prince, so it seemed, made the likelihood of a throne remote.

Marie Mallet, the former Miss Marie Adeane, noted in her diary (29 October 1895) that Maud's engagement 'caused much excitement' at Balmoral, 'and has been the cause of endless telegraphing. . . . The Queen is delighted and healths were drunk at dinner.'[8]

Maud delightedly informed the Queen (27 October):

Though I know that Papa and Mama have already written to you to announce my engagement to my cousin Carl, I thought you would like to hear from me myself dear Grandmama, as you have always been so very kind to me and I wanted to tell you how happy I am and I hope you approve of my choice. All the dear relations in Denmark were delighted when it took place but it was very sad parting from them all on Wednesday and particularly for me as I was only just engaged the day before! However I hope that dear Carl will be able to come to Sandringham in November for a few days as his ship stops in England on its way to the West Indies and will be away for five months. But after his journey he means to come here and thus I hope he may see you dear Grandmama as he has never seen you yet though he has been here several times some years ago.[9]

She confessed herself overwhelmed in a letter to Prince Alexander of Teck (8 January 1896):

Charles really liked me three years ago but I never thought that it would last and that he would forget everything when he went to sea, but instead of that when he met me in the autumn again it became more so, and finally ended in this happy way![10]

Charles was due to set off for a five-month cruise in the West Indies, so the wedding was scheduled for the following summer. It was celebrated on 22 July 1896 in the chapel at Buckingham Palace as more of a family gathering than a state occasion. The King and Queen of Denmark, both in their late seventies, declined to make the journey, but the groom's parents, Crown Prince and Princess Frederick, both attended; from Athens came Crown Prince and Princess Constantine, as well as the immediate British relatives.

One of the Princess of Wales's great gifts, it was said by contemporaries, was her knack of dressing simply without affectation. Maud was likewise attired in very simple fashion, with her mother's wedding veil, a dress of ivory satin without jewels, and a bouquet of orange blossom. All the guests thought this far more effective than anything too elaborate. The bridesmaids all wore white trimmed with red geraniums.

Charles, in uniform and escorted into the chapel by his brothers Princes Christian and Harald, had recently been promoted to first lieutenant. Always modest about his abilities, when asked why he had remained a second lieutenant for so long, he attributed it to 'lack of strings and influence'. It was owing to his marriage, he answered, that he had achieved senior rank.

Archbishop Benson, who officiated at the wedding, was not alone in his verdict when he remarked that Maud was 'the brightest of the Princesses', and said that she looked almost as young as when he had confirmed her. Even Queen Victoria, whose opinion of weddings at the time of her eldest son's nuptials had been such a gloomy one, seemed rejuvenated. After embracing her granddaughter and the groom tenderly, and joining fifty other royalties in signing the register, she talked spiritedly for several minutes. An Indian servant wheeled her chair into the chapel, but she waved it back. 'Behind the door!' she commanded, hobbling determinedly on her stick across the room.

After the ceremony, a luncheon was given in the state ballroom at Buckingham Palace. The guests were presented in turn to Queen Victoria, and that afternoon the Prince and Princess of Wales hosted a garden party at Marlborough House.

Appleton House, the Prince of Wales's wedding present to Princess Maud

The couple left from St Pancras for what was to be a short honeymoon at Appleton on the Sandringham estate. Appleton was a wedding present from the Prince of Wales to his daughter, given with the stipulation that she should visit it at least once a year. It had formerly been a farmhouse rented by Louise Cresswell, whose brave defence of her land and crops against the Prince's sporting obsession had resulted in her bankruptcy and flight to America.*

In fact, the honeymoon of Prince and Princess Charles lasted for five months. The Duchess of Teck's observations that Maud dreaded leaving England were soon realized. She was too accustomed to life at Sandringham, with regular visits to Cowes, London and the Scottish Highlands, under the protective wing of her mother and father. Her eldest sister had been fortunate enough to marry into the nobility and still live in Britain. Even though she had married into a family of cousins whom she had known and visited regularly since childhood, how would she adapt to making her home in a foreign country?

Three weeks after the wedding, the Danish royal family gathered at Bernstorff Castle to welcome the couple. At the end of August, 'Motherdear' and Princess Victoria joined them. Like heads of state attending an international summit meeting, more relations gradually appeared. 'We are going off to Denmark on the 1st (September) in the "Osborne",'[11] Maud wrote to Queen Victoria (20 August), but they did not. Early in September King George of

---

* The full story of this sordid business, recounted by Mrs Cresswell in *18 Years on the Sandringham estate* and more recently by David Duff in *Whisper Louise*, reflects the least creditable and most selfish aspect of the future King Edward VII's character.

Greece made his way to Bernstorff, to be followed a few days later by Tsar Nicholas and Tsarina Alexandra.

Yet still Maud could not bring herself to leave Appleton. She and her adoring, yet increasingly anxious, husband stayed on at Sandringham receiving congratulatory addresses, riding their ponies, cycling round the estate, and inspecting schools. In London they paid visits to the Duke and Duchess of Fife, attended the theatre, and visited Green Park to hear the band play. They visited Queen Victoria at Windsor, Osborne and Balmoral. As autumn gave way to winter, the welcoming committee returned to their respective homes in disbelief. Maud and Charles were still in England on 14 December, and joined the rest of the family at the Prince Consort's anniversary service at Frogmore.

By now, Charles's six months' leave from the navy was nearly over. Maud was persuaded that she must steel herself to leave England, and although nothing would have pleased her more than to spend Christmas at Sandringham, she and Charles set off for Copenhagen on 21 December.

Driving through the streets of Copenhagen from the station to their married home close to Amalienborg Palace, the crowds welcomed them effusively, though their enthusiasm was doubtless tempered by questions as to whether the new Princess, half-Danish by birth, would take her adopted country to her heart. They attended a state banquet on their first night in Copenhagen and their grandfather, King Christian IX, proposed her health; 'as my dear daughter Alexandra has won all British hearts, so may my granddaughter win the hearts of the whole Danish nation.'

She described the proceedings in a letter to Queen Victoria (30 December):

> We had a grand reception on our arrival which was rather alarming and I had to go round and shake hands with everybody, and we drove in gold carriages in procession in the Streets which were gaily decorated in our honour. Several dinners have been given for us and we have had numerous deputations and charming presents – It has been great trouble in finding and arranging all our things, but now at last we have got our rooms tidy and comfortable and we like the house very much, though it is rather damp just now as the days are so short and the weather is abominable, so raw and damp and dreadful cold winds.[12]

The couple's first married home was a ten-room apartment in the Bernstorff Palace. Formerly the official residence of the Danish foreign minister and subsequently other members of the Danish royal family, it was bought in 1881 by King George of Greece, who converted part of the ground floor into an apartment for use on his frequent visits to Denmark. Its most picturesque feature was the garden with its Chinese pavilion, where Maud and Charles would later give regular tea parties to friends in the summer. The rooms had been furnished partly by King George, and to these were added items brought over by Maud to reflect her English tastes. In true Sandringham fashion, she loved to fill her rooms with family photographs and knick-knacks. She was also interested in Napoleonic memorabilia, and had collected several paintings and *objets d'art* connected with England's late arch-enemy.

Maud and Charles began their life together with a modest income, consisting largely of an allowance from Charles's mother. King Christian had asked his ministers to propose funds for Charles on the occasion of his marriage, but they were reluctant to breach the Danish tradition which restricted state financial provision to the sovereign, his children, and the heir apparent in the next generation. Not until the accession of Maud's father some four years later were their fortunes supplemented by her additional grant of £6,000 per annum in the British civil list, as a daughter of the sovereign.

Fortunately for them, their tastes were modest. Maud had almost as little appetite for society life as had her eldest sister, and Charles's upbringing and naval career had ingrained in him a spartan way of life. Expenditure on social obligations and travel was unavoidable, particularly as Charles's elder brother Christian was still a bachelor and the prospect of his eventual accession to the Danish throne was still theoretically possible, but they spent comparatively little on themselves. They employed a staff of fourteen, including one lady-in-waiting for Maud. She and Charles had a carriage and kept riding horses, though bicycles proved a more convenient mode of transport in the Copenhagen streets – notwithstanding a family joke 'that wind in the Danish capital was round, since one met it everywhere.'

Yet Maud's heart remained in the country of her birth. At first she disliked Denmark, and when Charles was away for long periods at a time on naval duties she was bored and lonely. The Princess of Wales, who recalled her mother-in-law's strictures about loyalty to England during the war of the duchies in 1864, had to remind her sharply that she must never forget she had married a Danish prince and a naval man, 'and *he owes* his first duty both to his country and his profession.'[13] It was a profound relief to her when she could return to Appleton each year, with or without Charles, walking and riding around the estates where she had been brought up, and attending official functions and theatres in London.

She still accompanied her family from time to time on visits abroad, largely for the sake of her health. March 1899 found her wintering *en famille* in the south of France. The Princess of Wales and her daughters, commented Marie Mallet, looked very seedy, and Maud had 'dyed her hair canary colour which makes her look quite improper and more like a little milliner than ever.'[14]

Part of Maud's perpetual longing for 'home' stemmed from less selfish causes – namely her concern for 'poor Toria'. She told Knollys that she hated the idea of leaving her unmarried sister '*alone* again as her life is not an easy one.'

Princess Victoria did not remain in what her grandmother called 'single blessedness' for want of suitors. The latter had hoped that 'Dolly', Prince Adolphus of Teck, might have married either her or Maud, until in 1894 he became betrothed to the daughter of the Duke of Westminster. Her name was also romantically linked at various times with a member of the Baring family, and with that of her father's equerry, Arthur Davidson. He was only twelve years older than Victoria, and a devoted friend to the Prince and Princess of Wales, but as a commoner he would have been ineligible.

Where Princess Victoria's heart was concerned, nobody was more important than the Liberal Prime Minister, Lord Rosebery. A widower, his marriage had been idyllic. According to his close friend Winston Churchill, his wife was 'a remarkable woman', and 'without her he was maimed.' The courtship was conducted with great discretion, but the Prince of Wales professed himself rather startled when Rosebery asked him for his daughter's hand. The Prince, who had objected on largely political grounds to the betrothal of his sister Louise to Lord Lorne in 1870, may have felt that it was constitutionally unwise for somebody so close to the throne to be thus linked with a prime minister, and therefore identified closely with one of the political parties. Alternatively, he might have deferred to the wishes of his wife.

In view of the Fife match, the argument that the Princess of Wales could not consent to her daughter's marriage with a commoner or another peer holds little weight. The real reason was almost certainly sheer possessiveness. In this, it must be admitted, she was following her mother-in-law's example. Queen Victoria had been loath to lose her youngest daughter Beatrice, whose engagement to Prince Henry of Battenberg when she was twenty-seven took place after vigorous resistance from her astonished Mama. She had only consented to the marriage on condition that Henry make his home under the eye of his mother-in-law, and he found his existence so irksome that he volunteered eagerly for the futile Ashanti expedition in Africa, during which he died of malaria.

Alexandra did not intend to lose her spinster daughter. She might have approved of a marriage between her and her nephew the future King Christian X of Denmark, who was still a bachelor, but he failed to kindle a flame in his cousin's heart. Described by some as the most intelligent of the Wales children, Victoria was denied a life of married bliss which her Aunt Beatrice had known but briefly. Rosebery likewise remained a lonely widower to the end of his eighty-two years.

Yet Princess Victoria's life was not totally devoid of excitement. Along with her Uncle Arthur, Duke of Connaught, and the Bishop of Peterborough, she was one of the select few English observers of the last Russian coronation, that of Tsar Nicholas II and Tsarina Alexandra, in May 1896. Knowing how protective Queen Victoria had always felt towards her motherless Hesse grandchildren since Alice's death in 1878, and towards Alicky in particular, the Princess wrote a detailed and graphic account of the poignant ceremony from Moscow a few hours later (26 May 1896):

> The coronation is over, every thing went off admirably and it was a most beautiful and impressive sight. We were up very early as we had to leave the house at 8 a.m. At a quarter to nine Aunt Minnie in her crown and robes headed our procession into church. She looked marvellously young, but I have never seen sadder eyes than hers and it was visible that only by a grand effort of will she kept back the tears that kept starting to her eyes. It was indeed a sad and sorrowing sight to see her standing all alone before her throne waiting for the new Emperor and Empress to come. I think her youthful looks made it all the more pathetic. We waited about an hour in church before Nicky and Alicky appeared, he looked very grave and serious and she remarkably handsome with hair unadorned and only a small string of pearls around her neck. She was flushed and a little trembling at first, but as the ceremony proceeded grew quite calm . . .[15]

Princess Victoria astride her bicycle

Still only in her late forties, 'Aunt Minnie' was to be a frequent visitor to Sandringham and Marlborough House in the years ahead. A telegram from the Duke of Connaught that same day confirmed that the coronation had been a 'most glorious and impressive ceremony.' Not until later that week were the festivities marred by the horror of Khodinsky Meadow, when what was to have been a free open-air feast turned into a mass stampede of drunken spectators fighting for their share of what was rumoured to be an insufficient supply of souvenir gifts and food. Around two thousand people were crushed to death in the panic.

After the triumph of Queen Victoria's Diamond Jubilee in June 1897, the last years of the longest reign in British history were sad ones for the family. The ailing Duchess of Teck, worn out by her endless charitable work and the strain of nursing her sick husband, died suddenly in October after an operation. In September 1898 Queen Louise of Denmark died, and the Empress Elizabeth of Austria was stabbed to death by a anarchist. The dawn of the twentieth century was overshadowed by the Boer war in South Africa, a conflict in which European sympathy was overwhelmingly on the side of the the Boers and not with the British empire, and by the passing of 'Uncle Teck' in January 1900. That April an anarchist fired at and narrowly missed the Prince and Princess of

Wales as they were leaving Brussels by train; three months later the Duke of Saxe-Coburg Gotha, Prince George's favourite uncle Affie, died of cancer of the throat, aggravated by heavy drinking. The Empress Frederick was slowly dying from cancer as well, and too ill to visit Britain. Prince Christian Victor of Schleswig-Holstein, elder son of Princess Helena, died of fever in South Africa that October, and soon after Christmas it was apparent that Queen Victoria herself was sinking. Surrounded to the last by her family in her bedroom at Osborne, she passed away on 22 January 1901.

CHILDREN OF THE KING
1901–10

7 'A Regiment, Not a Family'

Despite his mother's wish that her eldest son should reign as King Albert Edward, he very wisely chose to be known by the far more English name of Edward, one already borne by six previous Kings. Queen Victoria's coffin lay in state for ten days at Osborne, and was then brought over to the mainland where it initially lay for two nights in the Albert Memorial Chapel beside effigies of the Prince Consort and the Duke of Clarence. Her funeral, a dignified, awe-inspiring ceremony attended by several European heads of state, took place on 4 February.

So many sovereigns and princes were staying at Windsor Castle that Sir Frederick Ponsonby,* whose numerous duties included drafting the order of ceremonial, had inadvertently omitted the name of the new king's son-in-law, the Duke of Fife. While talking to Macduff one morning King Edward caught sight of Ponsonby and called him over to administer a severe reprimand. How could he have any confidence in a servant when such an error was made? After seeing the equerry thus brought to book, Macduff walked off satisfied. Once he was out of earshot, the King's tone instantly changed. He told Ponsonby that he realized what a magnificent job he had done, but Fife was so hurt at his name being left out that he felt he was not wanted.

One significant absence from the funeral ceremony was that of Prince George. The new heir to the throne had been present at his grandmother's deathbed; he travelled to London next day to St James's Palace to approve the royal proclamation and to take the oath of allegiance. After returning to Osborne

---

* Equerry to King Edward VII, and as such played a similar role as confidant to his sovereign as his father Sir Henry (who died in 1895) had to Queen Victoria.

House, he felt unwell and retired to bed with German measles. Anxious reporters and others, knowing that the King's elder sister was dying in Germany, wondered whether the life of his son was in danger as well. Fortunately, as in the case of his typhoid nine years earlier, he soon recovered.

Maud wrote consolingly (3 February) to May, to tell her how much they were missed, and:

> how sorry we *all* are that you and darling George are not with us now. I *do* hope he is *really* getting on satisfactorily and that Laking is satisfied, for you it must be *dreadful* being *quite* alone at Osborne all *so* empty and sad.[1]

As heir, George automatically became Duke of Cornwall in addition to his present title, Duke of York. Yet for the time being he was not to be Prince of Wales. King Edward's reason for not immediately bestowing this title on his son was sound enough. It had been associated with himself for nearly sixty years, and he saw that to confer it on another too soon would create confusion in the public mind. George was happy to accept this state of affairs, but with her passion for royal tradition May objected. Indignantly, she told her Aunt Augusta that it must be the first time that the heir apparent was not immediately created Prince of Wales.

King Edward VII and Queen Alexandra shortly after their accession

She suspected that Queen Alexandra was responsible for influencing the King's decision. Ever since the Duke and Duchess of York's wedding, Alexandra had been noticeably cool towards her daughter-in-law. Not only was she jealous of the woman who had displaced her as the first in Prince George's affections, but they were too dissimilar in character to have any instinctive mutual sympathy. The elder woman was invariably unpunctual, disorganized to a fault, largely devoid of intellectual and artistic tastes, but spontaneous and naturally charming in public. The younger was unfailingly businesslike, well-read and clever, if inclined to be stiff and ill-at-ease with strangers. It was a failing which King Edward sought to lessen by gentle chafing, and by telling May risqué stories which made her laugh in private. She was, however, able to give her husband the self-confidence he lacked owing to his mother's possessiveness and habit of treating her adult offspring as if they were still children. Queen Alexandra recognized this, and it was quite possible that she sought to deny her son and daughter-in-law their traditional title out of a sense of pique. May certainly believed as much, and strongly resented it. She never enjoyed the same rapport with Queen Alexandra as she had with the kindly, ageing Queen Victoria, who died with the knowledge that as the future king her grandson could not have found a better wife.

Those outside the family regarded May as the stronger personality of the two. Viscount Esher, Secretary to the Office of Works and later Keeper of the Royal Archives, had met them in 1899 and declared that, 'with her exceptional memory and intelligence,' the Duchess of York would be 'a woman of much importance one of these days.' Her husband was 'just a jolly sailor.'[2]

King Edward VII ascended the throne after almost a lifetime's experience of European diplomacy, yet handicapped by his comparative lack of knowledge of British statecraft. Queen Victoria had guarded her position as sovereign jealously, and refused to introduce her son to the duties and details of constitutional monarchy. Not until 1892 had he been presented with a key to official foreign office despatch boxes, ironically by the minister who might have become his son-in-law – Lord Rosebery.

The King was determined that his son should not be kept in such ignorance, and intended that there should be few secrets between them. He had suffered from his mother's persistent refusal to let him see state papers, and he would not subject his son and successor to the same treatment. Moreover, he knew that his own health was not good; his reign might be extremely short, and it was imperative that the shy and diffident Prince George should be well prepared for an inheritance which might come at any time.

King and heir thus had their desks side by side at Windsor. No greater contrast could be imagined between this willingness to share duties and Queen Victoria's initial reluctance to allow her much better-educated husband to do more than help her with the blotting paper. Furthermore, not only was George allowed to see all state papers, but his wife was as well. In many ways, May was already better prepared for the throne than her husband. Lacking his natural insularity, she had a wide knowledge of Germany and fluency with the language, and the charity work with which she had helped her mother had given her a fund of practical knowledge on social and welfare issues.

George and May were astonished that she should be permitted by the king to see papers that were firmly kept from the eyes of Queen Alexandra, 'Mama doesn't see them,' the Prince said. 'No, but that's a very different thing,' he was told. King Edward recognized that his daughter-in-law was much more impartial than his wife, who only considered the interests of countries where her closest relations – Denmark, Greece and Russia – lived and reigned, and loathed Germany with a vengeance. Her suspicions of Emperor William's sabre-rattling and personal instability were later proved to be fully justified, but her partisanship of Admiral Fisher and his desire to invade Germany or launch a surprise attack on the Second Reich's ever-growing navy were frowned on by the anxious king.

George had travelled little, except during naval service, and one of the priorities at the start of his father's reign was for him to acquire some experience of royal duties as well as first-hand knowledge of the British empire. Shortly before Queen Victoria's last illness, the government was making arrangements for George and May to visit Australia and open the first parliament of the new federation. When the matter was raised, soon after Queen Victoria's funeral, King Edward complained. He told Lord Salisbury and Arthur Balfour that he 'had only one son left out of three and he will not have his life unnecessarily endangered for any political purpose.'[3] Yet the ministers insisted. His Majesty the King, they pointed out, was 'the greatest constitutional bond uniting together in a single Empire communities of free men separated by half the circumference of the Globe', and that everything which 'emphasizes his personality' to his subjects throughout the empire was of benefit to the monarchy.

On 16 March 1901, the heir and his wife set sail from Portsmouth in HMS *Ophir*. It was an emotional occasion for all concerned; King Edward was visibly affected at the farewell luncheon on board ship, while Queen Alexandra and Princess Victoria were in floods of tears; and Prince George himself was so upset by these displays that he could barely speak when the time came for him to reply to the toast.

The cruise lasted seven and a half months. It was an undoubted success for the two royal ambassadors involved, particularly for May. No longer overshadowed by members of the older generation or teased mercilessly by her sisters-in-law, she relished this first opportunity to demonstrate how well she had absorbed the lessons of being born and brought up so close to the first family in the land. Her charm of manner and newly-found confidence helped her to undertake undertake all the public appointments, and to help her husband who was still noticeably ill at-ease in unfamiliar surroundings.

Throughout their journey they continued to write to, and receive letters from, the family back at home. A note from May to Charles in Copenhagen elicited a charmingly playful reply from Maud (19 May 1901):

I really *must* write to you this time to tell you I cannot allow this sudden correspondence with *my* Charles!! I nearly had a *fit* when he told me *you* had written to *him*! Naughty naughty! and yet you *never* write to *me*! and I never expected really to get a letter as I thought you had never *any* time!! Well! now I forgive you because you did write a *few* lines on a pretty postcard from Gibraltar which I believe I have never thanked you for.[4]

Later that summer (14 September) Victoria wrote to comment on the assassination of Thomas McKinley, President of the United States of America; 'when indeed can one be safe? While shaking you with one hand they shoot you with the other!!'[5] Meanwhile Louise enjoyed herself photographing the children and sending their parents the results, with a letter dated 30 September:

> I know that you have a very busy time just now, but I am sure you will do it all beautifully, and that everything will go off as well as all you have done already. *What heaps* you will have to tell us when we meet again – and I hope you will show me your presents too, it will be so interesting.[6]

Although the Duke and Duchess of York had been sad to leave their four young children behind for so long, the youngsters benefited from a break in their parents' strict upbringing. For *en famille* George and May conspicuously lacked the human touch of King Edward and Queen Alexandra. The latter both spoiled their grandchildren even more than they had their own children, allowing them to race pats of butter down the seams of Grandpapa's trousers, and roaring with laughter when Prince Edward, repeatedly told not to interrupt the King at luncheon, informed him triumphantly that it was too late anyway as he had just eaten a slug on his lettuce.

Lessons were cheerfully disregarded. Many an afternoon the King and Queen were too engrossed in playing with the children to allow their unfortunate governess Mlle Bricka to interfere. She was dimissed with a wave of the regal hand, and on one visit by the family to Sandringham she was left behind, fuming, in London. An angry letter of protest was quickly despatched overseas to May, who replied in similar tones of annoyance to Queen Alexandra. Needless to say, May could have spared herself the effort for all the effect it had.

George and May landed at Portsmouth on 1 November. Victoria had written to say how 'madly excited' the youngsters were at their imminent return;

> I do hope you will think them well and not spoilt though I think they are. The *best* and *dearest* children in the world – I shall be in utter despair when they leave us.[7]

With a twinkle in his eye, King Edward had told his grandchildren that their parents would return with black skins after their exposure to tropical heat, and their relief at seeing Mama and Papa tanned but still recognizable can be imagined. At last the King was prepared to make good the break in royal tradition which had so irked May, and on his sixtieth birthday, 9 November 1901, he created his heir and his wife Prince and Princess of Wales and Earl and Countess of Chester, 'in appreciation of the admirable manner' in which they had carried out their arduous colonial duties.

In January 1902 the Prince of Wales made another official visit abroad, this time to Berlin. Ostensibily it was to congratulate the German Emperor on his ·birthday, but the underlying reason was to attempt some kind of rapprochement

King Edward VII, Queen Alexandra, and Princess Victoria at ceremony to launch the battleship HMS Queen at Devonport 7 March 1902. This was typical of ceremonial functions at which the Princess appeared with her parents, making her more familiar to the British public than her sisters

with the imperial government. British suspicion over Germany's growing navy was at its height, and after some bitter remarks about the conduct of the British army in South Africa, King Edward wrote to the Emperor to cancel the visit; it would not do for Prince George to come to Berlin if he was to be insulted. At length he was persuaded to rescind the cancellation, and George proceeded to visit his cousin, making an excellent impression. Though he disliked travelling abroad to Europe and did not speak any German there was none of the animosity between both men that characterized relations between Emperor William and King Edward. The Emperor found his guest 'merry and genial'.

During spring and summer 1902, preparations were made for King Edward's coronation. The ceremony was held back until after the conclusion of the war in South Africa.

However, the Boer war did not cast the only shadow. King Edward took his work, new responsibilities and his programme of opening new buildings and launching battleships as seriously as his station demanded, but his health was plainly suffering. The already prodigious regal appetite for good food, vintage wine and strong cigars increased in proportion. His clothes suddenly ceased to fit; he became more short-tempered than ever; and he would drop off to sleep from sheer exhaustion at the theatre, opera and even meals. On 14 June he was taken seriously ill with stomach pains, but protested angrily to his doctors that he would attend his coronation as planned if it killed him. They warned him gravely that it almost certainly would. His condition worsened, and after a semi-state drive from Windsor to Buckingham Palace in considerable discomfort, it was clear that he was in great pain and the ceremony would have to be postponed while he underwent an operation for appendicitis.

Throughout London, where the decorations suddenly took on an appearance of irony, it was rumoured that His Majesty was sinking fast. In view of his state of health, tendency to excess weight and bronchitis, and particularly the high mortality rate for appendicitis, such fears were not unfounded. Nobody feared for the future more than the man who might find himself on the throne more quickly than he had expected – George, Prince of Wales. 'One could wish for him another two or three years of respite and preparation,' wrote his wife's lady-in-waiting, Lady Mary Lygon.

An operating theatre was prepared in one of the King's rooms at Buckingham Palace. Queen Alexandra had to be dissuaded from remaining present throughout the forty-minute operation. Instead she, her son and daughters waited quietly in an adjoining bedroom until his surgeon, Sir Frederick Treves, came to announce that it had been a complete success. For the second time in his life, King Edward had made a remarkable recovery. Overcome with relief, Treves told Princess Victoria that he had been convinced His Majesty would die during the operation.

Most of the coronation festivities were cancelled or postponed, but two reviews went ahead as scheduled, the Prince of Wales deputizing for his father. After his six weeks' convalescence on board the royal yacht at Cowes, King Edward and Queen Alexandra were crowned at Westminster Abbey on 9 August.

As parents, the Prince and Princess of Wales were much more strict than their own had been. The key to the way in which they chose to bring up their five sons and one daughter is to be found in their characters. As an adult, George was by nature less tolerant and less easy-going than his father had been. May gave the impression of being curiously unmaternal. With her earnest, serious-minded character, she probably reacted against the informal and carefree upbringing meted out by both her mother and her mother-in-law, and was determined that her own children would be treated differently.

Albert, Prince Consort, was not the cruel, over-exacting father of popular legend. The future King George V's reputation for strictness verging on bullying has been similarly exaggerated. The boys enjoyed many a rough-and-tumble, played riotous games of golf, and cycled around the Sandringham estates. They were not too afraid of their father to play the occasional practical joke on him. One day they bought a teaspoon, made of an alloy with a low melting-point, and were duly rewarded by watching their puzzled papa stirring his tea and seeing it dissolve.

Queen Alexandra (standing on left) with Prince George of Wales (in her arms) and other members of the family, 1903. Front row, from left: Prince Henry; Lady Alexandra Duff; Prince Albert; Lady Maud Duff; Prince Edward; Princess Mary. Back row, from left: the Duchess of Fife; Princess Victoria; the Duke of Fife

The fairest verdict on the Prince and Princess of Wales as parents must be that of the Princess's lady-in-waiting Mabel, Countess of Airlie. She praised them for conscientious devotion to their children's upbringing, but added that 'neither had any understanding of a child's mind'. For George, who was not a bully but simply lacked imagination, it was never too soon to try and inculcate the highest standards of behaviour and principle in his sons and daughter. Naval discipline had made him what he was; why should it not benefit his boys as well? Typical of this attitude was a letter he wrote his second son Albert ('Bertie') for his fifth birthday; 'I hope you will always try and be obedient and do at once what you are told, as you will find it will come much easier to you the sooner you begin.'[8] Even under the tutelage of Stockmar, it is hard to imagine Prince Albert addressing such a lofty missive to his son and heir; Prince Albert Edward, now King Edward VII, would have never considered addressing his sons thus.

'Very cold and stiff and very unmaternal,' was the Empress Frederick's judgment on May. As a mother, she was too ready to admonish her children – 'Don't do this, don't do that.' When Edward was aged but two, she decided that 'he begins to like me at last, he is most civil to me.'[9] In later years this same Prince Edward, then Duke of Windsor, paid tribute to the cultural interests which his mother had passed on to him. Her wide-ranging tastes in literature, her powers of observation, and the adolescent years she had spent abroad studying European art and civilization, gave her an enthusiasm which she was able to impart to them in a manner which their thoroughly philistine father could

Family group at Mar Lodge, 1904. From left: the Duke of Fife; Lady Maud Duff; the Duchess of Fife; King Edward VII; Lady Alexandra Duff; Princess Charles of Denmark

never emulate. Yet it was somewhat unimaginative of her to devise a special treat for her son at the age of twelve that consisted of a trip to see a gallery of watercolours in Bond Street.

After the arrival of Prince Henry on 31 March 1900, May told her Aunt Augusta that she had considered she had done her duty 'and may now stop, as having babies is highly distasteful to me.' Yet there were two more to come. On 20 December 1902 she gave birth to a fifth child, George. 'I shall soon have a regiment, not a family,' the father remarked good-naturedly.

His 'regiment' was completed with the birth of Prince John on 12 July 1905. At the age of thirty-eight, May decided that she had gone through the process for the last time. Unfortunately it was soon obvious that this last baby was mentally retarded, and at the age of four he began to suffer from epilepsy. Most of his short life was spent at Wood Farm, Wolferton, with his nurse Lalla Bill.

Maud continued to spend several weeks in Appleton each year. It was not merely affection for her childhood home that brought her back to Norfolk so often; Scandinavian winters were severe, and she suffered throughout her life from neuralgia and later bronchitis. Her husband Charles regularly accompanied her, when his naval duties permitted, though sometimes Danish fleet manoeuvres kept him closer to home.

After King Edward VII's accession, it was rumoured that 'Uncle Charlie', as he was affectionately known, planned to join the British navy, though as he was already firmly established in his own country's service, it was never more than a

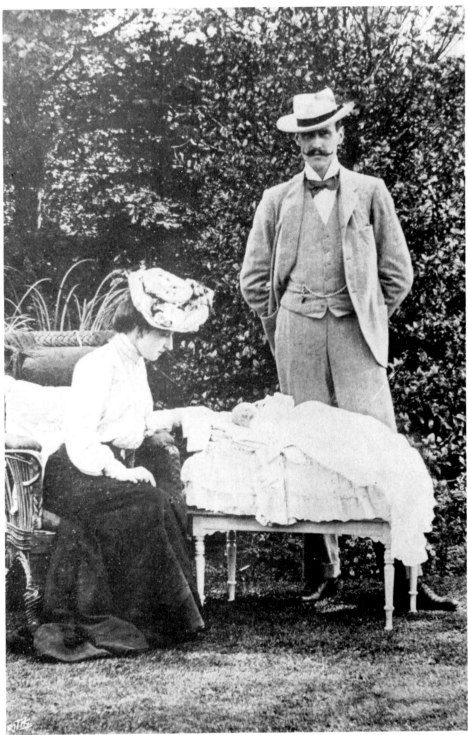

Prince and Princess Charles of Denmark with Prince Alexander, at Appleton, 1903

remote possibility. In 1900 he travelled to Norway for the first time, and at a dinner ashore on a subsequent visit, an enthusiastic shipowner convivially slapped him on the back, prophetically remarking: 'You really ought to be King of Norway.'

From October 1901 until the following February, Maud and Charles wintered at Appleton, and returned that summer for the coronation festivities in London. Charles resumed his naval duties in September, but joined her in England again at Christmas. Next spring they returned to Copenhagen together to join the rest of the Danish royal family for an official visit by the German Emperor, a duty neither of them relished. Anglo-German relations were deteriorating as a result of the Reich's insistence on building a fleet designed to eclipse British naval supremacy, and in any case Maud, like her parents, distrusted her bombastic imperial cousin and found it hard to forgive him his callous treatment of his mother the Empress Frederick, whose unhappy life had come to an end after a brave struggle against cancer of the spine and dropsy eighteen months earlier.

Yet their sojourn in Copenhagen was curtailed on medical advice. After nearly seven years of marriage, Maud was expecting a child and it was felt that the event should take place in England, where she would be more comfortable. On 2 July 1903 she gave birth to a son, christened Alexander Edward Christian Frederick. As befitted a prince of Denmark born to a princess of Great Britain, he was given names from both royal families. It was in England, however, that he and his mother remained for the winter.

Outwardly, marriage had made little difference to Maud. She still dressed just like her mother, and retained her affection for the English countryside. Gardening, riding and cycling remained her favourite activities. Though life in Denmark had made her no less ill-at-ease in public, she still had a boisterous sense of humour when with the family or with small groups of intimate friends. Unlike the Duchess of Fife, who preferred to spend her time with her husband and daughters, Maud was still on close terms with her mother and Victoria.

In April 1905 Maud and Victoria accompanied their parents on a Mediterranean cruise. After three weeks of sedate visits to such places as Algiers, Sardinia and Corsica by day, and endless games of bridge in the evening, Sir Frederick Ponsonby recalled, 'it was not to be wondered at that the time had arrived for a practical joke of some sort.'[10] The commodore of the royal yacht, Sir Archibald Milne, had a horror of monkeys on board ship. When he heard in casual conversation that one of the crew was thinking of buying a monkey to take home, he gave strict instructions to all his officers that they were to ensure no such animal was brought on board. Nobody ever found out how the rumour began, but Maud was on deck when the orders were being given, and she could not resist asking Ponsonby to devise some joke to be played on the commodore.

Ponsonby agreed with reluctance. As he admitted, he was not subject to naval discipline, but he was afraid that the rather pompous commodore might not appreciate having his leg pulled, and the joke could fall flat. However, he hesitated to disobey what almost amounted to a royal command. Later that day, on his return after a trip ashore, he noticed that an officer was eyeing all parcels being brought on board ship with care. None was large enough to contain a monkey, however, and nobody was stopped. So the equerry sent for Mr

Hammond, the head steward, and said he wished to have a packing-case made, but instead of a top it had to have bars of wood like a cage. Not surprisingly, this information soon reached the commodore, and stricter orders were circulated, an officer being placed on each gangway with orders to inspect whatever was brought on board. Ponsonby talked loudly about 'a new pet' to Maud in full hearing of the officers, and then it was only a matter of time before the yacht was being thoroughly searched for monkeys.

The situation was getting out of hand, and Milne realized that not even he could prevent King Edward's daughter from bringing one on board if she so wished. Deciding there was only one thing to be done, he went to see the King and asked him to forbid any of the party to purchase a monkey. His request provoked great astonishment, until Ponsonby told them it was all a joke and Maud had to explain everything. The King and Queen were most amused, and Sir Alexander was teased unmercifully at dinner that night for allowing himself to be taken in. Relieved at finding that nobody had any serious intention of obtaining a monkey in the first place, he took it in good part.

Little did Maud suspect at the time what fate, in the shape of Scandinavian politics, had in store for her.

8 'A Revolutionary Throne'

Since the congress of Vienna in 1815, Norway and Sweden had been joined together by an Act of Union. Norway had her own parliament, the Storting, but Sweden was the dominant partner and the King of Sweden reigned over both countries. Norwegian nationalism developed throughout the nineteenth century, and with the adoption of universal suffrage in 1898 she demanded complete independence.

Matters came to a head when Norway insisted on her own consular representation, and in March 1905 the Storting passed a bill (despite Swedish protests) affirming her right to do so. King Oscar II of Sweden refused to give his assent to this, and the Norwegian government resigned. Unable to form a new government, King Oscar refused to accept its resignation. The Norwegians argued that, as they had no government and as the King could not form one, the King of Sweden had ceased to function as King of Norway; the Act of Union was therefore dissolved. The Storting instructed the Norwegian council of state to take over the reins of government, and on 7 June 1905 the president of the Storting formally passed a resolution that union with Sweden under one king had ceased to exist.

As a gesture of goodwill, the Storting invited King Oscar to allow a prince from his family to become their independent sovereign. Not recognizing Norwegian independence, he declined the offer. Republican elements in Norway were overruled; in order to legitimize the peaceful revolution, other European countries would look with greater favour on her if her head of state was a monarch. A King of Norway would bring the country international recognition and strengthen her hand in negotiations with Sweden for amicable dissolution of the Act of Union.

King Oscar intimated that no member of his house would accept the crown, and maintained that the Storting had no right to offer it to anyone; so who was to occupy the newly-created throne? Political considerations ruled out a prince from the Great Powers. Anglo-German relations were in a state of mutual suspicion, and if a prince from one country was chosen, the other would be offended. Rumours that Emperor William was proposing to nominate one of his sons as a suitable candidate had already provoked alarm at the Foreign Office in London. Names of princes from Greece and Spain were suggested, but in the end the Storting agreed that only somebody from the houses of Sweden or Denmark would be acceptable. King Oscar's attitude made the former impracticable, so that only left the Danish House of Glucksburg.

There were two obvious candidates. The first was Prince Waldemar, youngest son of King Christian IX; the second was King Christian's grandson, Prince

Charles. Waldemar was aged forty-seven, with a Roman Catholic wife and adult children. Though favoured by Emperor William, he had as little enthusiasm for the prospect as Norway had for him. Charles was aged thirty-two, with a two-year-old son, and his mother, Louise (now Crown Princess Frederick of Denmark) was a niece of King Oscar. His father-in-law, of course, was King Edward VII. Except in the eyes of the ever-suspicious German Emperor, who looked askance at this last family connection, his claim could not be better.

Charles's immediate reaction was to decline the offer. He had before him the precedent of his Uncle William, elected to the throne of Greece in 1863 as King George I; his long and troubled reign was destined to end in assassination eight years later. Even less encouraging was the example of Prince Alexander of Battenberg, installed as Sovereign Prince of Bulgaria (another honour turned down by the prudent Prince Waldemar of Denmark as a young man) in 1879, only to be forced at gunpoint by agents of the Russian Tsar to abdicate seven years later and die, a broken-spirited exile, in his mid-thirties. Approached in confidence by Baron Wedel, Norwegian minister at Copenhagen, Charles protested that he was perfectly content as an officer in the Danish navy and had no desire to relinquish country or career.

Maud backed him to the hilt. She could not contemplate turning her back on a life divided between Copenhagen, cruises in the Mediterranean, and regular visits to Appleton, in exchange for that of queen consort of a country of which she knew nothing.

Yet their sense of royal duty did not permit them to refuse outright. Charles's father was Prince Regent of Denmark, and the octogenarian King Christian's death would bring him to the throne within less than a year. Maud's father had been heir apparent to the British throne from the moment of his birth until accession. Such an eventuality could not be avoided. All Charles could do was to stipulate that he would accept the crown if he could be of real service to Norway; if Sweden, Denmark, and Great Britain fully endorsed his accession; and, above all, if the Norwegian people gave their wholehearted consent.

The future looked uncertain while formal dissolution of the union was under negotiation. Norwegian republicanism was becoming more evident from week to week. The German Emperor, to whom the merest whiff of republicanism anywhere in Europe was a canker which called for an immediate remedy, entreated King Oscar to recognize Norwegian independence and accept the crown for a member of the Bernadotte dynasty. He had just returned from a meeting with Tsar Nicholas II of Russia at Björkö, and both Emperors had, among other matters, discussed the vacant throne. He informed his Chancellor, Count Bernhard von Bülow, that Tsar Nicholas was:

> very concerned about Norway; when he was told that King Oscar did not care in the least who was to be his neighbour, and cared not even if it were to be a Republic, he showed extreme consternation. He suggested also that if no Swedish prince were willing, Prince Waldemar might go in his place. I agreed with him, but remarked to him that, according to private information from Copenhagen, the King of England had declared his choice of his son-in-law. The Tsar was very unpleasantly surprised, seemed to know nothing about it, and said that his nephew Charles was

Prince and Princess Charles of Denmark

by no means suited to this post, since he had had no experience and was an insignificant and indolent man. By this means England would by 'fair or foul means' stretch forth hands towards Norway, gain influence there, and begin intrigue.[1]

It was unlikely that Tsar Nicholas had any real antipathy to Charles. Such objections as he may have had to his candidature were almost certainly inspired by his excitable 'cousin Willy', who had no wish to see one of his uncle's daughters on the Norwegian throne. To prevent this, he would not stop at putting words into the mouths of fellow-emperors, and his message to Bülow could not be taken at face value.

Likewise King Edward could hardly contain his jubilation, but in a different direction. On 29 June Sir Rennell Rodd, British minister at Sweden, confirmed to the King that a definite offer of the Norwegian crown was being made, and Wedel appealed through Rodd to the King to influence a favourable decision. On 1 July King Edward replied to a telegram from Stephen Leech, British *chargé d'affaires* in Copenhagen:

In answer to your telegram please inform the Crown Prince of Denmark, as Regent, that King Edward would gladly see Prince Charles of Denmark accept the throne of Norway (in which Queen Alexandra concurs) should the King of Sweden not wish any of his (Bernadotte) family to ascent the throne. But H.M. has no wish to interfere beyond letting his views be known and of course subject to the King of Denmark's entire approval.[2]

Charles declined to behave like an adventurer, going to claim a disputed crown like some medieval baron. He wired back to his father-in-law that he could not go to Norway without formal permission from his grandfather, King Christian IX. The latter would not grant such permission until King Oscar had formally renounced the crown, something he would not do until negotiations on the union's dissolution had been amicably concluded. To which King Edward replied (30 July):

Am quite aware of a double game going on to prevent your going to Norway. Pray warn your Grandfather and Father when the German Emperor comes to be firm. I strongly urge that you should go to Norway as soon as possible to prevent some one else taking your place.[3]

Later that week Emperor William visited Copenhagen, and was careful to give the impression that he would be happy to see Prince Charles assume the vacant throne. He gushingly lifted little Prince Alexander onto his knee and addressed him as 'Der Kronprinz Norwegens'.

Yet nobody was deceived at this sudden apparent change of attitude. Next Alan Johnstone, minister at Copenhagen, advised King Edward that the Storting was quite as ready to adopt a republic as it was to maintain a monarchy, and that the main chance of Prince Charles's adoption lay in an immediate visit to Christiania. The King telegraphed in reply to Johnstone to urge Charles to proceed to Norway as soon as possible, to forestall the proclamation of a republic or the selection of another candidate for the throne. To wait for any move from Sweden would be pointless.

Yet still Crown Prince Frederick of Denmark hesitated to incur King Oscar's displeasure by pressing his son's candidature until the King had issued an official proclamation of farewell. His deference to the latter's feelings, and his reluctance to give his assent to Charles's departure for Norway, made King Edward impatient. To him, the prospect of Norway declaring a republic simply because of a delay in which each of the parties concerned was waiting for the other to move was a galling one. Johnstone feared that even after legal dissolution of the union King Oscar might still nominate a Bernadotte prince to succeed him, and Baron Wedel thought that Norway would fight rather than have another Swedish king thrust on them without their consent.

Despite Johnstone's repeated urging, Charles declined to go to Norway without being formally elected king, and he was steadfast in his declaration that no Danish prince could accept a foreign throne without the King of Denmark's consent. Johnstone's insistence that everybody, including his own family, would treat him as an independent sovereign once he was in Norwegian waters, was to no avail.

Between Sweden and Norway, matters had reached deadlock. Neither country could agree on the precise terms by which separation should take place, and until such terms were settled Sweden thought it premature for Norway's provisional government to choose a new ruler. On the other hand, leading members of the provisional government thought it desirable to choose a new ruler as soon as possible, so that he could take part in the final settlement with Sweden. Because of this, Wedel suspected that in their haste the government might declare a republic at once and elect someone – perhaps even Wedel himself – as their first president.

The best way of preventing a republic, King Edward believed, was for Prince Charles to go there in person. He wrote to his son-in-law (11 August):

> The moment has now come for you to act or lose the Crown of Norway. On good authority I am informed your sister in Sweden* is now intriguing against you. I urge you to go at once to Norway, with or without the consent of the Danish government, and help in the negotiations between the two countries. Maud and Baby would do well to follow a little later. The Queen is quite of the same opinion.[4]

Still Prince Charles would not be swayed. He answered that he could not hurt the feelings of his grandfather the King of Denmark by going to Norway without his consent. However, he had been advised that Sweden would give an answer within ten days or so, and nothing was to be gained by not waiting till then. In vain did King Edward drum his fingers impatiently, hearing rumours that the German Emperor was intriguing after all for one of his sons to accept the throne. He wrote to Crown Prince Gustav of Sweden, urging him to cooperate with a view to a final settlement between both countries and requesting that Prince Charles be permitted to assume a leading role in them. To this the Crown Prince replied firmly, reiterating the official Swedish view that no candidature for the throne could be discussed until the union had been amicably dissolved. All King Edward could do was to hope that all would 'end satisfactorily for the different countries concerned.'

Though he recognized that the Scandinavian negotiations had to be allowed to take their own course, Wedel became impatient for King Edward to exert his influence once more. He sought a guarantee that Denmark would be granted protection from disturbance by sea in case Prince Charles was elected, in order to obtain the assent of Crown Prince Frederick.

Lord Lansdowne, British Foreign Secretary, deprecated this effort of Wedel to force Britain's hand. Sweden, he affirmed, was not contemplating war over the issue, and he refused to give any guarantee of British armed support to Denmark and Norway in the unlikely event of trouble with Sweden following any attempt to impose Prince Charles's candidature. With this King Edward concurred. The most Britain could do was to offer arbitration collectively with the Great Powers, should there be any possibility of what he could only look upon as the eventuality of civil war in the Scandinavian sub-continent.

---

* Princess Ingeborg, Crown Princess of Sweden.

By now, Sweden and Norway had agreed that the only solution to this impasse lay in a conference. Despite stormy arguments between ministers of both countries, and a half-hearted threat of war, agreement was reached within a few days and ratified by the Storting on 9 October. Formalities for the dissolution of the union were completed shortly afterwards, though not without further uncertainty for those most closely concerned. To her sister-in-law, Maud wrote from Copenhagen (12 October) to say how miserable she felt that she and Charles could not visit England for the time being:

> We had always *hoped* we could have come, *but*, alas! under the circumstances it is impossible and we are obliged to wait and see *how* events will turn out – the waiting is very tiresome and I do hope things may be settled one way or the other – there are a *lot* of intrigues going on which makes it *most* unpleasant for us.[5]

On 16 October the Swedish Riksdag passed an act acknowledging separation of the union, and eleven days later King Oscar addressed a letter to the Storting formally renouncing the Norwegian throne for himself and his heirs, and recognizing the country's independence.

Only one thing now stood in the way of Charles's immediate departure for Christiania – the apparent depth of Norwegian republicanism. He was being sent anti-monarchical literature regularly, and insisted on the offer being supported by a plebiscite. Despite objections from all sides, and none louder than those of his father-in-law, he had his own way. A referendum was held on 12 and 13 November, with a majority of 260,000 voting in favour of a monarchy and only 70,000 against. The Storting endorsed this verdict by meeting to elect Prince Charles of Denmark as King of Norway.

On 20 November Charles formally accepted the Norwegian crown at a ceremony held in the throne room of the Amalienborg Palace in Copenhagen, Maud standing beside him. He chose the regal name of King Haakon VII, and accorded his son the name Crown Prince Olav. After the ceremony, King and Queen drove through cheering crowds to their own rooms where they held a reception for members of the Norwegian delegation.

Four days later they sailed on board the *Dannebrog* into Christiania. Traditional Norwegian weather greeted them; the city was shrouded in thick grey mist, and bunting drooped disconsolately from red poles that lined the royal route to the palace, as it began to snow. During ceremonies and speeches that welcomed the first sovereign of independent Norway for six centuries, two-year-old Crown Prince Olav became bored. Looking around, he saw a group of boys waving flags. Running towards them, he fought the smallest boy, grasped his flag, and ran back triumphantly towards his father. The welcoming crowds were much amused by this diversion.

The following Sunday was Queen Maud's birthday. As she and King Haakon drove back from church, a little girl slipped and fell under their carriage. The King leapt down to help her up, and took her into the palace where it was found that she was more frightened than hurt. She was despatched home in a carriage with flowers and a present from the Queen.

Queen Maud of Norway

With his naval training, King Haakon had no difficulty in assuming a pleasant, kindly public manner. His father-in-law noted approvingly that he and Maud had both 'won golden opinions, and Charles's speeches are *very* good.'[6] May's Aunt Augusta was less pleased. She was affronted at the very thought of an English princess sitting on 'a Revolutionary Throne,' which was 'unsafe . . . to say the least of it,' while her husband went around making speeches thanking the revolutionary Norwegians for having elected him. To Augusta, the mere idea of an elected monarch was a contradiction in terms. Besides, she added spitefully, 'they have but that one *peaky* Boy.'[7]

Maud made a reluctant Queen. Though not so introverted as her sisters, she was still quite shy outside her domestic circle, and suffered from ill-health. In her case, premature deafness inherited from her mother, and persistent neuralgia, were her main afflictions.

One of her most immediate problems was moving house. The royal palace, Kongens Slot in Christiania, was vast by comparison with their Copenhagen apartments. The Swedish royal family had always lived in Stockholm, and built the palace in Norway merely for prestige and occasional ceremonial purposes. There was nothing remotely homely about this building with its stately rooms, one bath, and no lavatory. Meals and water had to be brought up from the basement kitchens, and slops carried down. Most of the furniture, the King of Sweden's personal property, had been removed and sent back to Stockholm. Maud's unpretentious furniture, purchased for their rooms in Copenhagen, was dwarfed in its new surroundings. The next year, however, a banker's mansion in Norway and its contents were sold, and its furniture was purchased for Kongens Slot by the state.

Not surprisingly, the palace soon took on a noticeable English flavour. Haakon and Maud spoke to each other in English, and Olav was looked after by two English nannies. Once suitably furnished, the family's private apartments were cluttered in true Sandringham style with family photographs and paintings. Maud made herself a rose garden, and kept several dogs and horses, brought over from England. Her favourite new residence, however, was their house in Kongseteren, a mountain chalet built in traditional Norwegian style, presented to them as a gift of welcome.

In order to identify herself more with her people, Maud took lessons in Norwegian and skiing. Her husband already spoke the language, but he likewise lost no time in familiarizing himself with his country's time-honoured sport.

On 17 December Maud wrote to May:

> Behold! I am a *Queen*!!! *Who* would have thought it! and *I* am the very *last* person to be stuck on a *throne*! I am actually getting accustomed to be [*sic*] called 'Your Majesty!' and yet often pinch myself to *feel* if I am not dreaming! We are very comfortably settled now, at least we are trying our utmost to get our rooms as we like. I think those who choose all these things must have been *extraordinarily* clever, to have discovered such a collection of monstrosities! The crowds always cheer. Little Olav gets tremendous ovations for himself. I never speak Danish very well as to the accent, but now just in Norwegian I get the right accent and they are delighted and think it is alright.[8]

As a nation Norway had accepted her monarch with reluctance, and radical elements in the Storting still harboured republican sympathies. Yet the people of Christiania were pleased to see lights at last in the royal palace which had stood dark and lifeless for so many years. At last they could take pride in having their own sovereign, instead of a King of Sweden and Norway who lived in Stockholm and appeared to take no interest in his second kingdom. King Haakon and Queen Maud were quick to announce that in the following summer they would undertake an extensive tour of the country.

With his youngest daughter elevated to a position of such worldly prestige, King Edward felt that it was time something was done for her retiring eldest sister. On 9 November 1905, therefore, Princess Louise, Duchess of Fife, headed the list of His Majesty's Birthday Honours, in being created, or 'declared', Princess Royal.

The style – rather than rank or title – of Princess Royal is not recognized by the British constitution, and there is no obligation for parliament to provide a princess royal with additional finance. It is one of the few remaining royal prerogatives, and within the sovereign's discretion, to grant the style for life to an eldest daughter who is unlikely to succeed to the throne. The first, Princess Mary, daughter of King Charles I, had been declared thus in 1640; the fourth, Louise's 'Aunt Vicky', Empress Frederick, had held the style from a few months after her birth, until her death in August 1901.

No less importantly, Louise's daughters were also elevated in title. Queen Victoria had liked Macduff and wished to see the line endure, with the dukedom passing to his daughters. In April 1900, she had granted him a fresh patent creating him Duke of Fife and Earl of Macduff, with the proviso that in default of male heirs these titles should pass to his daughters and their male issue. Yet she would not make his daughters 'royal' merely because their father had married a princess.

The then Prince of Wales had regretted this measure, and resolved to make this good at a future date. At the same time as declaring his daughter Princess Royal, King Edward conferred the style and title of 'Princess' and 'Highness' on his granddaughters Alexandra and Maud. Because of Louise's health, it was extremely unlikely that she would have any more children.

Yet if he hoped that by granting Louise such an honour it would make any difference to her, or persuade her to take a more prominent role in public life, he was disappointed. She continued a lead a life of seclusion with her husband and family, keeping her daughters away from the rest of her relations much of the time with a quiet stubbornness that Queen Alexandra, if not King Edward too, found rather hurtful.

Seven months after their arrival in Norway, King Haakon and Queen Maud were crowned. The ceremony was held in the Gothic cathedral at Trondheim, scene of the medieval Norwegian kings' coronations. Queen Maud dreaded the prospect, as a letter to May (22 March 1906) made clear:

> It all haunts me like an *awful* nightmare this Coronation and that it is *just* to be ours of all people. Think of me *alone* on my throne, having a crown to be shoved on my head which is very small and heavy by the aged Bishop, and a Minister and also has to be put on by them before the *whole* crowd!! and oil to be put on my head, hands and *bosom*!! Gracious, it will be awful![9]

It was preceded by a 'coronation journey', lasting one week, and gave the King and Queen their first opportunity to see the more remote areas of their kingdom. The streets of Trondheim were bedecked with flags, and stands had been built outside the cathedral. There was no palace, and the governor's residence had been refurbished to accommodate them for their stay. Visiting royalty, including the Prince and Princess of Wales, and dignitaries from other European nations, as well as Japan and the United States, had to stay on board their yachts anchored in the harbour. No representative came from Sweden, where the government had made it clear that no invitation was desired.

The coronation itself took place on 22 June; by English standards, it was very simple. King Haakon, in a mantle trimmed with ermine, and Queen Maud, in white satin, walked up the cathedral in solemn procession to their thrones as the

King Haakon VII and Queen Maud, from a colour postcard commemorating their coronation on 22 June 1906

King Haakon VII and Queen Maud in their coronation robes, from a Norwegian postage stamp of 1955 commemorating the King's Golden Jubilee

coronation march was played. After hymns, prayers, a sermon and litany, the King proceeded from throne to altar, where the crown was placed on his head jointly by the Bishop of Trondheim and the Prime Minister, Christian Michelsen. A similar procedure was adopted for the Queen, after which the president of the Storting declared them both truly crowned, calling out, 'Long live the King and Queen!'

Afterwards they left the cathedral in procession for their residence, where they showed themselves to the crowds wearing full regalia. Several steamers had been chartered to take tourists to Trondheim for the event, and at one point, remarked *The Times* correspondent, there was 'an outburst of unmistakable English cheering.' Their enthusiasm was in stark contrast to the verdict of the implacable Grand Duchess Augusta, who told her niece May petulantly how she objected to a '*revolutionary* Coronation . . . it looks like *sanctioning* all that nasty Revolution.' As tactful as ever, May agreed that it did seem curious, 'but we live in very modern days.'[10]

Celebrations continued in Trondheim and the surrounding area for several days. They included displays of *Heil-Gymnastik*, a choir of schoolchildren, and a *defilir cour* at which six hundred people passed in procession before the king and queen. Both stayed there until the second week of July to await a two-day visit from the German Emperor William.

By the time they arrived back at Christiania, neither they nor the government were in any doubt as to the popularity of the new independent Norwegian monarchy. The nation had received them with considerable warmth, and their enthusiasm at the sight of Crown Prince Olav was evident. It was observed that King Haakon was not merely interested in meeting the dignitaries from each town they passed, but he always made an effort to speak with his subjects and took a genuine interest in them and their living conditions.

Later that summer they moved into their seasonal residence at Bygdoy, where Queen Alexandra and Princess Victoria came to stay for a fortnight. The Bygdoy estate comprised an eighteenth-century house of modest size with English-style gardens, and a model farm. Its homely atmosphere reminded Maud and the family of Sandringham. In October they paid their first official visit abroad, to King Haakon's father, who had succeeded to the Danish throne as King Frederick VIII in January on the death at eighty-seven of King Christian IX.

In November King Haakon and Queen Maud were invited to the British court; they were received on their arrival in England at Portsmouth by the Prince of Wales and a guard of the Royal Marines. At Windsor King Haakon was installed as a Knight of the Garter, the first foreign sovereign thus honoured in person since Emperor Napoleon III during the Crimean war in 1855. The City of London invited them to a luncheon in the Guildhall, where eight hundred guests applauded a speech referring to the importance of good Anglo-Norwegian relations. They were also entertained at Buckingham Palace, and while there they were presented with England's coronation gift – a dinner service including twenty-four gold plates and one hundred and twenty pieces of table silver.

At Sandringham they celebrated Queen Alexandra's birthday on 1 December with a review of the Royal Norfolk Imperial Yeomanry Regiment in the presence of both kings, Haakon taking part as an honorary colonel. Three-year-old Prince Olav, who watched from the comfort of his mother's knee, made a great impression on all present when he solemnly saluted the British and Norwegian royal standards. Maud longed to remain there over Christmas, but they were due to visit Berlin and the Norwegian government felt that she would be snubbing the German Emperor if she did not accompany her husband.

It had been a busy year, in 1906, for the 'revolutionary' King and Queen, but they had succeeded in creating goodwill and positive interest in Norway throughout the world. Republicans in the country graciously conceded that their sovereign and his consort had won them much sympathy, and proved that the monarchy could play a vital role in furthering their national interests.

Yet Maud never relinquished her annual routine at Appleton. One of the conditions of accepting their throne had been that she should still be permitted to spend a certain period of each year in England for health reasons. In view of Norway's bitter winter climate, it was not an unreasonable request.

In the spring of 1907 King Haakon and Queen Maud made a three-day visit to Paris. Neither of them looked forward to it, as Maud confessed, in a spirit of apprehension mingled with mischief, 'as everything is so stiff, and I am certain I will never be able to be on my best behaviour for so long!'[11] In particular she dreaded the first prolonged separation from her young son, as well as her inevitable public appearances. However, their Parisian sojourn was a great success, not least for their self-control when the carriage horses fell off a low bridge during a drive in the park at Versailles. Maud's presence of mind and prompt concern for the slightly injured coachman and his team made a favourable contrast with the hysterics of Madame Fallières, wife of the French President, seated beside her.

Although shy, Queen Maud's sense of humour was never far from the surface. Fridtjof Nansen, Norwegian Ambassador to London at the beginning of King Haakon's reign, and well known to posterity as an Arctic explorer, attended an official function with them at Vadsø in the early years. After the party had eaten and were ready to go upstairs for the reception, it was found that the stairs on their way were almost blocked with half-empty beer bottles. They had been left by the band, who had been in a hurry to leave. Servants set about moving them as quickly as possible, with the result that bottles were knocked over and the stairs were awash with beer. The Queen had to exercise her utmost self-control not to burst out laughing.

When they had cautiously negotiated their way upstairs without slipping, King Haakon turned and whispered gravely to Nansen that there was a special seat for him. In front of them was an old-fashioned commode. It took up so much space that everybody, including the King and Queen, had to walk past in single file to reach the reception room. By the time they arrived Queen Maud was choking and Nansen, much to the disgust of an indignant lady-in-waiting who failed to appreciate the joke, was almost doubled up with mirth.

King Edward VII was indeed now the 'uncle of Europe', and his regular visits to courts on the continent increasingly took on the air of family reunions. His and Queen Alexandra's round of Scandinavian journeys in the spring of 1908 was

Queen Alexandra with the Duchess of Fife (left) and Princess Victoria, 1905

especially so, for Alix's brother was now King Frederick VIII of Denmark; and Princess Margaret of Connaught, daughter of Duke Arthur, the King's only surviving brother, was married to Gustav Adolf, Crown Prince of Sweden. The court of Copenhagen was just as homely and unpretentious, if dull to some, as it had been under King Christian IX, and only at Stockholm was there anything substantial in the way of pomp and ceremony.

By contrast, that at Christiania was simple in the extreme. To Sir Frederick Ponsonby, with its absence of an aristocracy, it appeared 'so socialistic that a King and Queen seemed out of place.' He believed that had the Left been in government during the 1905 revolution instead of the Right, Norway would have become a republic. However, with King Haakon's skill in maintaining the Glucksburg family's democratic traditions, and by keeping the Crown free of partisan associations, it was apparent that he was securing the love and respect of the majority of his subjects. Though the palace at Christiania was large and still uncomfortable, a considerable start had been made on installing modern plumbing and more homely furniture. The reception banquet for the English guests, though, was 'very indifferently done, as the suite were new to the game and the staff had never done a big dinner.'

Princess Victoria

King Haakon was careful not to underestimate the Left and its republican elements in the Storting. He asked Ponsonby whether he felt it would be appreciated if he and Queen Maud used the tramways instead of travelling by car. Ponsonby answered that he thought this would be a big mistake, as familiarity bred contempt. As a naval officer, he knew that a ship's captain never had his meals with the other officers. The King of Norway had to 'get up on a pedestal and remain there.' If the Norwegians saw him going about his business like an ordinary man in the street, they were bound to be disappointed.[12]

While Maud presided over the more domestic aspects of Europe's newest royal court, and Louise led a life of seclusion with her husband, daughters and their fishing rods, Victoria was the sister who remained most in the public eye at home. Increasingly a victim of her mother's selfishness, she grew ever more sharp-tongued, bitter and more of a hypochondriac. Her health had not improved, and in January 1905, like her father before her, she caused some anxiety prior to undergoing an operation for appendicitis. At almost every royal visit, reception, or cruise, it was duly noted that Princess Victoria accompanied Their Majesties like a faithful servant, or as her Russian cousin Grand Duchess Olga expressed it, 'just a glorified maid to her mother.' Olga saw how many a conversation or game between cousins would be interrupted by a message from the Queen, and Toria would run like lightning, only to find out that 'Motherdear' could not remember why she had sent for her in the first place.

Toria's unhappy situation caused most of the family no little anxiety. Like her father, brother and sister-in-law, she found Denmark unutterably tedious and dreaded having to accompany her mother on regular visits to Fredensborg and Bernstorff. Neither palace had ever been the same since those carefree days when Uncle Sasha ruled the roost with his hosepipe. Queen Alexandra adored her childhood homes 'much more than anything else', nonetheless, and resented the fact that everybody else apparently disliked them. Her children, she complained, were 'so spoilt' because they could not go shooting or do exactly as they liked there; it was 'too selfish' of them. That it was equally selfish of her to drag her daughter across the North Sea to what the Princess of Wales privately called 'that vile D . . . k', with monotonous regularity, never occurred to her.

Grand Duchess Augusta took Toria's side wholeheartedly. She found that the Princess was 'glad to have a rest by herself alone' whenever her mother was not around, and how odd it was that Queen Alexandra did not feel she was entitled to a little freedom, being a grown woman in her thirties. When the Duke of Cambridge died in 1904, leaving a house at Kew untenanted, the Grand Duchess thought it would be ideal as a retreat for Victoria. More in hope than in expectation, she suggested as much to Queen Alexandra, but to no avail.

Such simple pleasures as were available to her, Toria enjoyed to the full. At Windsor one evening when she was aged about forty, she and the diplomatist Lord Granville danced for hours after dinner, the servants having rolled up the carpet. One guest thought censoriously that such behaviour was 'not quite approved of,' but it would have taken more than disapproving whispers or glances to rob the spinster Princess of her occasional harmless fun.

She relished Maud's visits to Sandringham and Appleton almost as much as did Maud herself. The sisters knew every inch of the country for miles around, and loved to go out riding. Maud always persuaded Toria and Ponsonby to jump hedges, no matter how disinclined their horses might be. 'That's rot,' she retorted once when the equerry told her that his horse did not jump, 'it's because you funk.' Not wishing to disobey Her Majesty the Queen of Norway, he gave his mount a crack of the whip, dug his spurs in – and it did indeed jump, much to Maud's amusement. On their return to the stables, Queen Alexandra recognized the animal as one of her favourite hacks. Victoria whispered to him conspiratorially that it would be prudent not to say anything about the jumping, as the Queen would not be pleased if she knew.

Whenever Victoria came to stay with her newly-elevated sister and brother-in-law, they worked hard to provide extra entertainments for her as they liked to see her enjoying herself more than she did at home. 'Toria amused herself and danced a good deal,'[13] Maud wrote to May (23 May 1908) from Bygdoy approvingly as she described a party they had laid on for her benefit the previous evening.

King Edward VII's zest for life was legendary, and his travels at home and abroad continued unabated throughout his nine-year reign. Still the undisputed

Queen Maud of Norway with Crown Prince Olav, photographed by Downey, 1907

Family group at Sandringham, 1907. From left: Prince Albert; Queen Maud of Norway, holding Crown Prince Olav by the hand; Prince Henry; Queen Alexandra; King Haakon VII of Norway; Prince George; King Edward VII; Princess Mary; Prince Edward; Princess Victoria, holding Prince John

The Duke of York

Princess Victoria (left) and Queen Alexandra, photographed by Downey, 1909

'The late King Edward VII, and Royal Family at Home', from a montage postcard produced shortly after his death. The group includes King George V's sisters, as well as King Haakon VII and the Duke of Fife, but not the children of the latter two. Note also Winterhalter's 1846 family group of Queen Victoria, Angeli's Golden Jubilee portrait, a bust of Prince Albert and an oval portrait of the Duke of Clarence in background

leader of society, he was seen regularly at the theatre, opera, Cowes, and the race course. In 1909 his horse won the Derby, and his boyish delight was witnessed by hundreds. Each year he visited Marienbad, Homburg and Biarritz. A state visit to Russia in 1908 to meet Tsar Nicholas II at Reval was followed by one to Berlin the following spring.

Yet there was no disguising the decline in his health. In bad weather he suffered from bronchial colds, sometimes accompanied by fainting fits. After a luncheon at the British embassy in Berlin he had such a violent attack of coughing that the company were horrified lest he might succumb to a heart attack there and then. Chronically unfit, he refused to cut down on his gargantuan meals or cigars.

In March 1910, gravely worried by an impending constitutional crisis between the Commons and the Lords over a controversial budget, the King left England for his customary holiday at Biarritz. Already suffering from a chill, he collapsed soon after arrival. Queen Alexandra and Princess Victoria were on a Mediterranean cruise at the time; distressed by reports of his health, the Queen begged him to join them. Unable to be so far away while the political outlook was so uncertain, he declined their invitation, returning to England on 27 April, and left London at once for Sandringham.

Despite the cold damp weather he took his customary Sunday walk around the farm, and when he returned to Buckingham Palace the doctors were quite alarmed at his condition. Queen Alexandra and Princess Victoria, who had reached Corfu, were summoned home by telegram, but even they had no idea of how seriously ill he was until the Prince and Princess of Wales met them at Victoria station on 5 May. When they reached the palace they found the King hunched in his chair, ashen-faced and fighting desperately for breath. A bulletin was issued to warn the people that their sovereign was indisposed. On 6 May he suffered a heart attack, slipped into a coma, and died at a quarter to midnight.

Several members of the immediate family had been notified. The Prince and Princess of Wales, the Princess Royal and the Duke of Fife, and their Aunt Louise, Duchess of Argyll, were among those who joined Queen Alexandra and Princess Victoria in the Archbishop of Canterbury's vigil of prayer.

In spite of Queen Alexandra's annoyance Mrs Alice Keppel, the last of King Edward's mistresses, came to say her farewell to him, but the experience completely unnerved her. King Edward was barely conscious by the time she arrived. Escorted out gently by Princess Victoria, Mrs Keppel left the room almost shrieking, and repeatedly said, 'I never did any harm, there was nothing wrong between us,' and then, 'What is to become of me?' Victoria's attempts to calm her had no effect, and she became hysterical. Eventually she was carried into Sir Frederick Ponsonby's room and stayed there for some hours in a state of exhaustion. As Esher remarked, it was 'a painful and theatrical exhibition, and never ought to have happened.'[14]

'I have lost my best friend and the best of fathers,' wrote his son, now King George V, in his diary. 'I never had a word with him in my life. I am heartbroken and overwhelmed with grief but God will help me in my great responsibilities and darling May will be my comfort as she always has been.'[15]

THE KING AND HIS SISTERS
1910–38

9 *'Our Awful Shipwreck'*

King George V's moral character was beyond reproach. One of his first biographers, Sir Harold Nicolson, was moved to remark despairingly that for several years Prince George apparently did nothing but shoot and attend to his stamps.

It was ironic, therefore, that he should have been the victim of two persistent, totally unfounded slanders at the beginning of his reign. According to one, he was a drunkard. Typhoid fever at the age of twenty-six had left him with a red face, and his years in the Royal Navy had endowed him with a loud voice. These characteristics seemingly gave the more imaginative of his contemporaries licence to suggest that he drank too freely. Count Mensdorff, Austrian Ambassador, heard rumours that prayers were said at meetings in the East End of London for Queen Mary and the royal children, calling on Heaven to protect the drunkard's unhappy family.

Equally false was the legend of his bigamy. On the day of his engagement in May 1893, a less reputable London newspaper declared that the Duke of York had contracted a marriage in Malta with the daughter of a British naval officer. Rumours persisted throughout the years, and multiplied on his accession to the throne. Later in 1910 a republican paper, *The Liberator*, published in Paris but circulated widely in Britain, featured an article by E.F. Mylius purporting to give full details of Prince George's marriage in 1890 to a daughter of Admiral Sir Michael Culme-Seymour, and stating that he abandoned his wife and children born of the union once his brother's death had placed him in direct line of succession to the throne. Mylius was arrested for libel, tried, found guilty and sentenced to twelve months' imprisonment.

There had been much uncertainty on Queen Victoria's death and the beginning of a new era. In the same way, there was a mood of national unease at the passing of King Edward VII. Some of this reflected on the personality of the late King who, in Victoria Sackville-West's succinct phrase, 'kept things together somehow' in the first decade of the new century, and the comparative

The funeral procession of King Edward VII, High Street, Windsor, 20 May 1910

The funeral procession of King Edward VII, 20 May 1910. From left: the Duke of Connaught; German Emperor William II and King George V

The nine crowned heads who attended King Edward VII's funeral, in the white drawing-room, Windsor Castle, May 1910. Seated, from left: Alfonso XIII, King of Spain; King George V; King Frederick VIII of Denmark. Standing, from left: Haakon VII, King of Norway; Ferdinand, Tsar of Bulgaria; Manoel II, King of Portugal; William II, German Emperor; George I, King of the Hellenes; Albert, King of Belgium

shortcomings of his successor. For a couple of years, Lord Esher had pondered on the inadequacy of an heir to the throne who had 'all the domestic merit and political demerit of George III.'[1]

King George V was certainly handicapped by a sense of his own inadequacy for the position. Such was his lack of confidence that for several nights after his accession he could not sleep properly, and he was fully awake by five in the morning to make notes on the coming day's work.

He felt his limited education keenly. Not only was his knowledge of foreign languages almost non-existent, but he knew and cared little for science, history and the arts. In conversation with Esher, the Duchess of York (as she then was) had remarked how anxious she was that her eldest son should learn German, despite his father's objections. The Duke, she said, had suffered from not knowing French or German, or indeed anything of art and history. 'The other day in Paris I enjoyed everything,' she commented, 'but he was not really amused. . . He is told something about Francis I, and it conveys nothing to him.'[2] It was only thanks to his father's equerries that he had received some grounding in English constitutional practice.

In addition, the new King was to some extent a prisoner of his ingrained conservatism. King Edward VII had delighted in foreign travel, and was fascinated by the progress of modern science. He was keenly interested in inventions such as the motor car, and it was one of his dearest wishes to live until a cure for cancer had been discovered. King George V had travelled to India as Prince of Wales, and to Australia shortly before, but though he enjoyed the experience he disliked travel for its own sake, and he shared little of his father's enthusiasm for the march of progress.

Though he would brook no criticism of his father's moral lapses, he was not in the least ashamed of the quiet domesticity – or as the 'smart set' acidly commented, dullness – of his and Queen Mary's life together. He remarked to Mensdorff that they had all seen enough of what he termed the intrigue and meddling of certain ladies; 'I'm not interested in any wife except my own'. A quiet time by the fireside was infinitely preferable to the whirlwind of ceremonial and society functions.

His good relations with royalty did not last for long, but when David Lloyd George, Chancellor of the Exchequer, stayed at Balmoral for several days in September 1910, letters to his wife recorded a favourable impression. The King, he noted, was 'a very jolly chap,' and the family were 'simple, very, very ordinary people.' At lunch he sat between Queen Mary and the Prince of Wales, 'quite a nice little fellow.' After they had eaten, cigars and cigarettes were handed out, and the boys began a game of blowing out the cigar lights; then Princess Mary wanted to join in. Lloyd George, Queen Mary and everybody else threw dignity to the winds and joined in, till the noise was deafening. Only when Princess Mary set her lamp on fire did they decide it was time to stop.

Within thirteen months of his accession, King George V was required to undertake two ceremonial duties which he found most trying. In February 1911 he addressed the assembled Lords and Commons at his first State Opening of Parliament, which he called 'the most terrible ordeal I have ever gone through'. The second was his coronation on 22 June.

Almost from the day of his father's funeral (20 May 1910), a gathering at which eight other crowned heads were present, the King had been involved in what seemed to be never-ending arrangements for the ceremony at Westminster Abbey. Which foreign royalties were to be invited, and where would they be housed? What colours would be princesses' mantles be? Who was to bear Queen Mary's train? Despite her ill-health, the Princess Royal never shrank from claiming what she asserted were the rights of her recently-elevated daughters. Queen Alexandra claimed that dear Louise was deeply hurt because her girls could not wear proper princesses' robes; surely they ought to wear trains and each have a young lady to carry them? The King replied sharply that he could not help it if his sister was offended at her daughters not being allowed to wear robes, but it would be contrary to tradition; 'What a lot of trouble everyone seems to give.'

At the coronation, the Liberal minister Alexander Murray, Master of Elibank noted that King George V 'behaved throughout as those who knew him expected him to act; evidently profoundly impressed with the importance and sacredness of the occasion, but with the calmness and quiet dignity of a perfect English gentleman.' Queen Mary, he thought, 'was almost shrinking as she walked up the aisle,' but the very symbolic act of being crowned produced a complete transformation; 'one saw her emerge from the ceremony with a bearing and dignity.'[3]

From King George's own strictly factual account afterwards, there was one very emotional moment. 'I nearly broke down when dear David came to do homage to me, as it reminded me so much when I did the same thing to beloved Papa.'

Yet three of the King's closest relatives were absent. Queen Maud was not there, for protocol forbade her and her husband, as crowned heads, to attend another monarch's coronation. Instead they attended a service at Christiania, leaving the Norwegian Foreign Minister, Johannes Irgens, to represent them at Westminster. Queen Alexandra and Princess Victoria, accompanied by the former's widowed sister Dowager Tsarina Marie, spent the day quietly at Sandringham. She seemed unable to come to terms with her widowhood and with her son, not husband, occupying the throne. Her letters to him were addressed 'King George', not 'The King'. Suffering from depression and a severe cough, she decided not to attend (which admittedly conformed with tradition that a Dowager Queen did not attend the coronation of her husband's successor), or indeed stay in London at the time. While the nation rejoiced that their new King and Queen were being crowned, and perhaps gave thanks that the unsatisfactory Prince Albert Victor had been taken from them prematurely, his ghost still haunted his grieving mother. 'Eddy should be King, not Georgie,' she repeated tearfully to herself as she wandered round the garden at Sandringham.

With the death of her husband, Queen Alexandra's hold on 'poor Toria' tightened. Princess Victoria's life became ever more wretched; she suffered more and more from numerous ailments, some probably psychosomatic in origin, and from time to time she 'escaped' to boarding houses and hotels, ostensibly for the good of her health. One of the few regular simple pleasures of her routine was to ring her brother at 9.30 a.m. every day. 'Good morning, you old fool,' (or something less repeatable) she would greet him cheerily. Once the voice of the operator broke in with a hesitant 'Beg pardon, Your Royal Highness, His Majesty is not yet on the line.' The King never grew tired of relating the story to his family and friends. 'Of course, we're not always too polite,' he would chuckle.[4]

Much as she sympathized with her lonely sister-in-law, Queen Mary dreaded these 'chats', which gave her a lifelong hatred of the telephone. To her, it was an echo of the bad old days at Sandringham when young Georgie and Toria were mischievous children, telling tales and exchanging malicious gossip about their nearest and dearest.

As Toria became older and more bitter, so her tongue sharpened. Her letters to Queen Mary whenever the two were apart suggest an affectionate relationship, but when thrown together by circumstances both women, who were so very different in personality, evidently grated on each other's nerves. Toria

The children of King George V, photographed by Downey, 1910. Front row, from left: Prince John; Prince Henry; Prince George. Back row, from left: Prince Albert; Princess Mary; the Prince of Wales

King George V and Queen Mary in their coronation robes, June 1911

would take delight in making trouble by claiming back items of jewellery and furniture from George and Mary on the grounds that 'Motherdear or Papa said I should have that'. She knew Queen Mary was upset by such tactics.

Her sister-in-law was not the only butt of Princess Victoria's meddlesome behaviour. Prince Christopher of Greece, twenty-two-year-old son of King George, related how a certain unmarried princess who was said to have been 'disappointed in love' decided on his visit to Britain at about this time that she ought to find him a wife. Though he does not name Victoria, the account in his memoirs makes her identity obvious. She was, he said, 'the typical maiden aunt', who adored young people, engagements and weddings, gossip of any sort, and 'most of all, meddling in other peoples' lives'.

Princess Alexandra of Fife was considered to be a suitable candidate for his hand. Victoria dropped thinly-veiled hints to him that an engagement between them would meet with family approval, and promised to make all preliminary arrangements for his proposal. A few days later she visited Christopher with an invitation for him to stay at Mar Lodge with the Duke and Duchess of Fife that August. What she omitted to add was that this had been wrung reluctantly from the Duke after she had assured him solemnly that Prince Christopher gave his word of honour not to propose to his daughter.

In blissful ignorance, Christopher duly went to Mar Lodge that summer, and before long the young couple were secretly betrothed. Soon it occurred to them that perhaps her parents should be informed. Christopher saw no problem in this, but Alexandra was fearful of her father's wrath, and it took all her courage to go to his study one evening, pale and trembling, to inform him. Next time the family saw her, at dinner, her eyes were red and she was looking at her cousin with a gesture of despair. The Duke of Fife sat at the head of the table, his face registering thunder.

After dinner the bold young suitor was summoned to the Duke's study for what would always remain one of the most painful interviews of his life. He was told in no uncertain terms that there was no question of his marrying Princess Alexandra, that he had behaved like a cad in breaking his word, and his explanation was abruptly brushed aside. The rest of the evening passed in an atmosphere of high comedy drama. Alexandra and her mother wept long and loud. Princess Victoria, who had been responsible, followed suit and 'became so tremulous and involved in her explanations that she was worse than useless as an ally'. Queen Alexandra ran round from one to the other, unable to hear more than a few words of the excited and hysterical conversation, but anxious to pacify them all.

It was past midnight when the tired and emotional relatives retired to bed, and Christopher made his discreet exit in the small hours before anyone else was awake. He went straight to Balmoral and explained everything to Lord Knollys, who proceeded to tell King George. The King and Queen immediately invited Christopher to stay, and when they heard his side of the story they rocked with laughter. However the King insisted that matters could not be left to rest there, and advised him to write to the Duke of Fife, apologizing and telling him the exact state of affairs.

A few hours after sending his letter, he received 'a very charming answer' and

Louise, Princess Royal (centre), with her daughters Princesses Alexandra (left) and Maud, 1911

an invitation to lunch at Mar Lodge. He and Alexandra met at the luncheon table, both somewhat embarrassed, but they were not left alone for a moment. As Christopher later recalled, the scars were not very deep, for they had been more 'in love with love' than with one another. When they met again some twenty years later at the wedding of Prince George, Duke of Kent, both looked back with amusement on the episode.[5]

Nonetheless Princess Victoria and Prince Christopher remained good friends. While he was staying at Sandringham on a later occasion, she presented him with a Scottie called Sandy. This disagreeable animal formed an unholy alliance with Billy, a large Aberdeen terrier belonging to Christopher's brother Andrew.* The two dogs would go hunting for cats in the palace gardens at Athens, each grabbing hold of an end until the unfortunate victim was torn in two. Poetic justice, however, brought Sandy to a well-deserved ending. A cat he took on one day scratched him in the eye, and fatal blood poisoning set in.

In her spinsterhood Princess Victoria was denied the tragedy that overtook her elder sister.

For the last few years, Louise and her family had gone south for the winter. Like many a chronic invalid of the time, she took medical advice and did not stay in Britain during the severe cold and damp of winter. In 1911 they decided to visit Egypt and Sudan. Louise had longed to see the area ever since

---

* Later father of Philip, Duke of Edinburgh.

'Motherdear' had fired her imagination with descriptions of the country which she had visited in 1869.

In November 1911 Louise, the Duke of Fife and their daughters boarded the Peninsular & Orient ship *Delhi* at Tilbury. Shortly after she left the Thames estuary, strong south-westerly gales began to blow. Most of the eighty-odd passengers remained below decks as the storm gathered force in the Bay of Biscay. As *Delhi* reached the south-western corner of the Iberian peninsula, she was half a day behind schedule. Buffeted by torrential rain, she was blown onto a sandbank as she approached Cape Trafalgar. The passengers thought they had run aground at Gibraltar, but were then informed that they were some fifty miles west, within sight of the rocky cliffs of Cape Spartel, on the Moroccan coast.

The Gibraltar port authorities became concerned when *Delhi* did not appear there on time on the afternoon of 12 December, and the Atlantic fleet was alerted. A combined contingent of British and French ships proceeded on a rescue operation.

Although Macduff had a reputation for being surly and unsocial, and his wife for appearing pathologically shy and retiring, this crisis brought out the best in them. The ship was rolling heavily as Louise sat reading in her cabin, then she felt her go aground. People rushed in to call her and Macduff to go up to the saloon at once. She quickly pulled a dress on over her nightclothes, clapped a

Princesses Alexandra and Maud of Fife, 1911

128

soft felt hat on her head and fixed it on with a silk tie, then both of them joined the remaining passengers. Macduff insisted that all the ladies must sit down. With Louise, who clung to her umbrella, he mingled cheerfully with the gathering, talking to the more anxious in order to reassure them and keep their spirits up. At intervals, fierce squalls of wind and rain blew; once the Duke walked out on deck to watch. Louise rushed after him, grabbing his hand and ordering him back under cover. 'If we are to be drowned,' she told him sternly, 'we will be drowned together.' Meanwhile William Hayward, ship captain, repeatedly assured them that all would be well.

At length they were told that a French flotilla had answered the radio distress signals, and a large number of British ships were also coming to the rescue. After what seemed an eternity, dawn came and the watchers from the saloon found themselves practically ashore in Africa, amidst the fiercest sea and surf they had ever seen. Those who had felt seasick soon recovered, and had such an appetite that breakfast was almost as welcome a sight as daylight. A lifeline was rigged up and the stewards helped passengers pack their hand luggage, but in the end only those who had valuables with them were allowed to carry them ashore. The French warships came as close to *Delhi* as they dared; believing her to be in imminent peril, they lowered steam-driven pinnaces to take the passengers off. The Duke and Duchess refused to leave until all the women and children had been removed to safety. Once most of them were off the ship, the weather and waves worsened again, and fears were entertained for the safety of the royal party.

Admiral Sir Christopher Cradock, who was directing the British forces in the rescue operation, boarded the *Delhi* and took the tiller of the ship's boat in which the remaining passengers – including the Fifes – were to land. Waves crashed down on the boat, and Louise's jewel case, also containing her diary, photographs and watches, was torn from her grasp. Another wave washed Maud into the sea; her parents took hold of one hand each, and all three waded ashore with the Admiral's assistance. Shortly before their boat was swamped, Alexandra saw that Gilbert Bell, a young civil engineer from Glasgow whom they had befriended *en route*, was not wearing a lifebelt. She found one in the water at the bottom of the boat and promptly tied it to him. In doing so, she saved her own life. A couple of seconds later she was washed over the side herself. Bell grasped her hand as she fell in and was himself washed overboard; nevertheless, he kept hold of her. Unconscious and knocked about by breakers, they drifted ashore and came round just as they were being assisted up the beach.

The ordeal was not yet over. Miraculously all the crew and passengers of the *Delhi* had survived; so far, the only casualties were three sailors from the French cruiser *Friant*, involved in the rescue operation. Now, however, the party was faced with a five-mile walk in fierce rain across rocks and soft sand to Cape Spartel. The Duke and his family were still in their nightclothes, all soaking wet, having lost their baggage and jewels. Moorish guides and four British sailors escorted them through the darkness across unfamiliar terrain, and after four wet, exhausting miles they were met by the German resident from Tangier. He lent them his horse, which Louise and the girls used in turn.

More than twenty-four hours after the shipwreck, they saw the welcoming lights from Cape Spartel. After stopping to dry and warm themselves, they proceeded a further ten miles through storms to the British legation at Tangier, on mules sent by the legation staff. There they were provided with rest, a change of clothing, and refreshment.

The Duke promptly cabled home to advise that his wife and daughters were suffering from fatigue and shock, but so far 'no serious consequences had supervened.' Five days later they honoured *The Times* correspondent at Tangier with a visit to his villa. Louise asked him to announce that the effects of her terrible experience had been much alleviated by the splendid courage she had witnessed, especially from all British and French seamen involved, and by the kindness and sympathy she had received from everyone.

King George and Queen Mary were in India at the time for the Delhi Durbar, a ceremonial paying of homage from their Indian subjects. They were told that the Fifes had been rescued, and Louise wrote long detailed letters home on their ordeal. To the actor Sir George Alexander, a close friend of several years' standing, Macduff wrote (3 January 1912):

> I thought that some of us if not all must be drowned! Yet one had to appear perfectly calm! If I live twenty years the memory of that night and day will live with me. I am relieved to say that the Princess Royal is fairly well though I think she is beginning to feel the reaction now – she and our children were wonderfully brave! I may add that in my opinion nothing but our excellent life belts saved us and of course the hand of Almighty God.[6]

To Queen Alexandra, the King remarked that Louise had behaved most bravely, 'and I am proud that she is my sister.'

After a few more days of rest and recovery, the Fifes went to Khartoum and Cairo. Princess Alexandra wrote an account of their experiences, *Egypt and Khartoum*, which was printed privately. She described the peace and contentment they found in steaming up the Nile reading, writing and sketching, 'which gave one the opportunity to collect one's thoughts and replenish one's mind.'

In the middle of January they set out for Khartoum a second time, to attend the consecration of the cathedral. Their journey was halted when Macduff was taken ill. His speculation at living another twenty years with the memory of their ordeal was beginning to look over-optimistic. Louise wrote to Lady Alexander (25 January):

> We have been steaming along up the Nile – the days are warm, but the nights very cold. Gales, and wind have followed us since we left. We have had high winds, and they have been very chilly too. Coughs and colds we had lasting some time. My husband has never been well since our awful shipwreck, the strain of which he felt more than we realized! He got a chill, and on reaching this furthest place on the Nile, Wadi Halfa, he had high fever and a hacking cough – He has been seriously ill – with pleurisy, and *just* missed pneumonia.[7]

Only now did it dawn on Louise how much his health had been undermined by their experience. Her personal physician, Dr Abbott Anderson, was summoned from London, but it was too late. Early in the morning of 29 January the Duke died, aged sixty-two.

Relations between Louise, her mother and sister-in-law had not been easy for several years, but this sorrow brought them all together. As they approached Gibraltar on their way home, King George and Queen Mary were told of Macduff's death. Terribly upset, the Queen could think of nothing but Louise's grief and despair, and of the fresh trial to 'Motherdear' who was just beginning to appear more cheerful than she had been since the death of King Edward. With admiration, Queen Alexandra wrote that Louise's '*great courage* and faith have changed her into this *strong soul* and being.'[8] Queen Maud wrote to her sister-in-law (1 February):

> How sad it all is this sudden death of poor Macduff – one cannot *bear* to think of dear Louise's grief, as fancy *what* a *loss* he is to *her*, she lived for *him* and their two children, *he* was her all – it seems somehow impossible to be true, how terribly quickly it was all over, I suppose he must have been ill some time without anyone understanding it was serious. We were *dreadfully* shocked here when we got the news and I have been *so* upset, and *know* in what *utter* misery poor dear Louise *must* be in, left *alone*, and *so* far away too, and after *all* they went through too in that ghastly shipwreck and *none* were drowned and now he dies, and she just wrote me such cheery letters that they were looking forward to go to Khartoum.[9]

In a state of deep shock, Louise unburdened her feelings to Lady Alexander (1 February):

> He had had a terrible shock in the shipwreck! He was brave and never complained. I saw that he had felt the shock more deeply than we ever knew! He kept on and on but I saw he was failing. He cheered up and looked better here. He was always languid, but cheery and so thoughtful for us. Then he had a cold, a chill, that awful cough, and pain, and fever. He always smiled when we helped him, but at last he grew so weak, it tore my heart to hear the sob in his cough. He felt he was slipping from us. He said he would fight his illness as he had fought the waves – he only wanted to wait to help me and our children – and was very tired. He was ready for Heaven and now is at peace! Doctors, nurses, oxygen, all was done, but of no avail, he always went down, nothing on earth could hold him up. We sat by him and saw his precious life pass peacefully away. He looked like a beautiful saint.[10]

With the royal family in deepest mourning, the service of thanksgiving for the Delhi Durbar and safe return home of King George and Queen Mary at St Paul's Cathedral on 6 February seemed more like a funeral service than one of rejoicing.

Louise found solace in her Christian faith. With resignation she wrote to Queen Mary (8 February):

> My children and I have been through great trials! but God is giving us this strength, to bear our great sorrow! My beloved Macduff had a beautiful and peaceful end, in this silent land. I am thankful to think of his peace, no more pain nor anxiety now, but my heart is aching for his dear dear presence as we were always together![11]

King George V shooting at Balmoral, 1912

King George V and Queen Mary arriving at Silverwood Colliery, 9 July 1912

Royal visit to Woolwich, 9 April 1913. King George V and Arthur, Duke of Connaught passing through the entrance of the Royal Military Academy after inspecting the cadets

King George V and Princess Victoria leaving Hyde Park on horseback, 15 May 1913

In similar vein, she told Lady Alexander five days later than 'God would never have taken him unless I were fit to help them the children and those whom he has left in our care.'[12]

At the end of the month, Louise and her daughters arrived at Portsmouth with Macduff's coffin aboard HMS *Powerful*. Queen Mary reported on the 'awfully sad meeting' with them, but how 'wonderfully composed' they were. To Queen Alexandra, her daughter had become 'a saintly heroine,' and 'a *changed being* who can bear every cross now!'[13]

Despite her initial apprehension, Maud had adapted herself to life as a Queen Consort in Norway well. Though she still shrank from publicity, especially in private life, and though her contemporaries were largely unaware of the fact, she was ahead of her time in Norway by tacitly championing the rights of women to participate in outdoor sports, something previously regarded as a male preserve. In summer she played tennis, and bathed when the water was warm enough. She had learnt to enjoy skiing and tobogganing in winter, activities which had appealed to very few women before the 1914–18 war. With her love of such pursuits it might indeed be said that she was a 'revolutionary Queen'. Photography remained a favourite hobby; she still took pictures regularly and exchanged copies with her relations in England.

During these early years Maud had few close friends besides her ladies-in-waiting. She still had problems with understanding Norwegian, except when it was spoken slowly and clearly, but she consoled herself with the realization that many Norwegians had similar difficulty with English.

Maud and Haakon nonetheless enjoyed dining out with various societies and groups in Christiania, and she always relished dancing afterwards. They attended concerts and art exhibitions in the capital, and – despite the language barrier – theatres, where she dealt with the problem by going briefly through the play's dialogue and plot with her companions before they took their seats. Although migraine and other ailments continued to give her trouble, she enjoyed better health in her new country than in Copenhagen.

One of her greatest pleasures at Christiania and Bygdoy was to arrange small parties and concerts for select groups of friends. She felt less shy in the presence of smaller groups; poor eyesight and increasing deafness made it difficult for her to recognize many people around her all at once. In more intimate gatherings she could feel at ease. Big dinner parties at Kongens Slot were a trial, as long-drawn-out receptions and pompous speeches bored and tired her quickly. Yet her marked preference for Norway over Denmark, and the official appearances which visits to the latter entailed, was evident in a letter to Queen Mary (26 May 1913):

> We go off to Copenhagen for our official visit on the 10th to 13th and I don't look forward to it at all, a lot of formal entertainments and much standing about, which tires me always greatly. Here we are very peaceful in our dear little country place and have continually people to lunch and dinner.[14]

Return holidays at Appleton, however, were more than an opportunity to revisit childhood haunts. Olav was an only child and needed the companionship of his contemporaries, particularly his English cousins. Being much of an age with King George V's younger sons, he spent many happy hours playing with them. As might be expected, their favourite toys were model soldiers. King George looked indulgently on their war games, but on one condition; their opposing armies must not represent different nations, but rather planets, such as 'Earth' and 'Mars'. In a continent which was slowly but surely dividing itself into two armed camps, it hardly augured well for the future to encourage nationalism and rivalry between the sons of two of her kings.

10 'How Appalling This War Is'

Princess Alexandra, who became second Duchess of Fife on her father's death, had long had a reputation for being one of the best-dressed members of the royal family, with a taste in clothes which was much copied in fashionable circles. She had inherited her mother's love of angling, and became just as accomplished at the sport. When she succeeded to the title she took on much of her father's work in looking after tenants on their Scottish estates, taking gifts of food and clothing to the sick and reading to the bedridden. She was totally at ease with their children, who never found her too busy to join in their games.

Although she hesitated to leave her widowed and ailing mother for too long at a time, Alexandra became engaged in the summer of 1913, to her cousin Prince Arthur of Connaught. They were married on 15 October in the Chapel Royal, St James's.

This proved to be the last family wedding during those uncertain years of peace, before war engulfed Europe and brought the curtain down on the old imperial order. Ironically it was the threatening Anglo-Irish situation, agitation for home rule and the militancy of Ulster Unionism, which gave King George V the greatest anxiety. 'Please God 1914 may be a brighter year for my Country,' he wrote to Lord Stamfordham (29 December 1913), 'and that anyhow peace may be maintained.'[1]

It was with trepidation that King George V and Queen Mary embarked on a state visit to Paris in April 1914, for they were conscious of how unsettled matters were at home and apprehensive about the state of British prestige abroad. Yet they need not have worried about the latter, for Parisians gave them a warm welcome. President and Madame Poincaré were unstinting in their hospitality, and they returned to London assured that the Entente Cordiale was alive and well.

Two months later the Balkan powder keg exploded. On 28 June Archduke Francis Ferdinand of Austria and his wife, who had stayed at Windsor Castle the previous November, paid their fateful visit to Sarajevo which ended in their assassination. Not for another month, after an Austrian ultimatum had been rejected by the Serbian government, did the implications for Europe fully dawn upon her heads of state and governments. On 4 August, Great Britain declared war on Germany.

With so many marriages binding British royalty to continental powers, it was inevitable that divisions of family loyalty would arise. Among those who reluctantly found themselves taking up arms on behalf of Germany were Queen Alexandra's nephew Prince Ernest of Cumberland, and Charles, Duke of

Prince and Princess Arthur (Alexandra, Duchess of Fife) of Connaught on their wedding day, 15 October 1913. The bridesmaids are, from left: Princess Mary; Princess Mary of Teck (seated); Princess Helena of Teck; Princess Maud of Fife; Princess May of Teck

Saxe-Coburg Gotha, only son of Queen Victoria's youngest son Leopold, Duke of Albany.

In Britain, hysterical hatred of all things German demanded the sacrifice of Prince Louis of Battenberg, First Sea Lord. Unjustly blamed for every British reverse at sea and vilified because of his German ancestry and birth, he was forced into resigning his post, a move bitterly regretted by the royal family. His enforced retirement from public life brought back his old adversary Admiral Fisher to the Admiralty. The bellicose Fisher was distrusted by King George but much admired by Queen Alexandra and Princess Victoria, who congratulated him on his return to office; he noted in his diary (1 November) that they were 'simply heavenly to me and they both looked quite lovely! I wish I could have married both of them!'[2]

The admiral was often fulsome in his praise of the unhappy spinster Princess. Only two years earlier, it was his verdict that she, 'who used to be scraggy, lanky and anaemic, has developed into an opulent figure with a rosy plump face! She looked very handsome and I told her so, and her tall figure makes her most imposing now.'[3] It was Princess Victoria's tragedy that she never found an eligible suitor to pay her such compliments and rescue her from the boredom which so embittered her in middle age.

King George sensibly refused to be swept along by the virulent Germanophobia which prevailed in Britain throughout the war, though he reacted with anger to such incidents as enemy warships bombarding the Yorkshire coast. 'So this is German *Kultur*!' he exclaimed sardonically after being told of the casualties and fatalities involved.

As a constitutional monarch in wartime, demands upon him were intensified. During the four years of conflict, he paid seven visits to British naval bases, held 450 inspections, personally conferred some 50,000 decorations, visited 300 hospitals, and regularly toured industrial regions, training grounds, and bombed areas. Unlike many of his peers in the ruling classes, he and Queen Mary had great sympathy for the poor, who suffered more than anyone else from food shortages. After a visit to Deptford, he was particularly moved by the sight of people queueing for food; richer members of the community, he observed, were immune from such trials. He warned Asquith, the Prime Minister, that there would be considerable anger among his subjects if the pension for a widow whose husband had been killed in action was set at a meagre five shillings.

During the spring of 1915 Lloyd George, now appointed Minister for Munitions, told the King that drunkenness among munitions workers was hampering the war effort. King George had always enjoyed a little wine with his meals and a glass of port after dinner, but he agreed to set an example to the nation by giving up all alcoholic liquor himself and throughout his household for the duration. Privately he admitted that total abstinence was 'a great bore'; it was a self-denial which most of his entourage would gladly have foregone. His visits to the fleet and to troops in France were no longer such convivial affairs when nothing stronger than barley water was permitted. Admiral Beatty complained that 'the old boys don't get communicative without drink of some form or other.' On being invited for lunch with the King at GHQ, General Joffre was dumbfounded when offered a choice between lemonade and ginger beer. To the King's annoyance, his example was not followed as readily in society as he would have liked. Brewers and spirits manufacturers continued to make handsome profits. Lloyd George, King George believed, had made him look foolish; Queen Mary declared they had been 'carted'.

Like other parents of young and able-bodied sons, the King and Queen had their share of family anxiety. At the outbreak of war the twenty-year-old Prince of Wales joined the Grenadier Guards and began training as an infantry officer. Prince Albert, aged eighteen, was already serving as a midshipman on board the battleship HMS *Collingwood*, part of the home fleet guarding the North Sea approaches. The other three were still much too young to serve. Prince Henry, thirteen, was at Eton; Prince George, eleven, at St Peter's, Broadstairs; and the handicapped nine-year-old Prince John was still at Wood Farm.

In peacetime, the Prince of Wales had shown the same zest for dinner parties and glittering balls as had two of the last princes to bear that title, his grandfather and the Prince Regent. On 10 July 1914, he noted that he had only enjoyed eight hours' sleep in the last seventy-two, the rest of his time being taken up with society functions. However, after the declaration of war, he was eager to play his part in the patriotic effort. On being instructed by the King to wait in London until suitable employment was found for him, he wrote to his father of his distress at not being allowed to serve his country, and begged for a commission in the Grenadier Guards.

The King granted this request without hesitation. But when the Prince found himself transferred to the 3rd Battalion, stationed at barracks in London with no immediate prospect of being sent overseas to fight, he called at the War Office and demanded to see Lord Kitchener, Minister for War, pleading to be allowed to go to France. 'What does it matter if I am killed?' he asked. 'I have four brothers.'[4] Kitchener replied sternly that the government could not risk his capture by the enemy as a prisoner. His persistence paid off, however, and in November he was attached to the staff of Field-Marshal Sir John French, Commander-in-Chief of the British Expeditionary Force. Yet he was kept away from the trenches and employed most of the time with harmless paperwork, such as the carrying of despatches. Whenever he managed to have himself transferred to divisional headquarters close to fighting, he was always removed from the remotest chance of shellfire.

King George and Queen Mary were proud of their son, yet this pride was tinged with impatience at what they termed his disobedience, which was born out of sheer frustration. The King looked forward to his dutiful, affectionate letters about the campaign in France, and read them out with pride to the family, later showing them to his ministers.

But the Prince was disgusted at being awarded the Military Cross and the French *Legion d'Honneur*. Having never served in the trenches, he told Lady Coke, he felt that he did not deserve such decorations in the least. There were many gallant yet undecorated officers far more worthy than he who had never been out of 'an office'. King George, who shared the monarch's traditional affection for the accoutrements of awards and decorations on uniform, was offended that his son should adopt such an apparently subversive attitude.

No such irritation disturbed the bonds between King George and his shy second son Prince Albert. Like his father, and Queen Victoria's second son Alfred before him, Albert had chosen the navy as a career, becoming a midshipman in September 1913. He spent the last few months of peace on manoeuvres in the Mediterranean, and was on board *Collingwood* during the test mobilization of July 1914, in which the entire fleet passed before her sovereign in the royal yacht at Spithead on their way towards Scapa Flow and the North Sea battle stations.

The King's first thoughts for his second son, on the declaration of war, were that the conflict would soon be over and that God would 'protect dear Bertie's life.' The main threat to the young Prince, however, came not from enemy action but from ill-health. At the end of August he suffered severe gastric trouble which was diagnosed as appendicitis, and he was sent back by sea in dense fog, through mined waters, to a nursing home in Aberdeen. He proved to be a considerate patient, though sorry to miss the excitement of witnessing the first fleet action of war. From his sickbed he commiserated with his father, who 'must be very tired after all this trying time with so much work to do, and so many people to see, and never getting a rest.'[5]

Further illness recurred several months later and the King's physician, Sir Frederick Treves, advised that he should not return to sea. However, the following year he was permitted to return to his duties at Scapa Flow, on patrol for submarines.

King George also suffered ill-health in 1915. That October while he was visiting troops in France, his horse took fright at the cheers of the men and the Royal Flying Corps. He fell and was pinned to the ground, breaking his pelvis in

Contemporary heads of state, from a Great War postcard, c. 1915. Top row: Sultan Mohammed V of Turkey; William II and Francis Joseph, German and Austrian Emperors; Ferdinand, Tsar of Bulgaria. Centre row: Nicholas II, Tsar of Russia; King George V; Raymond Poincaré, President of France. Bottom row includes Peter, King of Servia; Victor Emmanuel III, King of Italy; and Albert, King of Belgium

two places and suffering severe bruising. Taken to hospital at Aire, he could not sleep without the aid of pain-killing drugs for another ten days. Thereafter he was in regular pain, and his shooting companions considered that he was never the same again.

During the conflict Queen Maud was unable to join her relations in England, and had to rely on correspondence to keep in touch. Barely had war been declared before she realized what considerable inconvenience they would all encounter, as a letter to Queen Mary (27 August 1914) made clear:

Alas, I cannot do what you asked me to do in sending on your letter to dear Aunt Augusta so I return it to you, we made full inquiries, *our* Foreign Office etc. and they say *no* post is allowed in Germany unless the letter is written in German and *open*, so *what* is the use of that? Altogether 'they' behave *too* abominably in every way and are more like mad beasts than ordinary human beings – How appalling this war is, and how all my thoughts naturally return to 'home' and all you dear ones, I feel *so* far away and lonely, it is terrible being away from one's own beloved country at *such* a ghastly moment – With what pride one reads of the splendid way the dear old country has behaved.[6]

'The King at the front: a greeting from the troops', from a Great War postcard, c. 1915

The Scandinavian nations declared themselves neutral, though royal family ties made it evident on which sides in the conflict their respective sympathies lay. Denmark and Norway could not be anything other than pro-British. Sweden was regarded as being more friendly to Germany, for the House of Bernadotte had always harboured Teutonic leanings, reinforced by the marriage of Prince Gustav (who had succeeded his father as King Gustav V in 1907) to Princess Victoria of Baden.*

The Norwegian Prime Minister, Gunnar Knudsen, shared the German high command's optimism in thinking that the war would only last a few weeks, but King Haakon appreciated that it could drag on indefinitely, and with it the ever-increasing risk of pressure being exerted on his kingdom and government to aid either the entente or central powers. With his naval experience, he recognized the strategic value of naval bases along the Norwegian coast, and feared that either Britain or Germany would demand their use. All three Scandinavian kings held a meeting at Malmø which achieved no practical results, beyond its value as a public relations exercise – an apparent affirmation of solidarity and neutrality – but it did not lessen King Haakon's fears that the Swedish economy's dependence on exports to Germany would soon draw her into the fighting on the side of Berlin.

For Queen Maud, the war was an opportunity to throw herself wholeheartedly into charity work. In 1907 she had taken a leading role in subscribing to a home

---

* Daughter of Louise, Grand Duchess of Baden, only daughter of Emperor William I and sister of Frederick III.

for unmarried mothers and attending a public meeting on its behalf, a bold stand that flew in the face of 'respectable' opinion among those who considered such good works to be beneath their dignity. Now, on the outbreak of war throughout Europe, she placed herself at the head of a relief fund-raising drive. Committees were organized throughout Christiania, and she presided over a main committee made up of two ladies from every parish. They met fortnightly at the palace during the winter months, and the money raised was distributed annually for many years on her birthday for the purchase of food, fuel, clothing and medicines. It was Maud's wish that special attention should be given to the needs of large families and to single mothers.

By 1917 King George was as weary of the war as his subjects. Tired and often in pain from his riding accident injuries, that year he was called upon to make what turned out in retrospect to be probably the most distressing decision of his life – that regarding the fate of his cousin in Russia, Tsar Nicholas II, and his family.

In March, revolution had broken out in the Russian capital, and it was with anxiety that the King heard of Nicholas's enforced abdication. Lloyd George, who had succeeded Asquith as Prime Minister three months earlier, sent a telegram to the head of the new provisional government in Russia praising the people for this achievement in their struggle for a popular government as well as for liberty. These apparently republican sentiments irked the King, until it was tactfully pointed out to him that the British monarchy was likewise founded on revolution.

The traditional version of events – that King George's strong desire to give his dethroned cousin, wife and children asylum in Britain was overruled by Lloyd George – has recently been disproved. Within a few days of the Tsar's abdication, the provisional government made a formal suggestion that the imperial family should come to England. This, Lloyd George and his senior ministers maintained, could not be refused. But a series of delays between governments, ministers of both countries, and the King, who questioned 'on general grounds of expediency' whether this was the best course of action, proved fatal. Would France or Switzerland – or perhaps Denmark – not prove more suitable?

That King George V persuaded his government to withdraw their original offer of asylum is beyond doubt. Superficially it may be seen as a cowardly decision. It has, however, to be viewed in the context of its time. In 1917 Britain was exhausted by the war and vociferous, albeit unrepresentative, elements suggested that the spectre of republicanism was not altogether dead. As a sop to public opinion, the King had been prevailed upon to alter his house's dynastic name from Saxe-Coburg Gotha to the more patriotic Windsor. How, asked angry letters delivered to 10 Downing Street, could a sovereign with Hanoverian ancestors and a Queen descended from the House of Teck have sympathies with any nation other than Germany, and was it surprising that the war was lasting so long with a pro-German monarch on the throne?

Radical journalists warned of dire consequences if the Tsar was brought to England. The Tsarina posed an even greater problem; even the King believed her to be largely responsible for the downfall of the Romanovs, thanks to her

King George V with Field Marshal Joffre, President Poincaré, Field Marshal Foch and Sir Douglas Haig at Valvion, August 1916. They had met to discuss Anglo-French military strategy after heavy losses in the battle of the Somme; rather misleadingly, this group photo was published as a postcard captioned 'The smile of Victory'

reckless partisanship of the detested Rasputin and her attempts to bring about a rapprochement with Germany.

Britain seemed an unlikely theatre of revolution, but after three years of war with no end in sight, and with mutterings from the likes of H.G. Wells about 'an alien and uninspiring court,' it looked like tempting providence for a constitutional monarch to identify himself so blatantly with Russian imperial autocracy. King Edward VII had not attempted to conceal his anger in 1908 when a few outspoken radical and socialist members of the Commons had deprecated their sovereign's visit to Tsar Nicholas at Reval, regretting that he should be hobnobbing with 'a tyrant and a common murderer.'* But his son thought it prudent to tread more carefully. In 1917 the instinct for self-preservation, and maintenance of the British monarchy, was paramount.

Although King George was anxious for the ex-Tsar's safety and feared that if imprisoned in Russia it was doubtful whether he would come out alive, he probably believed that the Bolsheviks' anger would be satisfied by the execution of their former ruler at most. That they would show such flagrant disregard for international opinion by butchering the invalid Tsarevich and his four sisters as well as their wheelchair-bound mother was a possibility which could hardly have

---

* The King maintained that this visit was primarily a family business and not a political occasion. Among his critics was the Liberal member for Stirling Burghs, Arthur Ponsonby, son of Sir Henry, and brother of Frederick. The royal family thought that with his court connections he should have known better than to associate himself with such attacks.

been envisaged by any but the most pessimistic. In July 1918 the King was informed that 'dear Nicky' had been shot, but there were no further details to hand. Not for another month was he to be informed that all seven, and their remaining servants, had been murdered simultaneously at Ekaterinburg; 'It's too horrible and shows what fiends these Bolshevists are.'[7]

In Norway, Queen Maud felt increasingly isolated; 'it seems as if this awful war would never end as so many fresh complications arise daily!' she wrote to Queen Mary (16 March 1918). 'I long to see you *all* again and dear "home", my thoughts are so continually with you *all* and I often feel *very* lonely and forlorn as there are so few to talk to!'[8] Two months later (21 May), she inveighed once more against the nightmare of 'this ghastly war,' which imposed such a strain on them all; 'it seems now too as if it would *never* end – and I feel as if I can never come home, it *is* so hard not seeing any of you for nearly five years now! But still one must always hope for the best!'[9]

Everyone's 'hope for the best' brought its own reward, for by now the tide was beginning to turn. The final German offensive, launched early in 1918 on the western front although meeting with initial success, gradually faltered during the summer. On 1 October King George heard with relief that Bulgaria had unconditionally surrendered; later that month Turkey did likewise, followed in November by Austria and Germany. On 11 November Germany signed the Armistice.

Two days earlier, 'dear Papa's birthday', as King George noted sentimentally in his diary, Emperor William had abdicated. The King acknowledged with magnanimity that his cousin had done great things for his country, but his ambition was so great that he wished to dominate the world; 'now he has utterly ruined his Country and himself. I look upon him as the greatest criminal known for having plunged the world into this ghastly war . . .'[10]

When his second son Bertie met the widowed Princess Adolf of Schaumburg-Lippe (formerly Princess Victoria of Prussia) in December 1918, she astounded him by being quite unaware of German atrocities during the war. Although a sister of the ex-Emperor, she had always disliked him and taken the side of their mother, the Empress Frederick, in family arguments. She asked after King George and Queen Mary, and said she hoped they would all be friends again shortly. Bertie answered politely that he did not think that possible for a great many years. This reply, King George, told him, was quite correct; 'the sooner she knows the real feeling of bitterness which exists here against her country the better.'[11]

Yet the King was not one to crow over a fallen enemy. When the ex-Emperor slipped quietly into exile in the Netherlands, he was angered to hear that the wife of the British minister to that country had publicly jeered at him. A few months later, her husband was prematurely retired from the diplomatic service. Likewise Lloyd George's bombastic remarks about having the former Emperor extradited and put on trial as a war criminal, about which the King only learnt after reading them in the newspapers, moved him to 'a violent tirade' for half an hour. To his intense relief, the Dutch government refused all requests for the Emperor's extradition.

Now Queen Maud could look forward to seeing her beloved Appleton again. 'I *am* wild with excitement at the idea of *at last* coming home and seeing you all again!' she wrote to Queen Mary (30 November 1918). 'It seems all like a *dream* to me, everything has changed so quickly from the *awful* war into peace.'[12]

11 'Things Will be Very Different Here Now'

During the war years, Princess Victoria had followed her brother's example in visiting hospitals throughout the country, and camps in France. Louise was now a virtual recluse, rarely seen in public except at weddings and other family gatherings, and at the Braemar games. Ironically she was often confused in the public mind with her Aunt Louise, Duchess of Argyll, who was almost nineteen years older than her but still maintained a busy programme of appearances with the zest of a woman half her age.

The Dowager Duchess of Fife's elder daughter, Princess Arthur of Connaught, had wholeheartedly embraced the nursing profession. Soon after the birth of her only child Arthur, born five days after Britain's declaration of war on Germany, she joined the staff of St Mary's Hospital, Paddington. In 1919 she became a state registered nurse and was later awarded a first prize for her paper on eclampsia, or convulsions in late pregnancy.

Princess Victoria welcomed any diversions from her stultifying life with 'Motherdear', and the perpetual movement between Marlborough House and Sandringham. Queen Alexandra, who as the war drew to a close was approaching her seventy-fourth birthday, had aged fast. The loss of her legendary beauty, increasing deafness, lameness and blindness, anxiety about the fate of her sister Minnie and other relations in Russia and Greece, and a general mental decline, all contributed to her depression and querulousness. Because of the risk of enemy action at sea, she could not visit her family in Denmark or her holiday retreat at Hvidore, purchased jointly with Minnie after the death of their father, and by the time peace was declared she was too frail to travel abroad.

The brunt of all this fell on Victoria, who found herself more and more indispensable to her unhappy, tyrannical mother. In 1912 the Queen had helped to inaugurate Alexandra Rose Day, and every June she and Victoria drove through the London streets in a carriage, stopping to speak words of encouragement to the rose sellers. Yet the effort of keeping a smiling face to show the world during what she privately called 'that tiresome Alexandra day, which I *dread*,' became greater each year, and the work steadily devolved on her daughter.

Queen Alexandra still could not resist giving children's parties, and every July she held one at Marlborough House to celebrate Toria's birthday. Their young guests were regaled with generous quantities of food, and entertainment from a Punch and Judy show, conjurers, jugglers and comedians. The press paid fulsome tribute to Princess Victoria's understanding of, sympathy with, and affection for children. But it must have been hard for her not to dwell with some bitterness on a fate which had denied her a family of her own.

How much the youngsters took to this surrogate aunt is open to question. Queen Mary's niece Mary, later Duchess of Beaufort, later recalled that as children she, her sister and brothers 'absolutely *hated* Princess Victoria.'

When members of the household dared to suggest that economies in the running of Sandringham and Marlborough House would be much appreciated as part of the national war effort, Queen Alexandra announced firmly that 'if I get into debt *they* can pay.' Stung by her obstinacy, Arthur Davidson (who might once have become her son-in-law) asked her pointedly *who* would pay. The nation could not afford to; such a burden would fall on King George or Princess Victoria, and it was not fair on them. Not for the first time, the Queen protested that she had not heard one word of the conversation.[1]

In 1922 King George gave Victoria a set of apartments in Kensington Palace. It was a just reward for years of dutiful attention to her mother, but Queen Alexandra complained bitterly at being deprived of her company. By now she found London life too exhausting, and preferred the seclusion of Sandringham.

Once again Victoria had the consolation, interrupted by the war, of regular visits from her younger sister. Queen Maud suffered increasingly from intense headaches and neuralgia in the cold damp Norwegian climate, and found it more and more painful to take part in official functions there. She preferred living in Bygdoy to Kongens Slot, looking after her garden and pets, and writing regularly to her relations abroad. When possible she generally spent between six and eight weeks each time at Appleton in the autumn, and again early in the new year. She travelled with a modest entourage, usually consisting of just a lady-in-waiting and her secretary. King Haakon generally took the train to Bergen to bid her farewell and to welcome her back.

In November 1919 she celebrated her fiftieth birthday 'at home', in the Norfolk countryside, and described it in a letter to Queen Mary the following day (27 November):

> It was *joy* to spend the day *here* again after six years! I loved being with Motherdear and Toria and they all came and lunched and everyone was so kind and gave me charming presents and I got heaps of letters and masses of telegrams. Unfortunately Motherdear and Toria were neither well yesterday, both having colds so they only came to lunch and then went home.[2]

She would have liked to stay there for Christmas, but the Norwegian government and King Haakon thought it only right she should return to them for the festive season. But the memory of this first post-war visit to her childhood home was slow to fade. '*What* fun our dancing was,' she recalled in a letter from Christiania to Queen Mary (24 January 1920), 'and I am *sure* cheered Motherdear up as well as ourselves and did us *all* lots of good after our *six* years of misery!'[3]

Whenever she was back in Norfolk, her sense of humour and ready banter with the family always made for a cheery atmosphere. When King George heard that she kept a special handkerchief for her little spaniel, he enlivened a walk around the estate with comments like, 'Where are its galoshes?' and 'Don't forget its cough drops.'

The first new year of peace-time brought personal family sadness for King George and Queen Mary. Prince John died suddenly but peacefully in his sleep on 18 January 1919. For Queen Alexandra, his release from suffering and burial in Sandringham churchyard, brought back memories of her youngest son of the same name, who had made so fleeting an appearance in the world. 'Now our two darling Johnnies lie side by side,' she wrote to Queen Mary.

Of Prince John's four elder brothers and sister, all but the latter had become virtual strangers to their parents. Princess Mary alone had stayed at home with them throughout the war. One of her greatest assets was that she could be relied on to keep conversation going at the dinner table.

As for the Princes, in 1919 Edward set up his own establishment at York House, St James's. Bertie, invalided out of the Royal Navy, was now serving with the newly-founded Royal Air Force. Henry and George, who had been schoolboys at the outbreak of war, had joined the army and only returned home when on leave.

Inevitably, war-weary Britain and her people constituted a very different nation to that which they had been before Gavrilo Princip raised his revolver in the streets of Sarajevo in June 1914. The British had become more anti-European, and for insular as well as economic reasons there was a noticeable drop in the number of holidays taken abroad. In this their mood matched those of their sovereign. The cosmopolitan King Edward VII had adored Paris, Marienbad and Biarritz, while his son denounced aborad as 'awful – I know, because I have been there.' For the younger generation – and, again, the King's family reflected this – pleasure was a priority. Those men who had gone straight from school into the army at a time when their country was engaged in a struggle for survival, and who came through four years of bitter strife with physical and mental health unimpaired, were restless and wished to turn their backs on 'the old days'.

The British monarchy had also survived, unlike its Hohenzollern, Habsburg and Romanov peers on the continent, but events had shown that thrones could not be taken for granted. At Westminster, the Labour party was no longer a minority faction but on its way to becoming the official opposition, supplanting the declining Liberals and soon to form its first government. During the general election campaign less than a week after the armistice, a Labour meeting held ironically at the Albert Hall, Bob Williams, secretary of the Transport Workers' Union, was cheered loudly when he announced that he hoped to see the red flag flying over Buckingham Palace. At first glance, therefore, socialism and royalty made uneasy bedfellows, and many questioned whether both could accommodate each other amicably during the coming years.

Edward epitomized love of revelry and night life of the twenties, so dear to the 'gay young things' of fashionable society. In this he was following in the footsteps of his grandfather and to an extent the uncle he had never known, although unlike the Duke of Clarence he was no lethargic simpleton. A handsome young man despite his small stature, he had the star quality and panache that his solid, dependable parents lacked. Advisers close to the King and Queen saw that he

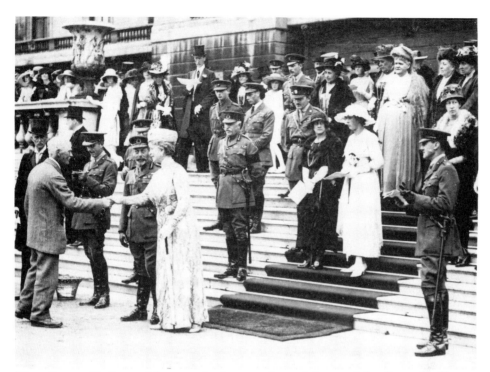

King George V, Queen Mary, and other members of the royal family at the Victoria Cross garden party, Buckingham Palace, 26 June 1920. They include the Duke of Connaught (behind the King and Queen); Princess Arthur of Connaught, and Princess Mary in white dress and hat (both standing, third step up); Prince Arthur of Connaught (behind them, to the left); Prince Henry, and the Duke of York (both fifth step up); the Princess Royal (far right); the Duchess of Albany (eighth step up); Princess Beatrice (behind, to the left); and the Duchess of Argyll (behind Prince Arthur of Connaught)

could be a valuable asset to the monarchy, and so began a series of tours throughout the United States, Canada and other imperial territories, rivalling in extent the travelling undertaken sixty years earlier by Queen Victoria's two elder sons.

Queen Mary was extremely proud of his success. Although she disapproved of his faddishness, particularly his taste in clothes, she was delighted at each successful reception he enjoyed abroad and the effusive headlines which followed. His aunt, Queen Maud also followed his progress with keen interest. 'You must indeed be a *proud* mother!' she wrote to her sister-in-law (27 November 1919), after the Prince's 'splendid success' in North America. 'He has such charm and wins all hearts and will get a tremendous reception in London.'[4]

King George, however, did not approve. He disliked the American way of life and the personal adulation accorded to his son. It seemed worlds away from the more dignified hero-worship given to monarchs and their heirs during his own formative years, and he was also more than a little jealous. Throughout his adult life he had been overshadowed – first by his elder brother, then his father, and since his accession by his mother, who even in widowhood refused to relinquish

Princess Victoria (centre) with the Hon. Violet Vivian and Sir Arthur Davidson after a garden party, Buckingham Palace, July 1921

privileges accorded to her as first lady of the land until she was too elderly and too frail to insist. Now, His Imperial Majesty King George V was being denied the spotlight by a handsome, dashing young rival who would obviously outlive him by many, many years – his eldest son.

Indeed, King George found it hard to come to terms with the prevailing mood of the twenties and the ceaseless pursuit of change for its own sake. Even Queen Mary was not spared her husband's temper as she experimented with modern fashions which appealed to her. His disgust after seeing her raise the hem of her skirts by a couple of inches, or his wrath on finding Sir Frederick Ponsonby teaching her new dance steps, ensured that she did not try again.

In Norway, King Haakon and Queen Maud proved themselves to be more flexible. No longer did it seem improper for them to wear more casual clothes in public. The quickstep and foxtrot were danced at palace parties, and the King did not feel obliged to observe Ponsonby's reservations about using a tram. But socialists still looked on the monarchy with a lack of enthusiasm, if not hostility. King Haakon was dismayed at the denunciations of capitalism and the upper classes that found their way into the press, often inspired by socialists and communists who sat in the Storting, and sometimes he asked his ministers whether the strong language used constituted anything more than empty rhetoric.

On occasion it took no more than good-humoured commonsense to solve such problems. When the Labour Mayor of Oslo* omitted to invite Their Majesties to the laying of the foundation stone for the new city hall, King Haakon sent his secretary to apply for two tickets to the ceremony on behalf of the palace. All those who had subscribed to the hall were entitled to request tickets, and by thus legitimately ensuring places for himself and his consort in the front row when the mayor bade his guests welcome was a more effective way for the King to make his point than any words of reproof.

Although she abhorred publicity and still spent several weeks of the autumn and winter in England, Queen Maud made her own contribution to the popularity of the monarchy which should not be underestimated. Like Queen Mary, she was genuinely interested in the welfare of the needy, and her tireless charity work did not go unnoticed by those who worked with her on committees. She never acquired much grasp of Norwegian politics, and always found it difficult to read and understand the papers, but she was proud of her husband and all that he had achieved. Her modest nature never allowed her to realize how much she helped him in securing the love and respect of a nation which had accepted its independent monarchy more for reasons of prestige than out of any great enthusiasm.

Victorian as he was in outlook, King George V adapted with success to certain landmarks of a changing world. Despite initial misgivings, he experienced no difficulty in working with the first British Labour government in 1924.[†] In time

---

* Christiania was renamed Oslo in 1925.

† See below, pp. 157–58.

Queen Maud of Norway attending a meet of the West Norfolk Hounds, January 1922

he came to help inaugurate the tradition of royal Christmas broadcasts on the radio, a new development which he initially viewed with feelings akin to horror.* As a father, if not as a husband, he was less successful, particularly where relations with his eldest son were concerned.

By coincidence, history had repeated itself. While King Edward VII's first son had been the despair of his father, and only escaped the worst manifestations of paternal wrath by dying young, his second son had been the industrious one who was to win his exacting parent's full approval. So it was to be with King George V's sons. His second son, created Duke of York in 1920, was handicapped by his diffidence, chronic ill-health and a speech impediment, yet Bertie's courage and determination to serve his country in wartime and beyond did not go unnoticed. Though he was still so in awe of his father that visits to the palace were a strain on his nervous system, his readiness to agree with him helped to avoid painful scenes.

All the same, he dreaded the dreariness of life at home. It become more so after the marriage of Princess Mary, who was engaged to Henry, Viscount Lascelles, eldest son of the Earl of Harewood, in 1921. Like the late Earl of Fife,

* see below, p. 167.

King George V and Queen Mary, with Viscount Lascelles and Princess Mary on their wedding day, 28 February 1922

King George V as Admiral of the Fleet

Lascelles was considerably older than his betrothed. What he lacked in youth, charm and good looks (behind his back he was known as 'that dismal bloodhound') he made up for in personal fortune, similar interests to both parents-in-law, namely shooting and a connoisseur's eye for fine paintings and antiques, and true British blue blood. Since the war, foreign princes and princesses were no longer so eligible, and it was inevitable that at least some of King George V's children-in-law would come from British families.

The wedding, the first great state occasion since peace was declared, took place at Westminster Abbey on 28 February 1922. As the family had predicted, Mary left 'a terrible blank behind her.' 'Things will be very different here now that Mary has left and mama will miss her too terribly,' Bertie wrote sadly to Edward.

For Bertie, however, wedding bells were soon to ring as well. Two years earlier, at the RAF ball at the Ritz, he had met a girl whom he vaguely remembered sitting next to at a children's party in 1905 – Lady Elizabeth Bowes-Lyon. In due course she became a close friend of Princess Mary, and a bridesmaid at the wedding.

King George and Queen Mary could not help noticing how Bertie was always talking about her. Though the Queen stoutly maintained that parents should never meddle in their children's love affairs, she was curious to find out more. While on a visit to Balmoral, she drove over to the Bowes-Lyon home, Glamis Castle. As Lady Strathmore was unwell, Elizabeth acted as host. She made a most favourable impression on Queen Mary, whose first reaction was that this young woman would make an ideal wife for Edward – he needed a steadying

King George V at work in his study. This was said to be one of his favourite photographs of himself

King George V as Marshal of the RAF

Four generations, 1923; King George V and Queen Alexandra with Princess Mary, Viscountess Lascelles, and her first son Gerald

155

influence. After being told by Lady Airlie that Edward, who had an uncomfortable penchant for married women, was not ready to settle down yet and that Bertie was passionately fond of Elizabeth, she changed her mind.

'You'll be a lucky fellow if she accepts you,' King George gruffly warned him, less from a desire to be pessimistic than from the intention to steel himself for disappointment if she did turn Bertie down. Lady Airlie thought Elizabeth was uncertain about her feelings, and afraid of the public life which would lie ahead for a King's daughter-in-law. Lady Strathmore was deeply sorry for the persistent suitor who sometimes seemed in despair at his lack of success; she liked him very much and realized that he was 'a man who will be made or marred by his wife.'

In the first week of 1923, newspapers carried a story that the Prince of Wales was soon to be betrothed; the next Queen of England was the daughter of a well-known Scottish peer, and one of the closest friends of Princess Mary, Viscountess Lascelles. In all details they were correct, save one; she was not destined to be Edward's bride. A few days later, Bertie went to stay with the Strathmores at their Hertfordshire home, St Paul's Walden Bury. He proposed and Elizabeth, reconciled to a royal future, accepted him. News of the engagement was received with delight by the family, though diarist Henry 'Chips' Channon suggested that the clubs were in gloom as there was not a man in England who did not envy him.

The wedding took place on 26 April, at Westminster Abbey. There had not been such a ceremony there for a prince of the royal house since that of King Richard II to Anne of Bohemia in 1383.

King George V, who had told Queen Mary the previous summer how he dreaded the idea of having daughters-in-law, was captivated by the Duchess of York. Whenever he felt the need to remonstrate with her, he did so very gently. Mildly disturbed by her willingness to cooperate with journalists, he sent an equerry round to the Yorks' London house at Bruton Street to request that there should be no more interviews. Yet he was happy to accept her habitual unpunctuality, much as he deprecated it in others. When his son and daughter-in-law arrived two minutes late for dinner one evening and she apologized, he astonished everyone by telling her genially that the rest of them must have sat down two minutes too early. To a courtier who remarked privately that the Duchess was sometimes unpunctual, he defended her by saying that if she was never late, she would be perfect, 'and how horrible that would be!'

On 12 November 1923 Louise came out of her seclusion briefly when her younger daughter Maud of Fife married Lord Carnegie, son of the Earl of Southesk, at the Guards Chapel, Wellington Barracks. 'All brides are beautiful,' wrote *The Times* correspondent effusively, 'but the Princess Maud made a Titania among brides – the daintiest of real fairy-tale princesses.'[5] Almost as striking in her appearance was Maud's grandmother, resplendent in purple with an ermine cape. Sixty years had elapsed since the eighteen-year-old Princess Alexandra of Denmark had captured a nation's heart as she arrived in England to wed the Prince of Wales. Now, becoming ever more frail, the Dowager Queen made her last major appearance in public at this family wedding.

For King George and his sisters, the next couple of years were to bring more than their fair share of trouble and personal sadness.

Shortly before Maud's wedding Earl Farquhar, a close family friend and former Lord Steward of the royal household, had died. Farquhar had entered royal circles through his friendship with the Duke of Fife. His connection with various financial scandals did not affect the regard in which he was held by King Edward VII and King George V, both of whom shot with him regularly on the Norfolk estates. He grew steadily more eccentric and less reliable in old age, and after his failure to account for large sums of money missing from the coffers of the Conservative party he was dismissed as treasurer by the Prime Minister, Andrew Bonar Law, ostensibly on grounds of ill-health.

It was no surprise to anyone when his will was published. A lifelong bachelor, his estate was provisionally valued at the then considerable sum of £400,000. Several members of the royal family, from the King and Queen downwards, were left generous bequests of jewellery and other *objets d'art*. The Dowager Duchess of Fife had been well provided for by her wealthy husband, so she received little, but Princess Victoria was left two Dresden quails, and Louise's daughters a diamond necklace each.

Farquhar's friends, royal and non-royal, were touched that he should have remembered them in such style, but King George thought the estimated value of his estate somewhat optimistic. Time proved him horribly right. Soon after publication of the will, it was revealed that Farquhar had left massive debts as well. Rumour had it that the spendthrift financier and art collector had invested recklessly in London and Paris theatres at a time of depressed conditions. The net value of his estates, it later transpired, was precisely nil. None of his legatees received anything.

That was not the end of the unhappy story. Next year it came to light that his trusteeship of the Fife estates had been exercised as irresponsibly as his share of Conservative party funds, and £80,000 of trust money was unaccounted for. His co-trustee, the Dowager Duchess of Fife, was legally obliged to make good the sum. 'She is open-mouthed in consequence,' noted Lord Lincolnshire. Part of the deficiency was raised by her sale of family pictures. Forty-five paintings, including portraits by Reynolds and Raeburn, and religious scenes by Mabuse and Matsys, once part of the collection formed by one of her husband's forebears in the seventeenth century, were sold by auction at Christie's on 18 July 1924, and raised over £13,000.

It was not only the Farquhar embarrassment that made 1924 an eventful year for King George V. In January, he had asked Ramsay MacDonald to form the first Labour administration of Britain. As he noted in his diary, he wondered what 'dear Grandmama' would have thought of a socialist government. However, he readily admitted to his new prime minister that he had served in the Navy for fourteen years, and thus had opportunities of seeing more of the world, and mixing with his future subjects, than if he had spent his formative years cocooned in a palace. A couple of years earlier, he had warned Lloyd George sternly that the two million unemployed in his kingdom wanted work, not dole, and that a government which had afforded the enormous daily cost of the war could be generous in peacetime as well. It was appropriate that such words should come from a King whose grandfather, Prince Albert of Saxe-Coburg Gotha, had irritated his wife's ministers by proclaiming freely that if socialism meant helping one's less fortunate fellow men, then he was proud to be a socialist.

Queen Mary had worked side by side during the war with Mary MacArthur, founder of the National Federation of Women Workers in 1906, helping to provide employment rather than charity for women thrown out of work as a result of the war. Consequently she already knew several of the new ministers' wives. Courtiers were astonished at the ease with which the King and Queen accepted their first, albeit short-lived, Labour government and its leaders.

As 1924 drew to a close, the royal family gathered as usual for Christmas at Sandringham. For three years Queen Alexandra had come to London only when family weddings or appearances on 'Alexandra Rose Day' demanded, preferring the seclusion of 'the Big House' in the Norfolk countryside where she and her husband had made their home together. Age and increasing infirmity made her a pitiful figure; her face was immaculately but heavily made up till she looked almost waxen, and she never stepped outside without the protection of a thick veil. 'It is hard to see that beautiful woman come to this,' Queen Mary noted poignantly.

King George, approaching his sixtieth birthday, was far from well at the time. That winter he suffered from colds, coughs and rheumatic complaints. Shortly after his return to London from Sandringham in the new year he took to his bed with influenza, followed by bronchitis and a high temperature. Although in great pain, he refused to neglect his duty of consulting the daily boxes of government papers, working in bed propped up by pillows, seeing as few people as possible outside the family.

The doctors ordered him to go abroad and convalesce as soon as he was well enough to travel. King Edward had made a point of avoiding the capricious British climate each winter; why should the same not hold good for his son and his bronchial trouble? King George received the idea with dismay, but his doctors were insistent. So was Queen Mary, whose last journeys to the continent had been filled from dawn to dusk with an unrelenting round of official duties. She relished the idea of visiting art galleries and places of historical interest. Naples, she suggested, would be ideal, till he snapped back that the harbour was full of dead dogs. Malta he likewise vetoed as 'a bloody place'. The libel action over assertions of his 'marriage' there still left a scar. Irritated by his wife's efforts to whet his appetite with the glories of European culture, and at a loss as to how he would fill his days of cruising around on the yacht as a semi-invalid, he asked Princess Victoria to accompany them.

For Victoria, the invitation was more than welcome. She received little enough thanks for looking after her mother, especially as her own health was far from good. The royal doctor, Lord Dawson of Penn, thought her a first-class hypochondriac, but the sheer tedium of her life at Sandringham and Marlborough House year in year out, with only rare 'escapes' to her apartments at

The family riding in Windsor Great Park, May 1923. From left: King George V; the Prince of Wales; Prince Albert; Prince Henry (almost hidden) and Prince George

Kensington or boarding-houses, afforded her precious little distraction. Sir Dighton Probyn, who had been comptroller to King Edward VII throughout most of his adult life and then to Queen Alexandra, died in June 1924 at the age of eighty-seven, leaving the ninety-year-old Charlotte Knollys as the sole survivor of the Dowager Queen's generation.

Once a lively house that rang with the echoes of a young and high-spirited family's laughter, Sandringham was now a virtual mausoleum. Queen Mary found the atmosphere of old age and illness so oppressive that it was an ordeal to step inside, let alone stay there. The effect of such surroundings on Princess Victoria can be easily imagined, as the ever-sympathetic Queen Maud appreciated. She realized how much she was missed every time she had to leave Appleton for Norway. To Queen Mary she wrote (11 January 1924):

> Poor Toria was in such a state to be left *alone* with all 'the old ones' (as we call them!) I do pity her, and her life is *awful*, no one to talk to, *do* urge her, like I wrote to George, to make her have someone to come and stay and go out with. She is in *such* a state of anxiety and nerves unstrung that I fear she might have a breakdown.[6]

Victoria had her hobbies; she was an enthusiastic patron of concerts, and shared the family love of photography. Gardening, needlework, art galleries, paintings, and collecting old glass and silver appealed to her. Most of all, she was a voracious reader, and took delight in binding books herself and designing bindings. Yet despite these interests – which she shared with many ladies of the time – it would have taken the disposition of a saint not to be soured by the life she was forced to lead; and Princess Victoria of Wales was no saint. To the Prince of Wales, who believed that she was part of an unofficial intelligence network responsible for reporting many of his indiscretions back to the King, his aunt was 'a bitch of the first order.' Her sisters, he later told biographer James Pope-Hennessy, were little better. They were not merely inferior in education and intellect to Queen Mary, 'they could just read and write, period. That was all.'[7]

With their common interests in art and collecting, the sisters-in-law should have been close friends. Unfortunately their temperaments clashed, and they drifted further apart with age. Though she had great sympathy for the unhappy spinster, Queen Mary resented the hold that Victoria had over her brother. There was no denying the Princess's concern for his welfare, as her letter to Queen Mary during his illness shows (26 February 1925):

> Of course he must not start too soon and be shaken about in trains or be sick. He used to do it just as a real pleasure trip avoiding any fuss at ports. With officials and tiresome people to visit – and never went to sea till real good weather – as so unnecessary to be in gales which do of course come up very quickly on the Mediterranean.[8]

Victoria's presence brought out the worst in George, and the two of them would behave almost like children again, fooling around and making fun of her as they had done in childhood. When the Queen heard that Victoria was to accompany them abroad, her heart sank.

Her worst expectations were soon confirmed. Soon after they set out for Genoa by train on 19 March, the weather broke and all caught colds as they cruised between Naples and Sicily. George and Victoria refused on principle to join in the sightseeing tours at ports – Pompeii, Messina, Syracuse and Palermo – where they stopped. When Mary put her foot down and insisted, they spoiled things for her by a continual stream of silly jokes and laughter. With grim determination, the Queen gleaned what pleasure she could out of ancient monuments and scenes of beauty on their way, and she was pleased that good weather did wonders for the King's health – but as they sailed homewards she was '*so* glad to be back.'

To do the irritable patient and his sister justice, they had a grave worry on their minds throughout the tour. Victoria's conscience probably reproached her for going abroad and leaving 'Motherdear' behind. 'I feel *completely* collapsed – I shall soon go,'[9] the Dowager Queen wrote pathetically to them, in a barely legible scrawl, while they were away.

When they returned to England that spring, they realized that she had not been exaggerating. Queen Alexandra was now too blind to lip-read. Since suffering a minor stroke, her speech was so impaired that it was impossible at times to understand what she was saying. 'It really is *too* sad,' Queen Maud commented, 'and her speech is going, and she wants to tell one things and can't.' Even attendance at Sandringham church was an ordeal, and she only went to services twice during the last months – on her eightieth birthday, and again the following April.

At the very same time, Louise's health also gave cause for alarm. Since her daughter Maud's marriage, she had retreated more into her own private world, much to the distress of her brother and sisters. The humiliation of having to sell off some of her husband's paintings was a further cross to bear. On 30 April, shortly after returning to her house at Portman Square from a visit to the Royal Academy, she complained to Princess Arthur of Connaught of feeling unwell. A doctor was sent for, and severe gastric haemorrhage was diagnosed. Queen Maud wrote anxiously to Queen Mary (6 May):

> Oh, I am *so* distraught and miserable about poor darling Louise, it gave me *such* a shock in getting George's telegram, and I was *terribly* upset, but thank God the latter telegrams seemed more satisfactory. Do you know I *always* feared that *some* day something *dreadful* would happen to her as she looked so *terribly* ill and delicate and suffering, and that odd far away look in her eyes, has *always* haunted me, and I have kept on writing to her to be careful and rest more etc. Poor dear, *how* sudden it all was, as she wrote on 30th to me and said she had just been to the Royal Academy which was *very* tiring, but *never* mentioned she felt ill. She *must* have hidden all she has been suffering.[10]

Living on her own, the widowed Louise was even more bereft of company than Victoria, a situation which was not lost on their happily-married sister in Norway. 'Poor poor thing,' Queen Maud commented in another letter next day, 'she is so lonely and has *no* one to look after her anymore. Hope *now* she will pull through if only her strength can be kept up.'[11] Within a week Louise's condition improved so much that bulletins on her illness were discontinued, but in her declining years she was to be a never-ending source of worry to them all.

For Queen Alexandra, there was to be no recovery. She lingered on throughout summer and autumn, being taken for regular car drives around the Sandringham estate, and twice a week through the streets of King's Lynn. In October the press reported that she watched a football match for several minutes, but it was no more than a public-spirited gesture of interest in an activity which she could no longer see or comprehend.

On 19 November she suffered a massive heart attack. The following day, King George and Queen Mary moved continuously between York Cottage and Sandringham House, and they were by her side when she died late in the afternoon. For the woman once acclaimed as the most beautiful princess in Europe, death could only be a release. The coffin rested in Sandringham church, and after a funeral service in Westminster Abbey on 27 November she was buried beside her husband and eldest son at Windsor.

To Princess Victoria fell the heartbreaking task of arranging for the removal of her mother's belongings and such of her own as she wished to place in her new home, Coppins, near Iver in Buckinghamshire. Coppins had the relaxed air of a holiday villa, with large bay windows and stone mullions. Its dark rooms were soon furnished Sandringham-style with heavy old furniture and walls hung with family portraits. The entrance hall was dominated by a large marble bust of King Edward VII. An indefatigable gardener, Victoria supervised the planting of her grounds with plentiful trees and shrubs.

At last King George and Queen Mary could move into the 'Big House' at Sandringham, leaving gloomy and cramped York Cottage behind them. In March 1926 Victoria, temporarily at Marlborough House, was thoroughly run down and had a severe attack of influenza which developed into pneumonia. For an anxious few days, the King wondered whether he might not lose a sister as well as their mother.

Victoria was assisted by Maud, and the King and Queen, in dividing their mother's personal jewellery, pictures and other possessions at Sandringham and Marlborough House. As Queen Mary put it brusquely, they were confronted with a motley collection of good and bad things – 'a warning to one not to keep too much' as nothing had been thrown away during the last sixty years.

One ray of sunshine came to cheer the family's sadness. On 21 April 1926 the Duchess of York gave birth to her first child, a daughter who was named Elizabeth Alexandra Mary. A little nervously, the Duke asked his father whether it was still necessary to include 'Victoria' among the child's names. Despite his love of tradition, the King said he hardly thought that necessary by now. Elizabeth, or 'Lilibet', his third grandchild, was quickly to become – and remain – his favourite.

In spite of failing health, Princess Victoria took a keen interest in the activities of her new neighbours in Buckinghamshire. The Iver Girl Guides were proud of the interest she took in them, as was her local dramatic society the Richings Players. She was regularly seen in antique shops, and at arts and crafts exhibitions in South Buckinghamshire. Sometimes she visited the local schools, though she did not often go inside and preferred to wave to children from outside the windows instead. Nevertheless, she was often invited to give away prizes at the end of term.

Like her mother she worked hard for hospitals, charities and welfare services, and her first public engagement was opening an extension to the Iver and District Cottage Hospital. She was appointed Lady Grand Patroness, frequently visiting the staff and patients thereafter.

Her public manner, however, did not always match her generosity. A story is told of her appearance at a senior citizens' home in Harrogate, where she struck up a conversation with one old lady who had lived there for about twenty years and assured Princess Victoria how happy she was, because she had known everybody for so long and they were all her friends. 'Poor soul,' murmured the Princess. 'You think you are happy, but you are not.' After repeating herself several times in this mournful vein, the 'poor soul' burst into tears. So did the people in the other wards addressed similarly by Princess Victoria, who told the staff solemnly as she left how good it was to come and bring comfort to the dear patients.

One of her favourite indulgences was a glass of whisky, and Coppins was never without a good supply. It was a commodity much appreciated by her chauffeur, who was not above making free with it when she was not around. To disguise the fumes on his breath he carried a packet of extra strong mints around with him, but his employer was not fooled. One day she told him sternly that she did not mind if he helped himself to her whisky; what she really objected to was the smell of his mints.

Still the Princess and her brother phoned each other every morning, and in various matters her opinions continued to influence him. In 1927 Sir Frederick Ponsonby asked the King if he might publish a selection of the Empress Frederick's letters. She had entrusted the equerry, her godson, with a large collection of her private correspondence a few months before she died, and he was infuriated by the stream of German memoirs and biographies – notably a life of the ex-Emperor William II by Emil Ludwig – which presented her as a scheming Englishwoman who despised her deformed son and ruthlessly dominated her husband. King George was doubtful, and recommended that Ponsonby should consult the empress's surviving brother and sisters. Princess Beatrice disapproved, but the Duke of Connaught and the Duchess of Argyll told him that they were sure their maligned sister had always intended to have her correspondence made available in book form, and the time was right.

When *Letters of the Empress Frederick* appeared in October 1928, King George refrained from expressing an opinion until Princess Victoria told him she thought it one of the most dreadful books ever published. Only then did he join her and Princess Beatrice in criticizing it, though less wholeheartedly. Queen Mary, on the other hand, supported Ponsonby in his motives, though she thought he should have been more selective in his choice of material.

12   'The People "Love" to See a Happy Family Life'

It was perhaps inevitable with their record of indifferent health that none of the children of King Edward VII and Queen Alexandra would live to enjoy a vigorous old age. All four survivors celebrated their sixtieth birthdays during the second half of the 1920s, but they appeared old before their time. By comparison, Queen Victoria's two youngest daughters and one surviving son were still comparatively active.

Louise, Dowager Duchess of Fife and Princess Royal, was immured in the relative seclusion of her late husband's Scottish estates. She had become ever more frail with increasing heart trouble, and had long since ceased to make anything but the most brief of public appearances.

It was only the high profile of her elder daughter, Princess Arthur of Connaught, who reminded the public of her existence. In 1920 her husband was appointed Governor-General of the Union of South Africa, a task which he discharged with great ability. Her tact and easy manner likewise made her many friends among the South Africans, who were grateful for her interest in hospitals, welfare work, child welfare and maternity work. On their return to London in 1923 she resumed her nursing career at the University College Hospital, where she was known as 'Nurse Marjorie' and at Charing Cross Hospital. She was a dependable and imperturbable theatre sister, capable of performing minor operations herself as well as instructing juniors in their duties, and she boasted of having once amputated a patient's thumb under general anaesthetic. In July 1925 she was awarded the badge of the Royal Red Cross.

King Edward VII's grandchildren included not only a distinguished nurse but also a sportsman who would have probably excelled in a professional capacity if he had not been a crown prince. At the age of fourteen, Olav delighted his parents by taking fourth place in a ski-jumping competition at school, and winning third prize in a ski rally against over three hundred competitors. A year later he was given his first boat, and by the time he left military college he was one of Norway's most distinguished amateur sailors. In 1928 he won a gold medal for sailing at the Amsterdam Olympic games.

Though King Haakon and Queen Maud thought it prudent to have him educated in Norway, no objection was raised to his completing his studies in England. He was sent to Balliol College, Oxford, where he successfully completed a two-year diploma course in political science and economics. While

Norwegian royal family group at the time of Crown Prince Olav's engagement to Princess Martha of Sweden (both on right), 1928. King Haakon VII and Queen Maud are on the left

in England he was invited to lay the foundation stone for the Norwegian Seamen's Church in London.

In August 1928 Olav became privately engaged to his cousin, Princess Martha of Sweden. The betrothal was announced early the following year; King Haakon wished to wait for a favourable moment to make the news public, as Norway was, in general, still suspicious of her neighbour, but it was received with general approval. Olav and Martha were married in March 1929 at St Saviour's Church, Oslo, with his cousin the Duke of York as best man.

King George's final years were marked by his struggle against one illness after another. On 21 November 1928 he complained of a feverish cold, and took to his bed. Septicaemia was diagnosed, necessitating an operation, the condition of his heart deteriorated, and for several days he was close to death. Over Christmas he showed slight but discernible signs of recovery, attributed in part to the fact that he had inherited much of his father's and grandmother's will to live. At the end of January 1929 he was permitted to leave his bed, and early next month he went to Craigwell House, Bognor, to recuperate, accompanied by Queen Mary.

In May, both returned to Windsor amid scenes of public rejoicing, but the King suffered two further relapses, each requiring an additional operation. In

July they took their seats at a national service of thanksgiving for his recovery at St Paul's Cathedral, but not for another two months did his doctors feel confident enough to announce that he was really recovered. In fact, he never enjoyed good health again. His nurse, Sister Catherine Black, remained close at hand and the family found him increasingly irascible and older than his years.

In the autumn of 1929 the Dowager Duchess of Fife was taken ill at Mar Lodge with another gastric haemorrhage, and was brought back to London. At her house in Portman Square she was given the best nursing and medical attention possible as befitted a king's sister, but all to no avail. She lingered on listlessly for another fifteen months, soothed by the solicitude of her family.

Her last letter to Queen Mary (27 November 1930) talked of going out of a morning, and then back to bed. Spending so much time resting, she was grateful for the regular gifts of flowers, 'which make my room so light.'[1] By Christmas 1930 she was obviously weaker; her daughters were summoned, and in the afternoon of 4 January 1931 she died after a heart attack in her sleep. Aged sixty-three, she was by the time of her death tenth in order of succession to the throne.

Louise and her brother had never been particularly close, and since her husband's death the two had seen little of each other. All the same, he felt this loss in the family deeply. Victoria missed her more. Writing to Queen Mary that same day, she saw her sister's passing as a release:

> Louise suffered *so terribly* these last few months that one can but thank God. She is at peace with her dear ones. But it's sad for us and the loss of a sister comes very near one's heart.[2]

With the King and Queen, she attended Louise's funeral service at Windsor, where her body was to rest until its removal to Mar in the spring. Queen Maud was denied this chance to pay her last respects, but she was deeply touched by Queen Mary's letter describing the obsequies. She replied from Kongseteren (14 January):

> It has been *dreadful* for me being *so* far away and I have been *most* miserable, and I just longed to hear many small details. You know *how* devoted I was to *her* and understood her, and she was *always* so sweet to me, and we have never had a row in our lives, we wrote to each other twice a week or more, and now there is such a blank and silence which is horrible. The news gave me an *awful* shock, though I expected it, and yet always *prayed* she would get stronger, but she never did and only got worse and far more than since I left.[3]

It was a sad start to the year for King George V. For him the thirties, the last decade of his life, gave no promise of contentment or lasting happiness. Old customs and fashions were receding further into the past; the sartorial slackness of politicians, outlandish modern fashions in dress and entertainment were the order of the day, much to his regret. 'Good God,' he exclaimed loudly from an open window while watching visitors on Windsor terrace one Easter Bank Holiday. 'Look at those short skirts, look at that bobbed hair!' Queen Mary promptly told him to keep quiet.

The changing styles of a changing world were the least of his worries. A world slump and escalating unemployment led to a political crisis in 1931; the King and Queen had just arrived at Balmoral that August when the exhausted monarch was summoned back to London by an urgent telegram. He advised that the solution to a national crisis was more important than party politics, and counselled the formation of a national government with Labour Prime Minister Ramsay MacDonald – whom he had come to admire greatly – at its head. Queen Mary was angry that he should be called back so soon, and disgruntled at being left alone. 'I will not be left sitting on a mountain,' she proclaimed emphatically.

The following year this most conservative and traditionally-minded of kings was at the centre of a startling new innovation – a Christmas radio broadcast to his people. King George was a reluctant broadcaster, but politicians urged him to cooperate in the experiment. His speech was written by Rudyard Kipling, and he was so nervous that a thick cloth had to be put on the table to muffle the sound of paper rustling in his shaking hands. Yet it was so favourably received as a seasonal greeting, throughout Britain and the Empire, that it immediately became an annual tradition.*

Queen Maud's health was deteriorating as well, and had she been given the choice she would have spent much more time at Appleton. Christmas 1928 had been the last that she and Charles (as she still referred to him in her letters) spent with Olav before his marriage, and she wrote happily to Queen Mary (28 December) of 'a quiet and nice Christmas "*à trois*" with our Xmas tree lit up, and our long table arranged for us three, where we spread out all our presents.'[4] Three years later, without their son, she lamented (25 December 1931) her homesickness at the festive season, 'and *long* to be at Appleton.'[5]

Next month winter aches and pains, and the death in exile from cancer of cousin Sophie, widow of ex-King Constantine of the Hellenes, lowered her spirits further. A letter to Queen Mary (22 January 1932) mentioned:

> The 'flu' caught me badly and I got *acute* bronchitis which I have had *only* once before *years* ago, and I felt *very* bad and an *awful* cough and aches in all my limbs. . . .
> It was *very* sad about poor Sophie, and *dreadful* for the three children, without any home or money – Also poor Mossy[†] wrote she was heartbroken, *adored* Sophie – What a lot of troubles and worries there are, and the new year has not begun well.[6]

But she took delight in the company of Olav's children, and ever the proud grandmother, regularly sent photographs of them to her relations in England. In June 1932 Princess Ragnhild celebrated her second birthday with a children's party organized by the Queen, who told Queen Mary (10 June):

---

* Some of King George V's subjects were somewhat perplexed by such manifestations of modern science. The present author was told of an elderly great-aunt who listened with due reverence as the first royal Christmas message was being transmitted. At one point she bowed to the wireless and spoke: 'I beg Your Majesty's pardon. Would you mind repeating that last bit, please?'

† The former Princess Margaret of Prussia, now married to Frederick Charles, Landgrave of Hesse.

King George V, with Princess Elizabeth, Queen Mary, and the Duchess of York (seated opposite), returning from Crathie Church, 1933

She *loved* her toys, and was really *very* good letting *all* the children play with her things. We gave them a *big* tea, and they ate enormously, which made *all* the mothers rather nervous![7]

Two ever-present worries darkened King George's remaining years; the threat of war, and the behaviour of his heir, still a bachelor.

In Europe, the rise of the dictators filled him with alarm. The growing menace of Hitler and Mussolini looked ominous, and when the latter sent his armies into Abyssinia in 1935 and Lloyd George commented belligerently on the news, the King angrily insisted that he would not have another war. The last had been none of his doing, and if his government threatened to bring him into it, he would personally join the pacifists in Trafalgar Square and with them wave a red flag for peace.

Meanwhile, the gulf was widening between father and son, until they could hardly bear to be in the same room as each other. Edward dreaded the gloom of Buckingham Palace, complained bitterly to friends how he and his brothers 'froze up' inside it, how they feared their crochety father's temper, and how the

Duchess of York was 'the one bright spot there.' His association with married women older than himself and his failure to find an eligible wife weighed heavily on the King, who dreaded the consequences for his kingdom and throne after his death. 'After I am dead,' he told his last Prime Minister, Stanley Baldwin despondently, 'the boy will ruin himself in twelve months.' One day he roared at Edward, 'You dress like a cad. You act like a cad. Get out!' Sometimes on car journeys the king was so irritable that Queen Mary threatened to get out at the next town and follow him back by train.

There was to be one more marriage in the family with a princess from the continent – that of the King's youngest surviving son George, recently created Duke of Kent. George was the most academically-minded of the King's children, and the only one who fully shared his mother's artistic interests. He had first met Princess Marina of the Hellenes, a granddaughter of Queen Alexandra's brother King George, on a visit to Windsor in 1923. Though he was immediately taken with her, she returned home before anything could come of it, and for a while he was inconsolable. The family were horrified when he took heavily to drink and became involved in some unfortunate affairs; and it was largely through the efforts of Edward that he was saved from self-destruction. When he met Marina again several years later, it was evident that they had eyes for nobody but each other.

Marina was thought by the elder generation to be eminently suitable for him, and Princess Victoria was particularly pleased with his choice. George had always been her favourite nephew, and she wrote with delight (31 August 1934) to Queen Mary after hearing of his betrothal:

> Of course it is the best thing for him. Marina is a sweet child and so pretty and I do hope she will look after him and give him a happy home. He seemed to wander about so much which was so bad for him. It was a tremendous surprise! What made him *think* of it suddenly?[8]

The wedding was celebrated at Westminster Abbey on 29 November. Before the ceremony, guests were much amused by the behaviour of 'dear old Princess Victoria, grown querulous with emotion.' To her annoyance, she discovered that she was to drive in the procession with certain others of whom she did not approve. As a result, everyone was kept waiting to start while she explained indignantly to an agitated equerry that she would not get into the carriage with 'those dreadful people.' At length an old and less easily-silenced friend, who had found it hard to suppress his laughter as he watched, came to the rescue. 'Can't you get into the carriage, Madam?' he asked Victoria. Before she had time to open her mouth in protest, he pushed her gently but firmly inside and shut the door on her.[9]

At the Prince of Wales's request, his friends Mr and Mrs Ernest Simpson were also invited to the wedding. During the reception afterwards the Prince brought Mrs Simpson to meet his mother, with the casual words, 'I want to introduce a great friend of mine.' Queen Mary shook hands with Mrs Simpson warmly. Later she would recall this as the only occasion on which she had received the woman who was to cause such bitterness among everyone involved.

To casual observers, the ageing Princess Victoria may have seemed unpleasant, but she had her generous side. In the summer of 1933, a lance-corporal of the 2nd City of London Regiment and a fusilier in camp at Roedean were knocked down and injured by a runaway horse at Rottingdean. They were taken to a house where she was staying at the time, and she supervised the first aid measures. After they had been properly cared for, she visited the men in hospital, and on being told that they would be very disappointed at not seeing their regiment march away from camp, she arranged with the commanding officer that the regiment should march past the hospital. It was a characteristic example of her kindness and sympathy.

The Duke and Duchess of Kent were regular visitors to Coppins, which Victoria later left them in her will. When their eldest child Edward was born in October 1935, she was one of the first to be allowed to see him.

Shortly before his seventieth birthday, King George V enjoyed one great swan song. At the end of April 1935, he and Queen Mary left Windsor for Buckingham Palace to prepare for their Silver Jubilee celebrations.

Looking increasingly aged, tired and bent, King George's personal appear-

Family group on balcony of Buckingham Palace during the Silver Jubilee celebrations, June 1935. From left: the Duke of York; Mary, Princess Royal; King George V; Princess Margaret; the Hon. Gerald Lascelles; the Earl of Harewood; Princess Elizabeth; the Hon. George Lascelles; Queen Mary; the Duke of Gloucester; the Duchess of Kent; the Duke of Kent; the Duchess of York

ance shocked his family and friends. He had taken to dining alone in his room because the effort of dressing for dinner each evening was too much. Some people wondered whether his failing strength was equal to the planned festivities, but it was recognized that to cancel or delay them would fuel rumours that he was dying. On 6 May, the twenty-fifth anniversary of their accession to the throne, the King and Queen took pride of place in a procession to St Paul's for a service of thanksgiving.

To the public, there was something touching in the domesticity of their monarch's home life, that made such an agreeable contrast to the aggressive image of the dictators abroad. The jubilee was also a way of paying tribute to the King and Queen who had seen them through four years of war and then the turbulent world ushered in by peace. King George and Queen Mary had evidently established a rapport with their subjects, and he in particular was quite overwhelmed by the reception accorded them. He noted afterwards that he had never seen so many people in the streets before and their enthusiasm was most touching; 'I'd no idea they felt like that about me. I am beginning to think they must really like me for myself.'

Nothing would have kept Queen Maud from joining the family in England, and she stayed for her brother's birthday a month later. Shortly after her return to Norway she wrote to Queen Mary (30 June):

> It was *very* sad leaving 'Home' and you *all*, but I was *so* delighted to have been present at the Jubilee, I *loved* the enthusiasm and devotion which the people have for dear George and you, it is *so* touching – and in no other country I am sure it is like that! One is *proud* to be *British*. I was glad to have been in London for G[eorge]'s birthday and could see you *all* once more. – I do hope both you and George are not *too* tired, with all you have to do. It *is* wonderful, all you have got through.
> I had a tiring journey, but quite good crossing and Charles met me at Bergen, looking *much* better and stronger than when I left, he was *rather* disappointed he could not come to the Jubilee, he *longed* to come and I only wished I had mentioned it to you and perhaps it could have been arranged, as after all he is George's *only* brother-in-law! I am telling him *all* about it and he is *greatly* interested.[10]

King George was ever more disturbed by the Prince of Wales's behaviour. The latter's public pronouncements in favour of peaceful co-existence with Nazi Germany were deeply embarrassing, and resulted in a confrontation between father and son. Never again, the King ordered him angrily, was he to speak on such controversial or political matters without consulting the government. No less worrying was his infatuation with Mrs Ernest Simpson. She had already divorced one husband, and her second marriage was apparently breaking down. Edward seemed determined to flaunt her before his parents, and he invited her to Buckingham Palace without their consent. When he was later told, the King was livid; 'That woman in my house!'

Neither he nor Queen Mary could bring themselves to speak to their son about his conduct. He made his wife promise that after his death she would not receive 'the American woman' at the palace. To Lady Algernon Gordon-Lennox, he remarked, 'I pray to God that my eldest son will never marry and have children, and that nothing will come between Bertie and Lilibet and the throne.'

The Prince of Wales was already adamant that nothing would part him from Mrs Simpson. Did he have before him the sorry example of his Aunt Toria, who had been forbidden to marry the man she loved? 'If you knew what royalties have to endure and never show it,' Mrs Crayshay later told her niece, biographer Anita Leslie, referring to an afternoon spent taking tea in the early thirties with Victoria and her divorced cousin, Princess Marie Louise. Princess Victoria, she said, told her that once there had been someone perfect for her, but 'they' would not let her marry him; "and if you could have heard her voice break when she said, 'and we could have been *so* happy".[11] Not for several years did Mrs Crayshay realize that the Princess had been speaking of Lord Rosebery.

Victoria's unhappy life was running out. After her appearance at the Silver Jubilee service in St Paul's, she was not seen in public again. She was already gravely ill as the family celebrated the wedding on 6 November of Prince Henry, Duke of Gloucester, to Lady Alice Montagu Douglas-Scott, an occasion already saddened by the sudden death of the bride's father Lord Buccleuch the previous month. The wedding was solemnized quietly in Buckingham Palace chapel. Now all the children, King George observed gloomily, were married – except Edward.

King George was also unwell, and the public thought it was an ominous sign that he did not attend the Armistice service at the Cenotaph on 11 November. The court then moved to Sandringham, and from there the King and Queen drove to visit Victoria at Coppins. They had not seen her for several weeks, and though they knew how ill she had been, she made light of her sufferings so convincingly that they came away thinking she was much better.

It was a false dawn. On 2 December, following an acute and severe haemorrhage of the stomach, she was given a blood transfusion, but to no avail. Lord Dawson of Penn was at her bedside during the night as her remaining strength ebbed quietly away. Shortly after three o'clock in the morning she died, aged sixty-seven.

Coming on top of his other worries and the strain of events during Jubilee year, King George was grief-stricken. Victoria had always been his favourite sister. For once he was too tired and upset to discharge his public duties. The State Opening of Parliament scheduled for the afternoon of 3 December was cancelled, as were several other functions during the six weeks of court mourning accordingly proclaimed.

The Times commented on her death:

> Partly no doubt from choice, partly owing to a certain delicacy of constitution, she seemed to fall naturally into the position of daughter of the house . . . she remained at home, making the family circle the centre of her quiet, useful life, and she will be more deeply and sincerely mourned than many a personage who has played a more conspicuous part in the eye of the world.[12]

With a heavy heart how Queen Mary must have wished that they could have found some common bond in their shared interests, and that the bitterness of her life as a spinster had not soured family relations to such an extent.

Despite his anxiety over foreign affairs and over his eldest son, it was undoubtedly the loss of his beloved sister that sounded the death knell for King George V. 'How I shall miss her and our daily talks on the telephone,' he wrote sadly in his diary. 'No one had a sister like her.'[13] Lord Dawson had already discerned in His Majesty 'an obvious diminution of energy and interest.' From that day onwards his handwriting became shaky and uncertain. Victoria's funeral at Windsor on 7 December, which the doctor vainly tried to have shortened in order to spare his sovereign's failing strength, was a severe ordeal. He was never seen in public again.

Queen Maud was at Appleton when her sister died, and on being informed of the news King Haakon left Oslo to join her for the funeral. Before they returned to Norway, she wrote to Queen Mary (13 December):

> It was *kind* of dear George sending me her tortoiseshell dressing set in case, gave me though *quite* a lump in my throat, as I *always* saw them on her dressing table and she always used them. Some day *do* let me have a *little* brooch as a remembrance or a miniature. I don't want to be grasping, it is *just* the *longing* to have something to *wear* which belonged to her. We are so grateful to you *both* for having had us at Buckingham Palace those *very* sad days, and I hope we were *not* in the way – You are *always* so *kind* and *dear* to me – I am *very* low and miss beloved Toria *more* and *more* as the days go by, *no* telephone message *nothing* – only silence I think *that* is the *worst* of all. . . . Let us all pray that there won't be *war*.[14]

On 21 December King George left for Sandringham, where he carried out his last duties as monarch; he received his new Foreign Secretary, Anthony Eden, and delivered his fourth Christmas message to the empire. 'We were so *thrilled* hearing dear George's Xmas message on the wireless and thought it *lovely*!'[15] wrote Queen Maud (4 January 1936). She must have realized that it would be the last.

During the next three weeks he played with his granddaughters, watched his youngest grandson, Prince Edward of Kent, being bathed, rode his pony Jock gently around the estate when weather permitted, and looked on as Queen Mary rearranged Queen Alexandra's collection of Fabergé animals, sent back to Sandringham from Coppins after Victoria's death.

By now it was evident that the slightest effort tired King George, and the end was not far away. On 15 January, after feeling particularly unwell, he retired to bed early, and next morning he stayed in his room. On 17 January, he made the final entry in his leather-bound diaries which had faithfully chronicled the events of more than half a century. The almost illegible handwriting referred to snow and wind, and to Dawson's arrival: 'I saw him and feel rotten.'

A series of cautiously-worded bulletins, preparing his subjects for the inevitable, was issued. During the next two days, as his sons and daughter arrived at Sandringham, he drifted in and out of consciousness. On the evening of 20 January, as Queen Mary and her children dined 'alone', Dawson wrote his celebrated announcement on a menu card in the dining room; 'The King's life is moving peacefully towards its close.' Five minutes before midnight, King George died.

The lying-in-state of King George V in Westminster Hall, January 1936

Queen Maud of Norway was now the sole surviving child of King Edward VII and Queen Alexandra. Though desolate at losing her sister and brother within the space of seven weeks, she was uniquely placed to give considerable moral support to Queen Mary in the trying months ahead. She had always been the Queen's favourite sister-in-law, having had no part in the petty jealousies harboured by Louise and Victoria that had made their relations uneasy with a kinswoman whom they regarded as dynastically inferior. Her presence, and that of King Haakon, were a great comfort to her in the funeral procession on 28 January.

Throughout the traumatic year of 1936, Maud never ceased to take a keen interest in the activities of her late brother's family, especially those of 'David', now King Edward VIII. She was shocked to read in the papers of an attempt on his life, as a letter from Bygdoy (19 July) related:

> My thoughts are so constantly with *you* and I think you are *so* brave. Glad you go about and see gardens and exhibitions and the people *love* to see you. I hope you did not see anything of that incident, as it *all* went so quickly – Thank God dear David was unharmed. I got *rather* a shock, reading all sorts of exaggerated reports in the evening papers here – but didn't like to write to you or David, not to bother you. *How* busy he is and *how* popular he is, thank goodness.[16]

She was also pleased to hear that the Duke and Duchess of Kent liked Coppins:

and have made it so comfortable and pretty and hope they have changed it, it was *my* good idea *really*, I told Toria to leave it to Georgie, as first she wanted to leave it to Maudie, but she has two places.[17]

Like the rest of the family, Queen Maud – whose husband had reluctantly but dutifully accepted a crown which he had never expected to wear – looked on in disbelief as she saw her nephew renounce his throne in order to marry Mrs Simpson. Had Princess Victoria, who had yearned for the hand of at least one man in marriage, lived another year, she too would have doubtless been indignant at his dereliction of duty. The Duke of Clarence had been prepared to give up his place in the line of succession for a French Catholic, though the case never quite arose; King Edward VIII relinquished the throne for the woman he loved, an American with two former husbands still living. True to the ailing King George V's wish, nothing would now come between the throne and 'Bertie and Lilibet'.

When King Edward VIII abdicated on 11 December in favour of the Duke of York, who now became King George VI, Maud sympathized with him. Yet she could never bring herself to mention Mrs Simpson by name in her letters, let alone say one word in her defence. Two days after Christmas she wrote to Queen Mary:

Wonder *if* you have heard from dear David, seems *so* sad and all *alone* out there with strangers, sure he misses you *all*. I got a dear telegram of thanks for mine which I sent to him to wish him a happy Xmas. Where is She? *Do* wish something *could* happen and prevent them from marrying. *How* sad it all is, that he has ruined his life, fear later he will be sorry what he has done and given up. Dear Bertie and Elizabeth will have *so* much to do, and I am *certain* will do *so* well and be *just* like dear George and you – the people *love* to see a happy family life.[18]

It was soon apparent that King George VI and Queen Elizabeth, who not only had two daughters but were also of a more conventional outlook than the ex-King, were worthy successors in every way to King George V. What they lacked in star quality, they more than made up for in dignity and reliability. King Edward VIII had not enhanced the standing of the monarchy abroad by posing for photographers on board his yacht dressed in nothing but shorts, and at home he had shown a distressing readiness to cancel long-standing public engagements without notice when it suited him. There was no possibility of his brother behaving in like fashion.

That winter was a particularly bitter one in Norway, and Queen Maud was quite unwell. While recovering she apologized to Queen Mary for not having kept in touch as regularly as usual (19 January 1937):

I meant to have written long ago, only have been laid up with influenza and felt *so* bad and weak that I was fit for nothing. Am still in fact not a *bit* well, *very* tired and have inflamed eyes and *awful* neuralgia and very depressed. It does take such ages to pick up after a sharp attack, and the weather being so cold makes it harder to get well. . . . Glad you get letters from dear David, I have heard *how* popular *he* is in Vienna, wish something *could* happen to her!![19]

Queen Maud's sympathy for the Duke of Windsor did not blind her to the realization that his brother's unexpected accession to the throne was extremely fortunate for the monarchy. She was particularly touched that the new King's domestic life revolved around the familiar old haunts, such a contrast to King Edward's shortlived court at Fort Belvedere, as her next letter (20 February 1937) made clear:

> Thank goodness dear Bertie and Elizabeth are also so devoted to each other, and great help to each other, and they are *so* popular, and so are the darling little children. Nice that Bertie likes George's old rooms at B.P. and also left many of the old people at Sandringham. Hope they will go there more often as the people do *love* to have them there, in the dear old home. Wonder what Mary told you about dear David, he *must* be *very* lonely, sad she couldn't have stayed a bit longer. *Do* pray still that something may happen to 'her' to prevent her from marrying *him*! It makes me *quite* low to think of *him* banished out there and that he has given up everything of his own free will all on account of one *bad* woman who has hypnotized him – I hear that *every* English and French person gets up at Monte Carlo whenever *she* comes in to a place. *Hope* she will *feel* it.[20]

Since Plantagenet days, no British Queen Dowager had attended the coronation of her husband's successor. Despite her respect for tradition, Queen Mary longed to watch her second son being crowned, and in the aftermath of the abdication, she wanted to make it evident that the family stood together as one.

When she left Marlborough House by glass coach for Westminster Abbey on the morning of 12 May 1937, Queen Maud sat beside her. In the royal box at the abbey, Queen Mary took her place with Maud on one side and eleven-year-old Princess Elizabeth on the other – two Queen Consorts, and a Princess who would be Queen regnant less than fifteen years hence.

Queen Maud stayed on at Appleton after the ceremony. She had heard murmurings that Bertie was regarded by some as inadequate for the crown, and knew that with his natural diffidence and speech impediment he lacked confidence in his own ability to be a successful king. Yet his reception, and that of Queen Elizabeth, had dispelled any lingering doubts she may have had about his popularity. To her it was just like 'the old days'. To Queen Mary she wrote (20 May):

> I *loved* seeing how devoted everyone was to you, and how *splendid* you have been through *all* the trying times. I can't get over how beautifully dear Bertie and Elizabeth did it *all* at the Coronation, *so* dignified and calm and so charming to everyone.[21]

Queen Maud returned to Norway that summer, but by October she was back at Appleton. The more she saw of King George and Queen Elizabeth, the more she was impressed with them. If she had ever heard her brother's prayer that nothing would come between them and the throne, she would have agreed wholeheartedly. From her letter to Queen Mary (1 November):

King Haakon VII and Queen Maud of Norway, with Crown Prince Olav and Crown Princess Martha on their way to dinner at the Royal Yacht Club, Oslo, 1938

. . . *all* are enchanted that dear Bertie is *so* fond of the dear old home, and *all* say that Sandringham will be like 'old times' if the King comes. He has been wonderful going *all* the rounds of the farms and estates and shooting besides. They were *such* dears to me yesterday, first we met in Church and then I walked with them back to the house, through a *huge* crowd of 8000 who clapped their hands as if we were actors![22]

Like her sisters, Queen Maud had never been of such robust health as Queen Mary; in particular her neuralgia and tendency to bronchitis became worse each winter. Yet there was no reason to think that she might not reach such a good age as had her mother. She certainly had more to live for than her sisters did; she had never known the loneliness of a spinster's existence, or been denied the opportunity to reach the evening of her days with her husband, enjoying with him the company of grandchildren. In England she was a familiar sight each winter staying at Appleton, or shopping in Bond Street, London, a dog at her heels.

When she returned to these old haunts in October 1938 – her departure from Norway postponed for a week, as her anxious husband wished her to remain behind with him until the outcome of Neville Chamberlain's meeting with Adolf

Hitler at Munich was known – she appeared to be her usual cheerful self. But on a shopping expedition in London the following month, she complained of feeling unwell. She was admitted to a nursing home, and after an X-ray examination the doctors decided to operate. Hearing of her illness, Queen Mary went to stay at Claridge's Hotel so that she could be close, and sat with her for several hours on the day before the operation, 16 November.

King Haakon was warned of possible complications, and he left for England at once. After the operation she had a disturbed night, but next day she appeared to be recovering well. It was illusory; at twenty-five minutes after midnight on the morning of Sunday, 20 November, she died suddenly in her sleep. Her death, thirteen years to the day after that of her mother and within six days of her sixty-ninth birthday, came so unexpectedly that only a nurse was present. King Haakon, staying at Buckingham Palace, was unable to reach her in time.

Later that day he issued a short statement:

> God has taken the Queen from me this night, and it is a heavy loss for me to bear, though I well understand it is His will. He has taken her because her work is finished, and He has, I know, spared her thus much suffering.[23]

King George VI telephoned the widower from St Paul's Walden Bury, where he and Queen Elizabeth were spending the weekend. The Norwegian Prime Minister, Johann Nygaardsvold, telegraphed a message of sympathy to his sovereign. In a public announcement he paid eloquent tribute to the English Princess who had so unexpectedly found herself a Scandinavian queen consort:

> All who knew her are aware what a warm-hearted and magnificent character she was, and the present Cabinet and I personally have learnt to value her burning interest in the people of this country and in many social undertakings. We sympathize in the sorrow which has fallen upon the Royal Family and feel sure that the whole Norwegian people takes part in that sorrow and sympathy.[24]

Queen Maud's body was brought back to the chapel at Marlborough House where she had been christened. The next morning Queen Mary, almost as stunned at the news as King Haakon himself, took her place in the procession behind her coffin to Victoria station, whence it went by train to Portsmouth to be placed aboard the battle cruiser *Royal Oak* for Oslo. The coffin lay in state for two days at Akershus Castle, and the funeral service was held in St Saviour's Church on 8 December. Later a mausoleum was built at Akershus, where her husband was eventually laid to rest by her side.

Among other tributes paid to her, two must be mentioned. In January 1939 the Norwegian government declared an area adjacent to Australian Antarctica to be Norwegian territory, and named it Queen Maud Land. That same year, the establishment of Queen Maud's Children's Fund was marked by a set of four postage stamps.

Less than seventy years had elapsed since Queen Victoria despaired at the mere thought of her eldest son's children, those 'poor, frail little fairies.' By royal

Queen Maud, from two Norwegian postage stamps. Left: one of four, each sold with a surcharge to aid the Queen's children fund, 1939. Right: one of two commemorating the centenary of her birth, 1969

standards, none of them enjoyed a particularly long life. Only King George V attained the Biblical threescore years and ten, and for the last few of those years he was a very sick man. It was ironic that all should have been survived by three of Queen Victoria's brood of nine.

Moreover, it was indeed fortunate that the two occupants of the nursery at Sandringham who showed the greatest strength of character were those who were called upon to wear a crown in later life.

King George V's achievements speak for themselves. A modest, retiring man who disliked, if not actively feared change, he shouldered the burdens of kingship in an era of instability when, to quote his advisers, 'thrones were at a discount.' 'I might be uninspiring,' he retorted in reply to H.G. Wells's celebrated criticism in April 1917 which called upon the British people to rid themselves of "the ancient trappings of throne and sceptre," 'but I'll be damned if I'm alien.' He was old-fashioned, insular, and not in the least intellectual; as such, he shared prejudices held by many of his subjects. Above all, he was the model of a constitutional monarch. King Edward VII was virtually his own foreign minister, much to his government's dismay, and to the end of her days Queen Victoria's partiality to certain prime ministers, and antipathy to others, could make matters uncomfortable for some of her secretaries of state. No such criticism could be levelled at their successor.

Queen Maud, likewise, helped to play her part in supporting King Haakon VII on the Norwegian throne with a sure touch. Despite shyness she responded well to the demands made on her, throwing herself wholeheartedly into charity work with enthusiasm and lack of prejudice – as demonstrated by her concern for unmarried mothers – which astonished the less open-minded. Her comparatively early death was both a fortune and a misfortune; it spared her the anxiety of living through another momentous war, something for which her bereaved husband was thankful, though it denied her the chance to see him lead Norway's heroic stand against Nazi Germany and offer him her support when perhaps he needed it most. Her role in helping to gain respect and popularity for the new Norwegian monarchy, which enabled King Haakon to bequeath a far safer throne to their son Olav in September 1957 than the one to which he had been elected, should not be underestimated.

The short-lived Duke of Clarence, the Duchess of Fife, and Princess Victoria of Wales all had a negligible impact on public life. Constitution and temperament denied them any alternative, though one cannot but wonder whether the unhappy Princess Victoria would have left behind a happier legacy of personal achievement if she had become Lady Rosebery, or Queen Consort of Denmark.

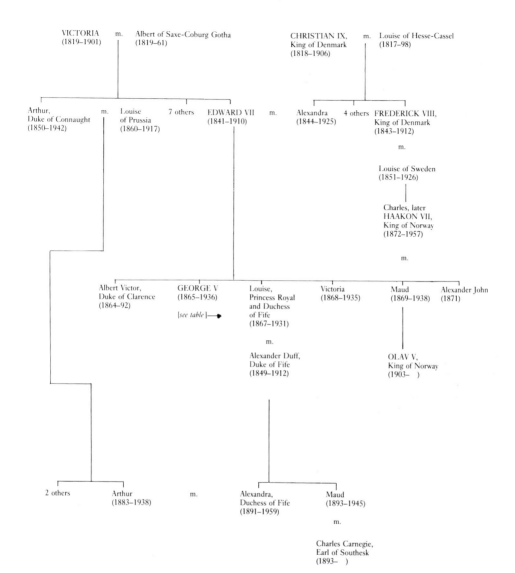

VICTORIA (1819–1901) m. Albert of Saxe-Coburg Gotha (1819–61)

CHRISTIAN IX, King of Denmark (1818–1906) m. Louise of Hesse-Cassel (1817–98)

Arthur, Duke of Connaught (1850–1942) m. Louise of Prussia (1860–1917)   7 others   EDWARD VII (1841–1910) m. Alexandra (1844–1925)   4 others   FREDERICK VIII, King of Denmark (1843–1912)

m.

Louise of Sweden (1851–1926)

Charles, later HAAKON VII, King of Norway (1872–1957)

m.

Albert Victor, Duke of Clarence (1864–92)   GEORGE V (1865–1936) [see table] →   Louise, Princess Royal and Duchess of Fife (1867–1931)   Victoria (1868–1935)   Maud (1869–1938)   Alexander John (1871)

m.

Alexander Duff, Duke of Fife (1849–1912)

OLAV V, King of Norway (1903–)

2 others   Arthur (1883–1938)   m.   Alexandra, Duchess of Fife (1891–1959)   Maud (1893–1945)

m.

Charles Carnegie, Earl of Southesk (1893–)

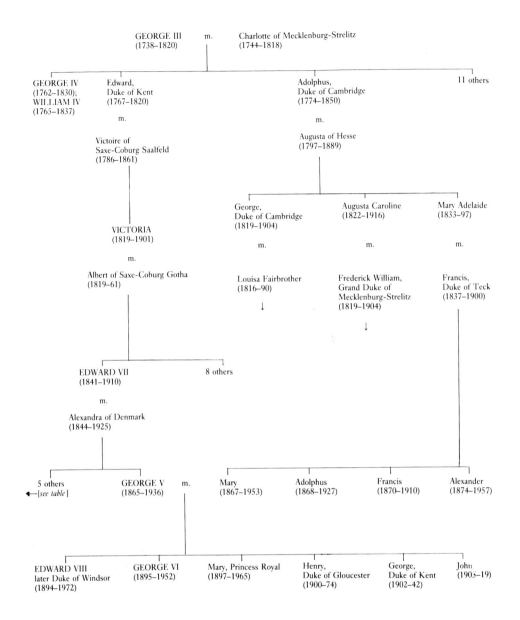

GEORGE III (1738–1820)   m.   Charlotte of Mecklenburg-Strelitz (1744–1818)

GEORGE IV (1762–1830); WILLIAM IV (1765–1837)

Edward, Duke of Kent (1767–1820)
m.
Victoire of Saxe-Coburg Saalfeld (1786–1861)

Adolphus, Duke of Cambridge (1774–1850)
m.
Augusta of Hesse (1797–1889)

11 others

VICTORIA (1819–1901)
m.
Albert of Saxe-Coburg Gotha (1819–61)

George, Duke of Cambridge (1819–1904)
m.
Louisa Fairbrother (1816–90)
↓

Augusta Caroline (1822–1916)
m.
Frederick William, Grand Duke of Mecklenburg-Strelitz (1819–1904)
↓

Mary Adelaide (1833–97)
m.
Francis, Duke of Teck (1837–1900)

EDWARD VII (1841–1910)
m.
Alexandra of Denmark (1844–1925)

8 others

5 others
◄—[see table]

GEORGE V (1865–1936)   m.

Mary (1867–1953)

Adolphus (1868–1927)

Francis (1870–1910)

Alexander (1874–1957)

EDWARD VIII later Duke of Windsor (1894–1972)

GEORGE VI (1895–1952)

Mary, Princess Royal (1897–1965)

Henry, Duke of Gloucester (1900–74)

George, Duke of Kent (1902–42)

John (1905–19)

King Edward VII's Children and Grandchildren

1. ALBERT Victor Christian Edward, born 8 January 1864 at Frogmore; created Duke of Clarence and Avondale, 1890; engaged to Princess Victoria Mary of Teck, 1891; died 14 January 1892 at Sandringham. No legitimate issue.

2. GEORGE Frederick Ernest Albert, born 3 June 1865 at Marlborough House; created Duke of York, Earl of Inverness and Baron Killarney, 1892; married Princess Victoria Mary of Teck (1867–1953), 6 July 1893; created Prince of Wales and Earl of Chester, 1901; ascended throne as King George V, 6 May 1910; crowned 22 June 1911 at Westminster Abbey; died 20 January 1936 at Sandringham. Issue:
   (1) Edward (1894–1972), reigned as King Edward VIII, January to December 1936; created Duke of Windsor on abdication
   (2) Albert (1895–1952), reigned as King George VI, 1936–52
   (3) Mary, Countess of Harewood and Princess Royal (1897–1965)
   (4) Henry, Duke of Gloucester (1900–74)
   (5) George, Duke of Kent (1902–42)
   (6) John (1905–19)

3. LOUISE Victoria Alexandra Dagmar, born 20 February 1867 at Marlborough House; married Alexander Duff, 1st Duke of Fife (1849–1912), 27 July 1889; declared Princess Royal, 1905; died 4 January 1931 at 11 Portman Square, London. Issue:
   (1) Alexandra, Duchess of Fife and Princess Arthur of Connaught (1891–1959)
   (2) Maud, Countess of Southesk (1893–1945)

4. VICTORIA Alexandra Olga Marie, Princess Victoria of Wales, born 6 July 1868 at Marlborough House; died unmarried 3 December 1935 at Coppins, Iver.

5. MAUD Charlotte Mary Victoria, born 26 November 1869 at Marlborough House; married Prince Charles of Denmark (1872–1957), 22 July 1896; became Queen of Norway on her husband's proclamation as King Haakon

VII, 20 November 1905; crowned at Trondheim Cathedral, 22 June 1906; died 20 November 1938 at London. Issue:
(1)   Alexander (known as Olav after his father's proclamation as King) (born 1903), reigns as King Olav V, 1957–   .

6.   ALEXANDER John Charles Albert, born 6 April 1871 and died next day at Sandringham.

Reference Notes

RA: Royal Archives, Windsor. BL: British Library.

PROLOGUE (pp. 1–11)
1. Magnus 26
2. Battiscombe 29
3. Magnus 59
4. Gernsheim 23
5. *Dearest Mama* 226

CHAPTER 1 (pp. 12–21)
1. *Dearest Mama* 289
2. Ibid 301
3. Ibid 312
4. *Your dear letter* 17
5. Battiscombe 79
6. Ibid 80
7. Nicolson 4
8. Battiscombe 65
9. *Your dear letter* 200–1
10. Magnus 100
11. Battiscombe 108
12. Weintraub 360–61
13. St Aubyn 155–59
14. James 6
15. Ibid 10

CHAPTER 2 (pp. 22–38)
1. Gore 14
2. Battiscombe 122
3. Gore 24
4. Marie of Roumania I 43
5. Nicolson 12–13
6. Ibid 14
7. Gore 31–32
8. St Aubyn, *Edward VII* 103
9. RA Z82/13
10. Gore 41
11. Rose, *King George V* 14
12. Gore 48
13. Stephenson 64
14. Magnus 178
15. *Letters of Queen Victoria* II iii 592
16. St Aubyn, *Royal George* 299
17. Gore 17

CHAPTER 3 (pp. 39–48)
1. Leslie 287
2. RA Z82/33
3. RA Z82/107
4. Pope-Hennessy, *Queen Mary* 56
5. Woodward 52
6. *Letters of Queen Victoria* III i 505–6
7. Ibid 506
8. Mallet 31
9. *The Illustrated London News* 2.8.1889
10. RA Z83/85
11. *The Times* 5.1.1931
12. RA Z83/89
13. BL Add MSS 48599/134
14. RA Z83/118

CHAPTER 4 (pp. 49–65)
1. Pope-Hennessy, *Lonely business* 259
2. Pope-Hennessy, *Queen Mary* 194
3. RA Z82/117
4. Pope-Hennessy, *Queen Mary* 196
5. Ibid 193
6. Battiscombe 185
7. Magnus 239
8. Battiscombe 185
9. Magnus 239
10. RA GV CC45/99
11. Pope-Hennessy, *Queen Mary* 222
12. Magnus 239
13. St Aubyn, *Edward VII* 112
14. RA Z95/14
15. RA Z95/17
16. Magnus 239
17. Ponsonby, Arthur 359

CHAPTER 5 (pp. 66–77)
1. Nicolson 46
2. RA Z84/79
3. RA Z84/82
4. Nicolson 47
5. Pope-Hennessy, *Lonely business* 242
6. Nicolson 47
7. RA Z84/63
8. RA Z84/109
9. RA GV CC45/126

10. Pope-Hennessy, *Queen Mary* 259
11. Weintraub 540
12. Battiscombe 196
13. Pope-Hennessy, *Queen Mary* 279
14. Battiscombe 199
15. Nicolson 54
16. Wheeler-Bennett 6
17. Ibid 7
18. *Morning Advertiser* 16.12.1895

CHAPTER 6 (pp. 78–88)
1. RA Z84/136
2. RA Z84/137
3. Battiscombe 199
4. *Empress Frederick writes to Sophie* 170–71
5. Michael 91
6. RA Z85/18
7. Pope-Hennessy, *Queen Mary* 322
8. Mallet 64
9. RA Z85/34
10. RA GV FF3/458
11. RA Z85/46
12. RA Z85/61
13. Battiscombe 200
14. Mallet 156
15. RA Z160/2

CHAPTER 7 (pp. 89–100)
1. RA GV CC45/229
2. Lees-Milne 119
3. Nicolson 67
4. RA GV CC45/240
5. RA GV CC45/249
6. RA GV CC45/252
7. RA GV CC45/253
8. Wheeler-Bennett 18
9. Pope-Hennessy, *Queen Mary* 292
10. Ponsonby, Frederick 214

CHAPTER 8 (pp. 101–19)
1. Lee II 317–18, quoting *Die Grosse Politik* XIX ii 461
2. Lee II 317
3. Ibid 318
4. Ibid 321
5. RA GV CC45/283
6. Magnus 346
7. Pope-Hennessy, *Queen Mary* 408
8. RA GV CC45/285
9. RA GV CC45/289
10. Pope-Hennessy, *Queen Mary* 408
11. RA GV CC45/289
12. Ponsonby, Frederick 193–94
13. RA GV CC45/310
14. Lees-Milne 206
15. Gore 237

CHAPTER 9 (pp. 120–35)
1. Lees-Milne 211
2. Ibid 188
3. Rose, *King George V* 103
4. Gore 436
5. Christopher of Greece 95–97
6. RA FF4/4
7. RA FF4/6
8. Battiscombe 280
9. RA GV CC45/388
10. RA FF4/7
11. RA GV CC45/389
12. RA FF4/8
13. Pope-Hennessy, *Queen Mary* 465
14. RA GV CC45/418

CHAPTER 10 (pp. 136–45)
1. Gore 281
2. Fisher II 65
3. *Ibid* II 470
4. Windsor, Duke of 108
5. Wheeler-Bennett 79
6. RA GV CC45/454
7. Rose, *King George V* 216
8. RA GV CC45/547
9. RA GV CC45/551
10. Gore 308
11. Wheeler-Bennett 120–21
12. RA GV CC45/560

CHAPTER 11 (pp. 146–63)
1. Battiscombe 293
2. RA GV CC45/578
3. RA GV CC45/580
4. RA GV CC45/578
5. *The Times* 13.11.1923
6. RA GV CC45/653
7. Pope-Hennessy, *Lonely business* 214
8. RA GV CC45/676
9. Pope-Hennessy, *Queen Mary* 537
10. RA GV CC45/686
11. RA GV CC45/687

CHAPTER 12 (pp. 164–80)
1. RA GV CC45/803
2. RA GV CC45/809
3. RA GV CC45/808
4. RA GV CC45/741
5. RA GV CC45/829
6. RA GV CC45/831
7. RA GV CC45/839
8. RA GV CC45/920
9. Christopher of Greece 166
10. RA GV CC45/965
11. Leslie 291
12. *The Times* 4.12.1935

13. Gore 436
14. RA GV CC45/977
15. RA GV CC45/979
16. RA GV CC45/1048
17. as 16
18. RA GV CC45/1073

19. RA GV CC45/1082
20. RA GV CC45/1092
21. RA GV CC45/1109
22. RA GV CC45/1115
23. *The Times* 21.11.1938
24. as 23

Bibliography

I MANUSCRIPT SOURCES

Royal Archives, Windsor. Letters from Princess Louise of Wales, later Duchess of Fife and Princess Royal; Princess Victoria of Wales; and Princess Maud of Wales, later Princess Charles of Denmark, and later Queen of Norway; to Queen Victoria and Queen Mary.
    Letters from the Duke and Duchess of Fife to Sir George and Lady Alexander.
Gladstone MSS. Letters from the Duchess of Fife to Edward Hamilton. Department of Manuscripts, British Library (Add MSS 48599).

II BOOKS

Aronson, Theo, *Grandmama of Europe: the crowned descendants of Queen Victoria*, Cassell, 1973.
Battiscombe, Georgina, *Queen Alexandra*, Constable, 1969.
Brook-Shepherd, Gordon, *Uncle of Europe: the social and diplomatic life of Edward VII*, Collins, 1975.
Cathcart, Helen, *Anne, the Princess Royal: a Princess for our times*, W.H. Allen, 1988.
Christopher of Greece, Prince, *Memoirs*, Right Book Club, 1938.
Derry, T.K., *A short history of Norway*, 2nd ed., Allen & Unwin, 1968.
Donaldson, Frances, *Edward VIII*, Weidenfeld & Nicolson, 1974.
Duff, David, *Queen Mary*, Collins, 1985.
    —, *Whisper Louise: Edward VII and Mrs Cresswell*, Frederick Muller, 1974.
Edwards, Anne, *Matriarch: Queen Mary and the House of Windsor*, Hodder & Stoughton, 1984.
Fisher, John Arbuthnot, Lord Fisher of Kilverstone, *Fear God and dread nought: the correspondence of Admiral of the Fleet Lord Fisher of Kilverstone*; selected and edited by Arthur J. Marder, 3 vols., Jonathan Cape, 1952–59.
Ford, Colin, (ed.) *Happy and Glorious: 130 years of royal photographs*, National Portrait Gallery, 1977.
Fulford, Roger, *Hanover to Windsor*, Batsford, 1960.
Gernsheim, Helmut & Alison, *Edward VII and Queen Alexandra: a biography in word and picture*, Frederick Muller, 1962.
Gore, John, *King George V: a personal memoir*, John Murray, 1941.
Greve, Tim, *Haakon VII of Norway: founder of a new monarchy*; translated from the Norwegian and edited by T.K. Derry, Hurst, 1983.
Harrison, Michael, *Clarence: the life of HRH the Duke of Clarence and Avondale, 1864–92*, W.H. Allen, 1972.
Hepworth, Philip, *Royal Sandringham*, Wensum, 1978.
James, Edward, *Swans reflecting elephants: my early years*; (ed.) George Melly, Weidenfeld & Nicolson, 1982.

Judd, Denis, *The life and times of George V*, Weidenfeld & Nicolson, 1973.

Knight, Stephen, *Jack the Ripper: the final solution*, Harrap, 1976.

Lee, Sir Sidney, *King Edward VII*, 2 vols., Macmillan, 1925–27.

Lees-Milne, James, *The enigmatic Edwardian: the life of Reginald, 2nd Viscount Esher*, Sidgwick & Jackson, 1986.

Leslie, Anita, *Edwardians in love*, Hutchinson, 1972.

Longford, Elizabeth, *Victoria RI*, Weidenfeld & Nicolson, 1964.

Lutyens, Mary (ed.), *Lady Lytton's court diary, 1895–1899*, Hart-Davis, 1961.

Magnus, Philip, *King Edward the Seventh*, John Murray, 1964.

Mallet, Victor, (ed.) *Life with Queen Victoria: Marie Mallet's letters from court, 1887–1901*, John Murray, 1968.

Marie, Queen of Roumania, *The story of my life*, 3 vols., Cassell, 1934–35.

Michael, Maurice, *Haakon, King of Norway*, Allen & Unwin, 1958.

Nicolson, Harold, *King George the Fifth: his life and reign*, Constable, 1952.

Ponsonby, Arthur, *Henry Ponsonby, Queen Victoria's private secretary: his life from his letters*, Macmillan, 1942.

Ponsonby, Sir Frederick, *Recollections of three reigns*; prepared for press with notes and an introductory memoir by Colin Welch, Eyre & Spottiswoode, 1951.

Pope-Hennessy, James, *A lonely business: a self-portrait of James Pope-Hennessy*; (ed.) Peter Quennell, Weidenfeld & Nicolson, 1981.

—, *Queen Mary, 1867–1953*, Allen & Unwin, 1959.

Rose, Kenneth, *King George V*, Weidenfeld & Nicolson, 1983.

—, *Kings, Queens & Courtiers: intimate portraits of the royal house of Windsor from its foundations to the present day*, Weidenfeld & Nicolson, 1985.

St Aubyn, Giles, *Edward VII, Prince and King*, Collins, 1979.

—, *The Royal George: the life of HRH Prince George, Duke of Cambridge, 1819–1904*, Constable, 1963.

Sanderson, Edgar and Melville, Lewis, *King Edward VII: his life and reign, the record of a noble career*, 6 vols., Gresham, 1910.

Stephenson, John, (ed.) *A royal correspondence: letters of King Edward VII and King George V to Admiral Sir Henry F. Stephenson*, Macmillan, 1938.

Thornton, Michael, *Royal feud: the Queen Mother and the Duchess of Windsor*, Michael Joseph, 1985.

Victoria, Consort of Frederick III, German Emperor, *The Empress Frederick writes to Sophie, her daughter, Crown Princess and later Queen of the Hellenes: letters, 1889–1901*, (ed.) Arthur Gould Lee, Faber, 1955.

Victoria, Queen, *The letters of Queen Victoria, second series: a selection from Her Majesty's correspondence and journal between the years 1862 and 1885*, (ed.) George Earl Buckle, 3 vols., John Murray, 1926–28.

—, *The letters of Queen Victoria, third series: a selection from Her Majesty's correspondence and journal between the years 1886 and 1901*, (ed.) G.E. Buckle, 3 vols., John Murray, 1930–32.

Victoria, Queen, and Victoria, Consort of Frederick III, *Dearest Mama: letters between Queen Victoria and the Crown Princess of Prussia, 1862–64*, (ed.) Roger Fulford, Evans Bros, 1968.

—, *Your dear letter: private correspondence between Queen Victoria and the Crown Princess of Prussia, 1865–1871*, (ed.) Roger Fulford, Evans Bros, 1971.

—, *Darling Child: private correspondence of Queen Victoria and the Crown Princess of Prussia, 1871–1878*, (ed.) Roger Fulford, Evans Bros, 1976.

—, *Beloved Mama: private correspondence of Queen Victoria and the German Crown Princess, 1878–1885*, (ed.) Roger Fulford, Evans Bros, 1981.

Wakeford, Geoffrey, *The Princesses Royal*, Robert Hale, 1973.
Weintraub, Stanley, *Victoria: biography of a Queen*, Unwin Hyman, 1987.
Wheeler-Bennett, John W., *King George VI: his life and reign*, Macmillan, 1958.
Whiting, Audrey, *The Kents*, Hutchinson, 1985.
Windsor, Duke of, formerly King Edward VIII, *A King's story: the memoirs of HRH the Duke of Windsor*, Cassell, 1951.
Woodward, Kathleen, *Queen Mary*, Hutchinson, 1927.

III PERIODICAL ARTICLES

Foot, M.R.D., 'Elected to the throne' (review of Greve's *Haakon VII of Norway*), *Times Literary Supplement*, 17 June 1983.
Hamilton, Alan, 'Royalty's unspoken fear', (royal family and mental illness), *The Times*, 7 April 1987.
'Ignota', 'Princess Charles of Denmark', *Lady's Realm*, October 1897.
Van der Kiste, John, 'Maud, Queen of Norway and Appleton', *East Anglia Monthly*, September 1980.
—, 'Poor Toria, Princess of Coppins', *Bucks & Berks Countryside*, June 1980.
—, 'A royal death at Sandringham', (Duke of Clarence), *East Anglia Monthly*, April 1980.
Watson, Francis, 'The death of George V', *History Today*, December 1986.

IV PERIODICALS – general references

Journal of the Commemorative Collectors Society
Morning Advertiser
The Illustrated London News
The Times
Western Morning News

Index